Politics and Economics in Contemporary Japan

Kodansha International Ltd.

Previously published by the Japan Culture Institute in 1979.
Edited by Murakami Hyōe and Johannes Hirschmeier.

Distributed in the United States by Kodansha International/ USA Ltd. through Harper & Row, Publishers, Inc., 10 East 53rd Street, New York, New York 10022. Published by Kodansha International Ltd., 12-21, Otowa 2-chome, Bunkyo-ku, Tokyo 112 and Kodansha International/USA Ltd., 10 East 53rd Street, New York, New York 10022 and The Hearst Building, 5 Third Street, Suite No. 430, San Francisco, California 94103. Copyright © 1983 by Kodansha International Ltd. All rights reserved. Printed in Japan.

LCC 83-80228
ISBN 0-87011-612-6
ISBN 4-7700-1112-1 (in Japan)

First paperback edition, 1983

CONTENTS

Contributors — vi

Preface — vii

PART I POLITICS

1. The Making of a Prime Minister — 3
   Murakami Hyōe

2. Parties, Factions, and the Diet — 21
   Hans H. Baerwald

3. The World of the *Zaikai* — 64
   Tanaka Yōnosuke

4. The Bureaucracy: Japan's Pool of Leadership — 79
   Japan Culture Institute

5. Case Study: Foreign Policy à la LDP
   (The 1956 Soviet-Japanese Peace Agreement) — 93
   Donald C. Hellmann

PART II ECONOMICS

6. "Japan, Inc.": Reality or Facade? — 111
   Namiki Nobuyoshi

7. Behind the "Made in Japan" Label — 127
   Yamamura Kōzō

8. Japan's Labor Unions: The Meeting of White and Blue Collar — 143
   Kōshiro Kazutoshi

9. The Unsung Mainstays (1): Small Businesses — 157
   Kiyonari Tadao

10. The Unsung Mainstays (2): Agriculture — 184
    Yanagi Susumu

11. Case Study: How to Go Bankrupt and Still Stay Afloat (The Ataka Affair) — 204
    Zushi Saburō

Appendix — 222
Bibliography — 225
Index — 227

Contributors

Hans H. Baerwald is Professor of Political Science, University of California at Los Angeles. He is the author of *Japan's Parliament* (1974).

Donald C. Hellmann is Professor of Political Science and International Studies, University of Washington. His works include *Japanese Domestic Politics and Foreign Policy: The Peace Agreement with the Soviet Union* (1969).

Johannes Hirschmeier is President of Nanzan University at Nagoya. He is the author of *The Origins of Entrepreneurship in Meiji Japan* (1964).

Kiyonari Tadao is Professor of Business Administration, Hōsei University. His works include *Nihon Chūshō Kigyō no Kōzō Hendō* ("Structural Changes in Japan's Small Business Sector," 1970).

Kōshiro Kazutoshi is Professor of Economics, Yokohama National University. He is the author of *Nihon no Chingin Kettei Kikō* ("Wage Setting in Japan," 1973).

Murakami Hyōe, former Managing Director of the Japan Culture Institute, is the author of *Sakura to Ken* ("The Cherry and the Sword," 1976).

Namiki Nobuyoshi is Director of the Japan Economic Research Center and the author of *Yōroppa Keizai-ron* ("The European Economy," 1968).

Tanaka Yōnosuke is an economic journalist and editorial advisor of Mainichi Shinbunsha.

Yamaji Susumu is an editor for the *Japan Economic Journal* and an expert on Japanese agriculture.

Yamamura Kōzō is Professor of Economic and Asian Studies, University of Washington. He is the author of *Economic and Demographic Change in Preindustrial Japan* (1977).

Zushi Saburō is on the editorial staff of *Ekonomisuto* ("Economist") published by Mainichi Shinbunsha.

Preface

When the classical economists fashioned their theories of "political economy," they set out from the explicit premise that government interference in the workings of the market was to be systematically avoided. Society would prosper best, it was felt, if each individual were permitted to pursue freely his own economic goals. The tacit underlying assumption was that society existed for the fulfillment of the individual.

Students of Japanese economics find themselves faced with a quite different set of circumstances and a starting point fundamentally opposed to that of the West. In Japan the goals of the individual are subordinated to the goals of the group to which he belongs, and ultimately to the state. Accordingly, Japan's political economy, far from championing the unhampered pursuit of private economic ambitions, presumes that the public realms of politics and economics cooperate toward a common goal. It is the aim of this book to show how this interrelationship operates and how differences in the political economies of Japan and the West can be seen to stem from differing cultural backgrounds.

The American sociologist Daniel Bell, in his *The Cultural Contradictions of Capitalism* (1976), has identified the three principal areas which interact with one another in a given society as: the techno-economic structure, the polity, and the culture. He goes on to argue that modern Western culture shows an increasing tendency to undermine the techno-economic structure. Applying his model to Japan, we find that throughout most of the post-Meiji period and up until recent times, all three realms have worked together in such a way as to be mutually reinforcing. Hence, the essays in this book, while focusing primarily on problems of polity and economy, must make frequent reference to the area of culture as it motivates and directs and also as it restrains and limits political and economic behavior in Japan.

The success of efforts to industrialize and modernize Japan's socio-economic structures at the beginning of the Meiji period (1868-1912) was the result of forceful government leadership, honest and dedicated bureaucratic controls, and entrepreneurial drive. Thriving businesses were given further guidance and subsidies inasmuch as they contributed considerably to the national aim of building a strong modern nation. In other words, the close cooperation among political leaders, top bureaucracy and big business grew out of Japan's need to answer the challenge posed by the superior Western power. At the same time as external structures and technology from the West were adopted almost indiscriminately, Japanese politicians demanded loyalty and obedience, and top managers introduced a system of labor-management drawn from cultural tradition: the notion of the "house" (*ie*) was transferred to the firm, and with it the vertical system of ranking continued within and among economic and political groups.

In spite of the postwar enthusiasm for democracy and individual freedoms and equality, the areas of techno-economic structure and polity retained the traditional elements of group-relatedness and vertical ranking. This in turn made possible the formation of enterprise unions. It enabled the disbanded *zaibatsu* to band together into *keiretsu*; it helped preserve or revive systems of permanent employment and seniority pay scales. And with the nation finding a common aspiration in the pursuit of economic growth, *zaikai* (business leaders), the top bureaucracy and the government party once again worked as one "for the good of Japan."

Recently several Western analysts have come to see much in the patterns of organization and human relationships in Japan's political economy worthy of adoption by the West. Of course, Japan's entire process of modernization could hardly be exported. But neither can individual parts of its system be so easily taken over and imitated. For it is based on a unique culture which—as the writers of this book point out—is in grave danger of coming apart at its seams. In order to work smoothly, the system requires a basic general consensus regarding overriding goals, and the willingness of individuals to rank duty and the exercise of their assigned role above personal rights and ambitions. At the present, signs of a serious erosion in these conditions lead people to speak of a spiritual crisis. Uneasiness concerning the future of Japan's social cohesion is spreading. Something seems to be happening which threatens to challenge Japan's future more seriously than her trade imbalance or her need to adjust to the new competitors within Asia. Indeed each of the three major components of Japan's "political economy" — the political leadership, the bureaucracy and the economic enterprises — has to cope with the backlash of hostility and contradiction following the long period of infatuation with the singleminded quest for national economic growth.

As Chapter 4 points out, the central bureaucracy is experiencing continued frustration through the weakening of the ruling government party and its need to accommodate conflicting demands. The elite-bureaucracy has, through its meticulous control and guidance system, certainly contributed toward the heavy concentration of socio-economic decision-making in Tokyo and thus to the expansion of the metropolitan area into a sprawling sea of people. Furthermore, the very ability of Japan's bureaucracy tends to diminish civic initiative. One readily relies on the state and trusts it to solve all problems. When this fails, discontent tends to concentrate itself on the state for having neglected its duty. In this way many problems over which it has little or no control are being classified as the responsibility of the state. And even as claims against the state increase, cooperation toward common goals decreases. Hostile groups oppose not only the construction of airports but also of railways, roads and electric power stations. Obviously, even an elite-bureaucracy can only function well as long as citizens and politicians agree on the priorities and are prepared to cooperate.

In the realm of politics, pragmatism rather than principle holds sway. The election of the Prime Minister (Chapter 1), the workings of political parties (Chapter 2), as well as the case-study of Japan's foreign policy (Chapter 5) all show how this dependence on general consensus is so great that when it is not attainable it quickly leads to compromise of principle, "horse-trading" deals between the *habatsu* (factions), and even various contradictory measures resulting from the need to satisfy different pressure groups. The perpetuation of the "one-hectare farm" agricultural system is a case in point (Chapter 10). This lack of political philosophy coupled with continual pragmatic compromising can only lead to a still greater disenchantment of the young with the state and politics. Of course, matters are not all that much better in Western democracies, perhaps because democracy tends by its very nature to thrive on pragmatic compromise. But at least in the West, opposition parties offer realistic alternatives which in turn permit reform and change of direction. The same cannot be said of the opposition parties in Japan, at least up until now.

Finally, in the realm of the firm, top-level management is clearly worried about what will happen once lower growth rates force a radical departure from the seniority system. Will the system of permanent employment be able to survive without it? Will permanent employment be regarded merely as the right of each employee but lose its motivational force for hard work and loyalty to the company? To be sure, much can still be done by the intensive educational efforts within the firm to foster pride in one's work and in the company. And group cohesiveness remains a vital element even among the young, despite the trend to individualism (a word which connotes egoism in Japanese). Today's youth may have been spoiled by the fruits of economic prosperity, but economic hardship may still lead them back into the fold of traditional cultural patterns.

Such are but a few of the questions which can be raised regarding the future of Japan's social fabric. This most interesting book uncovers the interplay among the techno-economic, the political and the bureaucratic structures, each chapter pinpointing one important aspect. The final chapter on the Ataka affair shows then, in a live-drama, how a solution to a serious problem was achieved within this accepted framework. To be sure, it was not all smoothness and "Japan, Inc."; the tensions and cross-purposes were strong. In the search for practical solutions, Japan's political economy may face growing tensions and contradictions, for it is caught up in the relentless dynamics of change. Will traditional culture keep providing that unique cohesiveness so characteristic of Japan's society or will its vanishing influence lead toward a disjoining of the political and economic realms? While not providing any answers, this book stimulates questions along these lines.

Johannes Hirschmeier

Editors' Note

The completion of any book depends on the cooperation of many individuals. The editors wish to express their deep gratitude to all who have helped make the publication of this book possible.

The editors would also like to thank Dr. Hans H. Baerwald and the Cambridge University Press for granting permission to include "Parties, Factions and the Diet," a chapter in Dr. Baerwald's book, *Japan's Parliament: An Introduction* (Cambridge, 1974), in this publication.

The Hepburn system of romanization is used for Japanese terms, which are italicized except for words included in the second edition of *Webster's New World Dictionary*.

PART I
POLITICS

The Making of a Prime Minister

MURAKAMI HYŌE

Introduction

During the thirty-three years between the end of World War II and 1978, thirteen men have served as Prime Minister of Japan. Except for a brief period immediately after the War, in each instance the Prime Minister was chosen by virtue of his being the leader of the majority political party, whose representatives in the Diet were elected under universal suffrage. Seven were bureaucrats before going into politics; one, an army general and member of the Imperial family; one, a journalist; and two, attorneys. The remaining two were career politicians.

The seven men with administrative (i.e. bureaucratic) backgrounds have served as Prime Minister for twenty-four of those thirty-three years. Those with other backgrounds have held the office for relatively brief periods — two months, for example, for Higashikuni Naruhiko immediately after the War, and nine months in the case of Katayama Tetsu (the only Socialist Party member to serve as Prime Minister). A further distinction is often made between the "enduring bureaucrats" and the "short-lived politicians." Postwar prime ministers with strictly political backgrounds — Hatoyama Ichirō (two years), Ishibashi Tanzan (two months), Tanaka Kakuei (two years and three months), and Miki Takeo (two years) — have served relatively short terms in contrast to the longer terms of such former bureaucrats as Yoshida Shigeru, Ikeda Hayato, and Satō Eisaku. Thus, it would seem that a bureaucratic background is an advantage both in seeking and retaining the prime ministership. All seven of the "bureaucrat" prime ministers were educated at former imperial universities, six from the University of Tokyo (Tōdai) and one from Kyoto University. Even the politician Hatoyama Ichirō and the Socialist Party's Katayama Tetsu were Tōdai graduates, which demonstrates how vital such a diploma is for a would-be Prime Minister.

Why are these two qualifications — being a graduate of a major university and having had a successful career as a bureaucrat — such important conditions for climbing the political ladder? The answer lies in the nation's social structure since the Meiji Restoration, or more specificly, in the high public regard for a solid academic background and the bureaucratic profession.

Beginning with the Meiji Restoration in 1868, Japan has undergone a sweeping transformation from a feudalistic, status-oriented society to a basically meritocratic one. The nucleus of leadership in the years after the Restoration was made up of young and revolutionary lower-ranking samurai who were instrumental in overthrowing the Tokugawa shogunate. To secure their hard-earned social position, these men created a new nobility, composed of themselves, former *kuge* (court nobles), and former *daimyō* (feudal lords). Other ex-samurai assumed the title of *shizoku* (descendants of samurai), to distinguish them from ordinary citizens (*heimin*). However, the new society was fundamentally a meritocracy based on educational achievement, and as a result an increasing number of capable men with university education moved in to fill the ranks of leadership.

A parliamentary system was inaugurated in 1885. The first Prime Minister, Itō Hirobumi, and his immediate successors were all men who had distinguished themselves during the Restoration. Katsura Tarō, the first Prime Minister in the twentieth century, represented a departure from this pattern, having made no notable contribution to the Restoration, although he had fought in the 1868 civil war. After studying in Germany, he became an officer in the army, eventually rising to the rank of General. His record as a capable military administrator was the important factor in his rise to the top office. Katsura's rise to power was assisted by the strong support given by his own *han* (fiefdom) of Chōshū (now Yamaguchi Prefecture) and Satsuma (now Kagoshima Prefecture). These two *han* exerted predominant influence in the newly formed Meiji government as well as in the struggle for Restoration. Indeed, so strong was the power of Satsuma and Chōshū that the new government was often referred to as the "Satsuma-Chōshū coalition government." It was not until Prime Minister Hara Takashi came to power in 1918 that *han*-based politics and Satsuma-Chōshū dominance were eliminated.

Hara boasted an unusual background for a Prime Minister: journalist, diplomat and businessman. He was also the first majority party leader of the Diet to become Prime Minister. Even though Hara was from a samurai family, he was known as the "commoner Prime Minister." He had probably the strongest public support of any government leader up to that time.

Inukai Tsuyoshi, who became Prime Minister in 1931, was also an exception, having come to the post from a journalistic background. Of the other twelve prime ministers from Katsura to Inukai (1901-32) not including Hara and Inukai, four were bureaucrats (including Wakatsuki Reijirō, a true commoner) and five were military leaders. One of the remaining three, Takahashi Korekiyo, had been a banker — another exception. Hara, Inukai, and Takahashi were all men of forceful personality, and all were victims of assassination. The remaining members of the group of 1901-32 prime ministers were Ōkuma Shigenobu and Saionji Kinmochi. Saionji was a pre-Restoration aristocrat and a distinguished activist during the Restoration itself. Saionji's longevity and liberalism made him the emperor's most trusted advisor, and he was one of the most influential of the so-called *genrō* (elder statesmen), who were instrumental in the selection of successors each time a cabinet was dissolved.

After Inukai's assassination in May of 1932, the country was swept up into a militarist current, which generated numerous cabinet shuffles. Of the eleven men who served as Prime Minister from 1932 until 1945, four were generals, four were admirals, two were bureaucrats, and one, Konoe Fumimaro, a liberal-minded man from a family closely related to the emperor. Konoe led three separate cabinets, all of which reflected popular hopes for reform and unity but none of which were successful in checking the ascendancy of the military.

In his book, *Nihon no Seiji Erīto* ("Japan's Political Elite", Chūō Kōronsha, 1976), Takane Masaaki demonstrates statistically that, given the same education, it was a definite advantage in pre-World War II Japan to be from a noble (*kuge*) family. Konoe is the prime example. Some doubt remains, however, as to whether the title of *shizoku* itself really was an advantage or not. It is probably more accurate to say that while the title did not directly insure a successful career, it did command respect. *Shizoku* advanced by virtue of a family upbringing that stressed academic excellence and the will to succeed. Be that as it may, the prime ministership from the Meiji era up to August, 1945 was held primarily by the heroes of the Meiji Restoration, followed by bureaucrats and military leaders. It was a reflection of the common public trust that no matter what his social status, a man could rise in the world if he graduated from a renowned university, Military or Naval Academy. (The military in peacetime might be regarded as a sort of bureaucracy. In postwar Japan, however, the downgrading of the military's social position has served to increase the chances of ex-bureaucrats becoming prime ministers.)

In what follows I should like to offer a brief sketch of the postwar prime ministers and of the circumstances that pushed them into the national spotlight. The drama of political maneuverings at the top should in turn provide not only an introduction to Japan's politico-economic system but also a vivid picture of the nation's postwar history.

The Yoshida Cabinets

On August 15, 1945, Japan accepted the Potsdam Declaration issued by the Allied Powers. The order to surrender was announced to the Japanese people and the Suzuki Cabinet resigned. General Higashikuni, a member of the Imperial Household, was chosen to handle the formalities of surrender. He had been recommended for the prime ministership during the World War II but the leadership decided not to nominate him, concerned that an Imperial prime minister might implicate the emperor himself should Japan be defeated. Once the War was over Higashikuni was able to become Prime Minister, the first from the Imperial Household. His selection was an attempt by the nation's leadership to invoke Imperial authority and thereby to reduce the shock accompanying Japan's defeat. At the War's end, millions of troops were still deployed throughout Asia and the Pacific, and it was thought that Imperial authority would be essential for carrying out orderly disarmament and demobilization.

Higashikuni's authority was soon rendered meaningless as the U.S.-dominated Allied forces began their Occupation of Japan. In October, Shidehara Kijūrō became Prime Minister. Shidehara possessed an impressive record as a diplomat before the War, having served as Minister of Foreign Affairs in four separate cabinets. He had lost influence as a result of opposing the adventurist foreign policies of the radical militarists and advocating harmonious relations with the United States and England. But now the Japanese saw in him someone who could cooperate with the Allied Powers — the perfect person to preside over a new era in Japanese history. This is not to say, however, that the Allies regarded him as a friend. In fact, they seem hardly to have paid any attention to him at all. When the Supreme Commander for the Allied Powers, General Douglas MacArthur, learned of Shidehara's appointment as Prime Minister, his first reaction was, "Does he speak English?"

Because the postwar Constitution had not yet been promulgated, the first two prime ministers after the War were chosen in the traditional way by the *genrō* — those former prime ministers and other elderly advisors who had occupied key government positions. Until his death in 1922, Yamagata Aritomo had been the *genrō* with the most decisive voice in selecting new prime ministers, and he was succeeded by Saionji Kinmochi. When the military came to power, however, its views had to be considered as well. At Saionji's death in 1940, the powerful role of mediator passed to Lord Keeper of the Privy Seal, Kido Kōichi. In October 1941, Kido endorsed Tōjō Hideki, who presided over the start of the U.S.-Japan conflict. At the time, Tōjō was thought to be the man most capable of controlling the radical military, and Kido hoped that as Prime Minister Tōjō would restrain the army until a peaceful option could be found. When Kido related the reasons for his choice to the emperor, the emperor responded with a Japanese proverb indicating that he knew the danger Tōjō posed: "To capture a tiger cub you must venture into the tiger's den."

The emperor had no veto power. Nonetheless, complying with his desire for peace, Tōjō vigorously sought to moderate the ambition of the military and to negotiate a way out of the impasse. But it was already too late. America, long suspicious of Japan, did not recognize the signs of change, and Japan reacted with the decision for war.

The first postwar general election was held in April 1946. When the votes were counted, the Liberal Party headed by Hatoyama Ichirō had won a plurality in the Diet, followed by Shidehara's Progressive Party and the Socialist Party. A conservative coalition government was expected to develop around Hatoyama, but SCAP (Supreme Commander Allied Powers) intervened and barred Hatoyama from office. Hatoyama then requested that Yoshida Shigeru, a former diplomat who had served as Foreign Minister, succeed him as head of the Liberal Party. Consequently, it was Yoshida who then formed a new cabinet in 1946.

With the exception of the period between May 1947 and October 1948, when a coalition of the Socialist Party and Democratic Party controlled the government, Yoshida guided Japan through the difficult Occupation years to the San Francisco Peace Treaty with the Allied Powers. Serving as Prime Minister for a total of seven years and two months, Yoshida was a strong leader. In choosing his ministers of state and making other appointments, a matter of major importance to Japanese politicians, he did not turn to *genrō* consensus but exercised his own authority. He was a man of aristocratic taste and disliked journalists. Because of his high-handed methods, including dissolution of the Diet when he was criticized for calling an opposition question "asinine," Yoshida's reign was characterized as a "one-man rule." On the other hand, he left behind a sparkling record in many areas, including tactful dealings with the Occupation forces, keeping the military budget at the lowest possible level, setting war-devastated industry back on its feet, and aligning Japan firmly with the Free World.

It was by sheer chance that Yoshida was chosen to succeed Hatoyama as head of the Liberal Party and as Prime Minister. Hatoyama had served before the War as Minister of Education and as secretary-general of one of the leading political parties. As a liberal, he was relegated to obscurity throughout the War. By the time Japan's defeat became a certainty, he believed himself destined to rise and lead the nation. He was also regarded by the majority of conservative Japanese politicians as the most capable man for this role. Nevertheless he was barred from office. The reason is still not clear, but it was probably because his anti-communist declarations prior to the 1946 election had irked SCAP's "new dealers," and because he had written an essay criticizing the use of the atomic bomb. Whatever the reasons, the Liberal Party was thrown into confusion by the sudden purge of Hatoyama. No one in the Hatoyama faction seemed qualified to take his place, but they needed a caretaker until Hatoyama could be cleared. Two other candidates for the post were quite elderly, one a journalist and the other a diplomat related to the Imperial family by marriage. The former declined because of his age, and party opposition to the latter was strong.

Ultimately, the party settled upon Yoshida, a career diplomat who had been on good terms with Hatoyama since the time he had served as Ambassador to Great Britain. Yoshida had served once as Foreign Minister, but he had little political ambition and had no base of support in the party. He became Prime Minister at Hatoyama's request, with the understanding that party finances and personnel affairs would be managed by Hatoyama, while Yoshida would have sole say over cabinet appointments. Hatoyama would resume formal leadership of the Liberal Party once he had been cleared. With these conditions, Yoshida officially joined the party, organized a cabinet, and was appointed party president.

Yoshida's father was Takeuchi Tsuna, an activist in the Tosa Liberal Party during the Meiji period. Yoshida himself married the daughter of an affluent Yokohama merchant and was adopted as the head of this household. After his graduation from the Political Science Department of Tokyo Imperial University, he entered the Ministry of Foreign Affairs and served as secretary and minister in several European embassies. He was a candidate for Minister of Foreign Affairs in the Hirota Cabinet (1936-37), but his appointment was vetoed by the military. Under the Tōjō Cabinet, he was regarded as a security risk and kept under close surveillance. His background made him the logical choice for Foreign Minister in the first and second postwar cabinets.

As Prime Minister, Yoshida's achievements were considerable. More than any other single individual, he was responsible for laying the foundations for Japan's economic rehabilitation, and he helped negotiate and signed the San Francisco Peace Treaty of 1951 which restored Japan's independence. He guided the nation out of the ruins of war, through the increasingly strident labor offensive and through the almost revolutionary changes in social institutions with minimal confusion. Throughout he was greatly helped by the SCAP Occupation forces. When the Cold War reached Asia, U.S. government policy began to change to Japan's advantage. SCAP increasingly recommended measures to revitalize the nation in order to keep it from slipping into communism. Japan's economic recovery was quickly accelerated, ironically, by the boom of special procurements that accompanied the Korean War. Circumstances helped, but Yoshida's skillful dealings with SCAP and his strong leadership were major factors in his political success. Party factionalism, often looked upon today as the chronic affliction of Japanese political parties, had not yet developed.

In the general election of 1947, the Socialist Party of Japan (SPJ), although failing to get a majority, won a plurality in the Diet. Katayama Tetsu, SPJ President, became Prime Minister in a coalition government of the Socialist Party of Japan, the Democratic Party, and the People's Cooperative Party—all the major political parties with the exception of the Liberal Party. Katayama was a Tōdai graduate, a Christian, and a humanist. He had served as Chairman of the Social Populace Party in 1926 and had been elected to the Diet.

Although Tōdai has produced most of the establishment leadership, especially its ranking bureaucrats, it has also produced many students who were committed to socialism and who later became leaders of revolutionary social movements. It is interesting to note that Katayama's chief Cabinet secretary, Nishio Suehiro, came from a working-class background, and that the next Prime Minister, Hatoyama (a Tōdai graduate) chose for his top advisor Miki Bukichi, who was without a university education. Such a combination is still common in the conservative and reformist parties.

The Katayama Cabinet collapsed after nine months, without any notable accomplishments. Its lackluster record was a direct result of left-wing opposition to formulating the budget. Ashida Hitoshi, president of the Democratic Party, then formed a coalition government of the SPJ,

Democratic Party and People's Cooperative Party. Ashida was also a Tōdai graduate and former diplomat who, upon retiring from the diplomatic corps in 1932, joined a major party called the Political Friends' Association (Seiyūkai) and ran successfully for a seat in the Lower House. Ashida had been mentioned as a candidate for the prime ministership when Hatoyama was purged, but by then he had already left the Liberal Party and was serving as Minister of Health and Welfare in the Shidehara Cabinet. By the time he formed his own cabinet, he was President of the Democratic Party.

The Ashida Cabinet also achieved little, primarily because several high-ranking cabinet members had become implicated in a financial scandal involving Showa Denko.* This failure of the coalition government gave the Liberal Party another chance, and Yoshida formed his second cabinet. Today, the Katayama and Ashida administrations have become an almost forgotten interlude in the tumultous postwar era.

From Hatoyama to Kishi

Hatoyama was depurged and returned to politics in 1951, but Yoshida was firmly installed as Prime Minister and gave no indication that he would withdraw. The situation gave rise to a feud between Hatoyama, who in effect demanded his old position back, and Yoshida, who was well established and did not want to return it. In 1954, Hatoyama finally left the party. Together with sympathetic conservative Dietmen he formed the new Democratic Party, destroying the Liberal Party's absolute majority. Yoshida was prepared to carry on the battle by dissolving the Diet and calling an election, but was dissuaded by Ogata Taketora, a former journalist whom Yoshida considered as his heir. Hatoyama received the support of the Socialist Party and became the next Prime Minister.

Ogata persuaded Yoshida to accept defeat in good grace, a strategy actually founded on Ogata's own need to build himself a base of support against Hatoyama. Had he lived, Ogata would no doubt have become a leading Prime Minister, but he died shortly thereafter of a heart ailment.

The transfer of power from Yoshida to Hatoyama was not a question of policy confrontation. Rather, it reflected a battle between individuals and changing factional alignments within the conservative bloc, as well as

---

*In 1948 certain politicians and bureaucrats were alleged to have received money from Showa Denko, a major chemical firm hoping for special government loans. Among those arrested was the incumbent Vice-premier. The affair led to the resignation of Prime Minister Ashida Hitoshi and his cabinet. However, none of the politicians later tried were found guilty.

a popular feeling that it was time for a change. When any one individual remains on top for more than a few years, groups outside the mainstream groups begin calling for a change. More than a dispute over specific policies, it is a demand for different people at the head of government. In Japan of the early 1950s, this feeling was bolstered by a desire to test the nation's post-Occupation independence by electing someone SCAP had not specifically approved.

Hatoyama Ichirō was born in Tokyo in 1883 to a prosperous, respected family. His father had been a Tōdai professor, lawyer, and Dietman. After graduating from Tōdai, Hatoyama qualified as an attorney, but instead of pursuing a legal career, he entered politics and was elected to the Tokyo Municipal Assembly at the age of twenty-nine, and to the House of Representatives at thirty-two. He rose rapidly and was appointed Minister of Education in 1931 at the age of forty-seven. His family background and political posts were major factors enabling Hatoyama to become Prime Minister. Kōno Ichirō, a Waseda graduate and one of the founders of the Liberal Party, was very helpful to Hatoyama after the War. Kōno aspired to the premiership himself, but he failed. Comparing his own fate to Hatoyama's, he once said ruefully, "The Prime Minister's place was reserved for Hatoyama the minute he was born."

Hatoyama retired in 1956 after engineering the normalization of diplomatic relations with the Soviet Union. Although friendly relations with the Soviet Union were an important issue since the Soviets had refused to sign the San Francisco Peace Treaty with Japan, public opinion was not necessarily behind Hatoyama. In announcing the 1956 Joint Declaration with the Soviet Union, Hatoyama deliberately attempted to demonstrate to the Japanese people the difference between himself and the "undeviatingly pro-American" Yoshida; he may have regarded the declaration itself as a political coup that would eclipse Yoshida's achievement in the San Francisco Peace Treaty. Hatoyama retired in satisfaction, having succeeded in the memorable feat of restoring ties with the Soviet Union.

Poor health was one factor behind Hatoyama's retirement, but more importantly, other politicians made it clear they expected him to give someone else a chance in the office, now that he had made his mark. The prospect of a change in administration stimulated anew the ambitions of a large number of politicians, and the general election which followed Hatoyama's retirement was the prototype for conservative factional struggles to come.

Only after the conservative party merger into the Liberal Democratic Party (LDP) did conservative party factions fully surface in postwar Japan.

Hatoyama was elected in the first LDP presidential election, even though the 69 members of the Yoshida faction cast blank ballots. Because the LDP has held the majority of seats in the Lower House since 1955, the party president automatically becomes Prime Minister. Accordingly, an LDP presidential election is in effect an election for the prime ministership. As a result, intra-party elections in which LDP representatives, councillors, and regional representatives cast ballots have become the setting for all-out struggles among individual candidates and factions.

In December of 1956, three candidates competed in the second LDP presidential election. The odds were in favor of Kishi Nobusuke, a Tōdai graduate who had been particularly influential in carrying out the Manchurian industrialization policies. Minister of Commerce and Industry in the Tōjō Cabinet, he had been designated a war criminal after World War II. For some time after his release from Sugamo Prison his activities were restrained, but he was immediately sought out once he returned to public life. The Yoshida-Hatoyama struggle provided him with a natural stage from which to campaign. Moving to support Hatoyama, he became Secretary-general of Hatoyama's Liberal Party and played a vital role behind the scenes in arranging the conservative coalition. When the LDP was formed, he became the new party's Secretary-general.

If we examine the qualifications for Prime Minister after 1960, we find that each successful candidate had served previously as minister in an economic-related ministry and as LDP Secretary-general. The ministry provides a proving ground for policy-making abilities, and the secretary-generalship is a lever with which to establish a following within the party. The Secretary-general controls both the party purse strings and the allocation of official support to candidates during a general election, and is thus an excellent post from which to help one's friends and impede one's foes.

Kishi was in an advantageous position to become the next Prime Minister. Furthermore, he had abundant political funds and spent more money on this party presidential election than any other candidate. While political campaigning had never been cheap, the standards rose sharply when Kishi entered. For the most part, Kishi's funds consisted of contributions from large corporations that were indebted to him for wartime favors when he was in the Ministry of Commerce and Industry.

In the LDP presidential election, Kishi's first-ballot lead was overturned in a runoff when Ishibashi Tanzan scored a narrow seven-vote triumph. Aiming at defeating Kishi, runner-up on the first ballot, Ishibashi faction had formed an alliance with the third-place candidate, in addition to promising one cabinet post to seven or eight influential people. Ishibashi quickly ran into trouble, however, because he was unable to fulfill all the promises made by his chief-of-staff during the campaign. His administration began with many cabinet posts empty.

Ishibashi was a Waseda University graduate and former economic journalist. In contrast to Kishi, who had had a long, successful career as a bureaucrat, Ishibashi had heaped criticism on prewar and wartime economic policies. His keen perception in economic matters was well known, and Prime Minister Yoshida selected him as Finance Minister. He also served as Minister of International Trade and Industry in the Hatoyama Cabinet. He was certainly qualified for the prime ministership, despite his unusual background.

Another candidate in the same LDP presidential election, Ishii Mitsujirō, was also a former journalist. His background was also unusual. However, Ishii had his own political faction which he inherited from Ogata. Ishibashi was unique in that he was elected on the basis of his character and insight, and not because of factional support. The Japanese people thus placed high hopes in Ishibashi as leader of the new conservative party. Not only did he come from a non-bureaucratic background, he was a long-time liberal with political courage. But fate was not kind to this distinctive Prime Minister. Soon after assuming office, Ishibashi suffered a stroke and had to retire after a mere three months. His replacement was Kishi.

Japan's Conservative Mainstream

Kishi was an advocate of rearmament, but he became increasingly discreet about voicing such opinion as he rose within the LDP. Politicians everywhere are prone to weigh their own convictions against public opinion, but this tendency is particularly conspicuous in Japan. Even people who attract attention for their forthright statements of principle when they are young, tend to speak out less and less often, and with increasing equivocation, as they become established. Rather than form alliances of principle, the accent is on broad consensus and avoiding conflict. Because of his record, Kishi was considered dangerous by some, and his speeches indeed contained traces of the prewar national socialism. The domestic troubles over the U.S.-Japan Security Treaty in 1960 stemmed partly from Kishi's attitude.

The Japanese government delayed renewing the Security Treaty, which had been ratified at the same time as the San Francisco Peace Treaty, in order to consider revisions that would put Japan on a more balanced footing with the United States. This policy, and the expanded military responsibilities which it would entail, met with extensive opposition from the Socialist Party of Japan and the Japanese press. The SPJ demanded total abrogation of the treaty and the adoption of unarmed neutrality. It may have been over-idealistic, but this stand appealed to the public, which was still wary of military involvement. The resulting furor over renewal of the Security Treaty increased general distrust of the Kishi Cabinet until it led to widespread popular opposition. With proceedings in the Diet obstructed by an unruly opposition minority, Kishi saw little option but to invoke his party's majority to force through the renewal of the treaty. His heavy-handed legislative coup was sensationalized by the media, and the Diet was besieged by thousands of angry, sometimes violent protestors for several days running. The demonstrations made it necessary to cancel a scheduled visit by President Eisenhower to Japan, and Kishi was forced to step down as soon as the revised treaty came into effect.

In the January, 1959 LDP presidential election, Kishi had defeated Matsumura Kenzō by a 320-166 margin for his third two-year term, but in 1960 there was no speculation that Matsumura would replace Kishi. Besides being highly respected, with wide support from the Japanese people, Matsumura was an old friend of Chou En-Lai. But these qualifications were not enough to bring support from conservative Dietmen. Although he had been in the Ministry of Agriculture and Forestry, he did not have the polish of a seasoned bureaucrat. He had the air of a mayor from a rural village, not that of a potential Prime Minister.

The LDP presidential melee after Kishi's withdrawal created even more turmoil than had the Kishi-Ishibashi struggle of 1956. Going into the election, there were four candidates and eight major factions. Of these, the Ikeda faction joined the Kishi and Satō factions, while the Ishii faction was backed by the Ōno, Kōno and Miki-Matsumura factions. The leaders of the former group (Ikeda, Kishi, Satō) were all former bureaucrats, and those of the latter group (Ishii, Ōno, Kōno), all politicians who had worked their way up the ranks. This election became a clearly-marked battle between bureaucrats and the party politicians. In addition to Ikeda and Ishii, the other candidate was Fujiyama Aiichirō, a former businessman who commanded too small a faction to compete. When the dust had finally settled, it was Ikeda who was elected on the second ballot.

This election demonstrated the strength of the bureaucrat-based factions. Ōno Banboku had risen as a regional politician and had become an extremely experienced, powerful politician, but his rural background worked against any hopes he had of becoming Prime Minister. When the Kishi Cabinet ran into dissent within the party, Kishi sought Ōno's support and promised to back him as the next Prime Minister. When Kishi blithely ignored his promise later, Ōno angrily withdrew from the race. Such vacillation by politician-based factions was a definite advantage for the bureaucrats.

Fujiyama Aiichirō ran twice more in party presidential elections but never managed to gain more than 25% of the total vote. He came from the Mitsui financial conglomerate, and was the wealthy owner of several companies. However, no individual financial resources could compete with the ability of bureaucrats to draw repeatedly on big business. Among the requirements for a would-be prime minister is the ability to procure funds, preferably from large enterprises, and to distribute them strategically on a continuing basis. Of course, charisma and talent are major requirements, but in sharp contrast to the many former bureaucrats who have been political successes, practically no one has successfully made the transition from financial to political leadership.

Ikeda Hayato, who succeeded Kishi, was a graduate of Kyoto University and former Vice-minister in the Ministry of Finance. In 1949, the year he was first elected to the House of Representatives, he was appointed Minister of Finance in the Yoshida Cabinet. This was a remarkable appointment, made all the more so if one realizes that a Dietman's political career, especially the number of times he has been returned to office, is of prime importance in the selection of cabinet members. Yoshida enjoyed the exercise of his powers of appointment to the fullest, and had a penchant for putting academics in government posts and promising young newcomers to his cabinet. Another "bright young man" whom Yoshida propelled to the limelight was Satō Eisaku, a former Ministry of Transportation bureaucrat. Since Satō succeeded Ikeda and stayed in power for an extended period, these men and their followers came to be referred to as the "Yoshida school," the conservative mainstream of Japanese politics.

Ikeda's appointment as Minister of Finance in the Yoshida Cabinet had strong business backing, particularly from the industrialist Miyajima Seijirō. As a bureaucrat in the Finance Ministry, Ikeda had wide-reaching business contacts. When he was asked by Yoshida for a recommendation for the minister's post, Miyajima invited Ikeda to his office one day in 1949 and questioned him on his basic political beliefs. As a result of this meeting, Miyajima endorsed Ikeda but said to Yoshida, "You know, though, he's a pretty headstrong young man, and he'll want a free hand in economic questions if you make him Minister of Finance." Yoshida reportedly replied, "He'd *better* wield a free hand. I don't know the first thing about economics!"

Ikeda's surprise selection for this post was the start of a brilliant political career. After achieving a distinguished record as Finance Minister, he continued to expand his influence within the LDP until he eventually became Prime Minister. As head of the government, he adopted two major policies: one was the famous National Income Doubling Plan masterminded by Shimomura Osamu, and the other was the "low-profile" political posture. In contrast to Kishi's reputation for riding roughshod over the Opposition, Ikeda made every effort to avoid political controversy.

Ikeda was honest, but he lacked the veteran politician's sophistication. He enraged the Opposition as Minister of Finance when he blurted out, "Let the poor eat barley," a comment that recalls the remark of a reported German bureaucrat, "Let the poor grub for roots." Once he became Prime Minister, he kept such remarks to himself and worked patiently to gain the Opposition's cooperation in economic development. If the keeping of campaign promises is the sign of a successful Prime Minister, Ikeda may be said to have succeeded many times over.

Ikeda organized his first cabinet in 1960. In the sixth LDP presidential election, he ran unopposed. In 1964 he defeated both Satō and Fujiyama to triumph on the first ballot. In this particular election, Ikeda's majority was said to have cost him close to one billion yen. Fortunately, the incumbent Prime Minister generally has easy access to party slush funds.

Soon after election to his third term, Ikeda developed cancer and resigned on November 9, 1964. Rather than throw the post open to another bruising intra-party fight, the party elders met to choose a successor. The main contenders were Satō, runner-up in the presidential election just four months earlier, and Kōno, who had supported Ikeda. Satō won, in part because business did not entirely trust Kōno. Kōno was a capable and influential politician, but he was of the Hatoyama school and not a mainstream conservative. He advocated Japan-Soviet negotiations, had built a power base in the Ministry of Agriculture and Forestry, and had obvious political skills, which only made business all the more wary. If Ikeda and Satō were honor students in the race, Kōno was the failure. Kōno later made peace with Satō, thinking that such a move would help his future, but he died soon thereafter.

Satō Eisaku was Kishi's younger brother. With Prime Minister Yoshida's support, he had early distinguished himself by serving in a number of important party and cabinet posts. After succeeding Ikeda, Satō remained in office for a record seven years and eight months. The fast growth of the Japanese economy continued at a steady pace, and there were no conspicuous domestic or foreign issues affecting the nation during his term. Although his job security was enhanced when Kōno died on July 8, 1965, there was no dearth of rivals in the 1964-72 period. Nevertheless, Satō was able to hold on to the post for nearly eight years because of his political skills and adroit management of personnel. Nicknamed "Mr.

Quickears," he had an uncanny knack for hearing even the smallest bit of political gossip and then using that information to defuse, disarm, and turn discontent to his own uses.

Perhaps Satō's most outstanding success was the negotiations for Okinawa's return to Japanese rule. Although Okinawa had been under U.S. military rule since World War II, Satō made its return a top-priority objective. When he first mentioned negotiating Okinawa's return, not even his own cabinet believed it could be done, but Satō persevered until Japan had peacefully regained full sovereignty over Okinawa. It was an achievement rarely matched in the annals of international diplomacy.

From 1972 to the Present

As the Satō government seemed to run on and on, calls for his retirement began to emerge from within the LDP. The most likely successors were Fukuda Takeo and Tanaka Kakuei, two men of extremely different backgrounds.

Fukuda seemed ideally qualified. Having risen rapidly in the Ministry of Finance hierarchy before going into politics, he had served as LDP Secretary-general, Minister of Finance, and Minister of Foreign Affairs. Tanaka, on the other hand, had only a gradeschool education and had risen to prominence in the construction business. He was, however, a veteran politician, having first been elected to the House of Representatives at the age of 30. He had equally abundant experience as LDP Secretary-general and in such cabinet posts as Minister of Finance. Fukuda was a bureaucrat by background, but belonged to the Kishi school of politics. Tanaka was a politician through and through, but he was from the Satō faction. Tanaka was only fifty-four, while Fukuda was sixty-seven, and there were strong public hopes that he could rejuvenate Japanese politics.

Speculation was that Satō favored Fukuda, a man with whom he had much in common, rather than Tanaka who was from his own faction. Fukuda had often been referred to as "the crown prince" of the Satō Cabinets, and had apparently expected that Satō would convince Tanaka to withdraw. But Satō declined to state any preference. Perhaps he hoped to maintain a Yoshida-like power behind the throne after his retirement, and felt that overt support for either side would alienate the other and run counter to his own long-term interests.

Whatever his reasons, Satō remained an impartial spectator as the battle for succession unfolded. The Tanaka faction quickly lined up with the Ōhira faction, an allegiance which had been useful since the Ikeda years, and when they received the added support of the Nakasone faction, which had been straddling the fence, a majority was secured. The Tanaka faction also spent far more on its campaign than Fukuda. Rumors circulated that amounts spent surpassed all previous limits, but in retrospect the incident now appears only typical of Tanaka's "money" politics. Business secretly hoped that the tide would turn in Fukuda's favor, but no one spoke out during the election, preferring to watch from a discreet distance. When Tanaka was elected, the mass media played up his youth and forcefulness, creating a minor "Tanaka boom." Big business also moved immediately to establish friendly relations with the new Prime Minister, and Tanaka, with his grandiose plan for building a new Japan, was off to a triumphant start.

Tanaka's 1972 victory is directly related to his liberal use of the private fortune he had made in land speculation. His power was enhanced with business donations as he rose within the party and government. While he had none of the connections that came with graduation from Tōdai and a stint in the bureaucracy, he did have the very best friends that money could buy. With the advent of modern public relations, Diet elections have come to be more and more expensive. Criticism of this has continued unabated, but the situation remains unchanged and Japanese politicians are chronically strapped for funds. When Tanaka moved boldly to fill their coffers, the politicians quickly became addicted to massive injections of cash, and became proportionately indebted.

Disaster struck when the widely-read and highly-respected monthly *Bungei Shunjū* put out a comprehensive report on Tanaka's financial operations. This exposé sparked a storm of popular sentiment against Tanaka, until he was finally forced to step down in December 1974, after only two years and five months in office. Tanaka was still young, and, unlike Richard Nixon, decided to yield peacefully in the hope of someday making a comeback.

The Tanaka plan for remodeling and redeveloping the Japanese archipelago was not in itself reprehensible, but it was announced with such fanfare that land prices skyrocketed all over Japan as trading companies and other large corporations rushed to buy choice locations. In addition, the Japanese people's confidence in politics and business had been rocked by the oil crisis of 1973 and the resultant "stagflation." Faced with scandal, discontent, and suspicion, the LDP needed a new image if it was to maintain even a minimum of public trust.

The two candidates favored to succeed Tanaka were Fukuda and Ōhira Masayoshi. However, to conduct an LDP presidential election at that point would have been to concede too much publicly, and it was decided to have the party elders nominate one person whom the others would accept. Out of this process emerged an unexpected compromise candidate: Miki

Takeo. Miki was the leader of his own faction, but had the reputation of being "the perennial also-run," partly because of his lack of political strength, which in turn stemmed from his ineptitude in collecting and distributing funds. But the same weakness was also a strength, for it meant that he had a clean political image, a necessary qualification for following Tanaka. Miki was also helped by the power stalemate between Fukuda and Ōhira. Selection of either Fukuda or Ōhira would have split the LDP, but the relatively weak Miki was acceptable to all sides, and he was quickly elected in an attempt to refurbish the LDP's image.

Miki graduated from Meiji University and spent his entire adult life in politics. Originally elected to the House of Representatives in 1937 at the age of 30, he was consistently reelected throughout the War, even though he did not have military backing in these campaigns. After the War, he belonged to the People's Cooperative Party, later maneuvering himself into an advantageous position with the subsequent party realignments. In addition to being an experienced politician, he also had an extensive background of service in major party and cabinet posts.

However, dissatisfaction with Miki's performance surfaced almost as soon as he assumed office, and there was constant unrest in the LDP during his two years as Prime Minister. Rightly or wrongly, he was held responsible for large LDP losses in the 1975 general election and subsequently had to yield to Fukuda in December of 1976.

Fukuda's position was anything but secure, as Ōhira remained a dangerous competitor for the prime ministership. Nonetheless, he was open to attack on very few counts. Not only did he manage the post-oil crisis economy adroitly, he also concluded negotiations for the China-Japan Treaty of Peace and Friendship.

Ōhira graduated from Tokyo University of Commerce (now Hitotsubashi University), rising through the Ministry of Finance ranks and serving as private secretary to Ikeda when the latter was Minister of Finance. He has compiled an impressive record as Minister of Finance, Minister of International Trade and Industry, and Minister of Foreign Affairs. He is a child of the conservative mainstream, and has every qualification for the office of Prime Minister.

At present, Ōhira is the likely successor to Fukuda, but nothing is ever certain in politics. Now sixty-eight years old, Ōhira could easily lose his chance at the office were Fukuda to hang on for any extended period. Other events could also intervene. For example, the LDP's young Dietmen are very resentful of the party's domination by its old leaders. While this resentment seldom flares up, it smolders constantly beneath the surface. This danger was illustrated strikingly when Kōno Yōhei, Kōno Ichirō's son and a promising figure in his own right, bolted the party in 1976 to found a new political party of people disenchanted with the LDP. Besides Ōhira, some of the other men presently being watched as likely candidates for Prime Minister are party-politician Nakasone Yasuhiro (b. 1918), former Finance Ministry bureaucrat Miyazawa Kiichi (b. 1919), and former businessman Kōmoto Toshio (b. 1910). Yet there is no telling who will occupy the office of the Prime Minister next. As LDP strategist Kawashima Shōjirō (1890-1970) once remarked, "In politics, tomorrow is always a mystery."

Editor's Note

On December 1, 1978, Ōhira Masayoshi was elected president of the Liberal Democratic Party in the first party primary ever held in Japan. For some time many LDP party members had been calling for changes in the election procedures, whose widespread corruption was an open secret. Under the new election rules, the LDP's one and a half million members would limit the field of candidates to the two top vote-getters in a nationwide primary, after which the LDP Diet members would determine the winner in a runoff election.

Prime Minister Fukuda Takeo and Ōhira were the top contenders in a field of four candidates. As the incumbent, Fukuda was naturally expected to gain a plurality in the primary and go on to win the runoff. But the top vote-getter in the primary turned out to be Ōhira — and this by a large margin, thanks to the solid backing of the Tanaka faction. A dumb-founded Fukuda not only conceded defeat but also announced his decision not to enter the runoff election. Ōhira became party president and de facto Prime Minister from that moment.

On June 3, 1980, Ōhira suffered a heart attack and died suddenly in the middle of the election campaign. The LDP made significant and unexpected gains in the July election and, led by the Ōhira and Tanaka factions, chose Suzuki Zenkō as party president without a primary.

At the expiration of his two-year term as Prime Minister, Suzuki formally declared his decision not to come forward as a candidate. In October 1982, in the second primary of the LDP, Nakasone Yasuhiro was elected president and de facto Prime Minister with the strong backing of the Tanaka faction.

Parties, Factions, and the Diet

HANS H. BAERWALD

In the byways of Tokyo's Akasaka district just down the hill from the Diet Building are to be found numerous *ryōtei*, a term which is inadequately translated as "restaurants." Delicious food is served, and possibly far more importantly private rooms are provided for discreet conversations among Japan's political elite. In the last quarter century a sprinkling of political party leaders has always been included; it was not always so. In prewar Japan, effective power was in the hands of higher-class civilian bureaucrats (*buchō* – department manager upwards), corporation executives and senior echelons of the military. Today, the civilian bureaucracy may still constitute Japan's governing class, but it is the political party leaders who rule. Lest it be forgotten, the Diet is the instrument through which these politicians exercise their power.

Japan's political party system has undergone a number of transformations since the end of the Pacific War. In the immediate aftermath of defeat, a multi-party system emerged. There were two major conservative parties which adopted the names "Liberal" and "Progressive" (also "Democratic") and were the descendants of the prewar Seiyūkai and Minseitō respectively. Around the center of the ideological spectrum a number of minor parties emerged, of which the most significant was the "Cooperative Party" (later called the "People's Cooperative Party") under the leadership of Miki Takeo. He and his followers ultimately joined the conservatives. The Socialist Party of Japan (SPJ) quickly established itself as the major left-wing force by bringing together various strands of the prewar non-Communist left. In addition to the Japanese Communist Party (JCP), which for the first time was accorded legal status, a large number of splinter parties ran a substantial number of candidates (most of whom were unsuccessful) in the three elections held under the Occupation (1946, 1947, and 1949). Of these, only the Communists established a foothold, but one which they soon lost. It took more than twenty years for them to recover and to become a national party again.

This multi-party structure lasted until 1955 when, during a banner year, the conservatives merged into a unified Liberal Democratic Party (LDP) six months after the Socialists (who had split into "Right" and "Left" parties) in 1951 had reunited. Japan's political party system seemed to be evolving into a relatively stable two-party structure during the last half of the 1950s. Power, as measured in number of seats in the Diet, was notably unequal between the two parties, with the LDP coming close to winning two-thirds and the Socialist not quite one-third of the seats, the remainder going to a small offshoot of the SPJ and to the Communists. It was, as Scalapino and Masumi have pointed out, more properly labeled a one-and-a-half party system.[1]

A new and far more permanent split in the Socialist Party — from which the Japan Democratic Socialist Party (DSP) under Nishio Suehiro emerged as a separate entity — ushered in the 1960s. And by the middle of the decade, Sōka-Gakkai (Value-Creation Society), a neo-Buddhist religious group, spawned Kōmeitō (Clean Government Party), which carved out a distinctive but ideologically imprecise niche for itself. In the interim, the Communist Party had been slowly and painfully rehabilitating itself from the debacles of Cominform criticism and the "Red" Purge as a force in Japanese politics. These efforts paid off handsomely in the December 1972 House of Representatives election, when it won the largest number of seats ever (39 plus one "Independent"), thereby surpassing both the Kōmeitō and the Democratic Socialists. These developments did not alter the basic shape of Japan's party system, however. As has been the case for nearly the entire postwar period, and most definitely so since 1955, the conservatives in the LDP held a preponderant share of power and the Opposition was, by comparison, weak and fragmented. Table 2-1 gives a detailed overview.

Japanese newspapers tend to classify the voting public into two major groupings, the *hoshu-kei* ("conservative group") and the *kakushin-kei* ("progressive" or "reformist group"). Election results provide a somewhat different picture when viewed from this perspective rather than from one based entirely on the strengths of the various parties in the Diet. While it is virtually impossible to be completely precise about the popular vote classification in the immediate postwar years because of the multiplicity of minor parties and the large number of "Independents" who ran, it is reasonable to assert that the popular vote supporting conservative candi-

---

[1] Robert A. Scalapino and Masumi Junnosuke, *Parties and Politics in Contemporary Japan* (Berkeley and Los Angeles: University of California Press, 1962).

dates did not fall below 60% of the total, and in several elections (1949, 1952, 1953, and 1955) exceeded 65%. Since then there has been a steady, if unspectacular, decline in the percentage of conservative voters. Thus, in the 1967 election for the House of Representatives, LDP candidates for the first time collected less than 50% (offset by the votes cast for conservative candidates running without the benefit of official LDP endorsement, that is, running as Independents and aligning themselves with the LDP after the election), and in 1972 the popular vote cast for progressive candidates actually exceeded that cast for conservatives, excluding Independents.

These trends in the popular vote have been somewhat obscured by the LDP leadership's superior tactical abilities. For example, in the 1969 election the LDP won 59.2% of the seats in the House of Representatives with only 47.6% of the popular vote and 55.2% of the seats with 46.6% of the vote in 1972. Achieving these results, given the vagaries of Japan's medium-sized multiple-member constituency system (which will be discussed in detail below), places a premium on a party's capacity to endorse just the right number of candidates and to organize the voters in each district to support the party's endorsees in an even-handed fashion. Obviously, the LDP has been more adept at this than the "progressive" parties, in part because the latter contains a multiplicity of parties, not just warring factions as is the case in the LDP (though the SPJ too suffers from this kind of intramural strife), and in part because the population shift from county to city has resulted in substantial — and growing — disparities in the size of electoral districts. The latter factor has increased the voting strength of the rural and semi-rural voters, who tend to support the LDP, at the expense of the urban voters, who are more likely to support Opposition party candidates. For example, in Chiba's 1st district, which has become one of Tokyo's suburbs, an Opposition (Kōmeitō) candidate lost despite receiving 140,622 votes; while in Chiba's more rural 2nd district an Independent (LDP) candidate was elected with only 41,488 votes in the 1972 election. So long as the LDP manages to win more than 50% of the seats in the House of Representatives it is unlikely that a rapid adjustment of this kind of disparity can be anticipated; it is the Diet which controls amendments to the existing electoral law. Thus far the judiciary has avoided the issue by refusing to rule on it as a "political question."

An unevenly-shaped tripod supports the LDP. Financiers and industrialists provide financial support, either directly or through such organizations as the Keidanren (Federation of Economic Organizations), Nikkeiren (Japan Federation of Employers' Associations), and Keizai Dōyūkai (Japan Committee for Economic Development). Farmers, fishermen,

Table 2-1. House of Representatives Election Results: Seats Won

Election: year	Liberal	Party Progressive (Shinpo)	Cooperative	Independent	Minor Parties
22nd: 1946	140 (30.2%)	94 (20.3%)	14 (3.0%)	81 (17.4%)	38 (8.2%)
23rd: 1947	131 (28.1)	Democratic (Minshu) 121 (26.0)	People's Coop. 29 (6.2)	13 (2.8)	25 (5.4)
24th: 1949	Democratic Liberal 264 (56.7)	69 (14.8)	14 (3.0)	12 (2.6)	17 (3.6)
25th: 1952	Liberal 240 (51.5)	Progressive 85 (18.2)		19 (4.1)	7 (1.5)

Election					
26th: 1953	Yoshida 199 (42.7)	Hatoyama 35 (7.5)	76 (16.3)	11 (2.4)	1 (0.2)
27th: 1955	Liberal 112 (24.0)	Democratic 185 (39.6)		6 (1.3)	2 (0.4)
28th: 1958	Liberal Democratic 287 (61.5)			12 (2.6)	1 (0.2)
29th: 1960	296 (63.4)			5 (1.1)	1 (0.2)
30th: 1963	283 (60.6)			12 (2.6)	
31st: 1967	277 (57.0)			9 (1.9)	
32nd: 1969	288 (59.2)			16 (3.2)	
33rd: 1972*	271 (55.2)			14 (2.8)	2 (0.4)

Source: Adapted from Nishihara Shigeki, *Nihon no Senkyo* [Japan's Elections] (Tokyo: Shiseidō, 1972).
Asahi Shinbun, December 12, 1972.

Table 2-1. (cont.)

Election: year	Party					
	Socialist			Labor-Farmer	Communist	Total
22nd: 1946	92 (19.8%)				5 (1.1%)	464
23rd: 1947	143 (30.7)				4 (0.8)	466
24th: 1949	48 (10.3)			7 (1.5)	35 (7.5)	466
		Right Soc.	Left Soc.			
25th: 1952		57 (12.2)	54 (11.6)	4 (0.9)	0 (0)	466
26th: 1953		66 (14.2)	72 (15.4)	5 (1.1)	1 (0.2)	466
27th: 1955		67 (14.3)	89 (19.1) →Socialist	4 (0.9)	2 (0.4)	467
28th: 1958	Socialist 166 (35.5)				1 (0.2)	467

	Kōmeitō	Democratic Socialist	Socialist		
29th: 1960		17 (3.7)	145 (31.0)	3 (0.6)	467
30th: 1963		23 (4.9)	144 (30.8)	5 (1.1)	467
31st: 1967	25 (5.1)	30 (6.2)	140 (28.8)	5 (1.0)	486
32nd: 1969	47 (9.9)	31 (6.3)	90 (18.5)	14 (2.9)	486
33rd: 1972*	29 (5.9)	19 (3.9)	118 (24.0)	38 (7.7)	491

Table 2-2. House of Representatives Election Results: Popular Vote (1=1,000)

Election: year	Party				
	Progressive	Liberal		Cooperative	Independent
22nd: 1946	10,351 (18.7%)	13,506 (24.4%)		1,800 (32%)	11,325 (20.4%)
23rd: 1947	Democratic 6,840 (25.0)	7,356 (26.9)		People's Coop. 1,916 (7.0)	1,581 (5.8)
24th: 1949	4,798 (15.7)	Democratic Liberal 13,420 (43.9)		1,042 (3.4)	2,008 (6.6)
25th: 1952	Progressive 6,429 (18.2)	Liberal 16,938 (47.9)			2,355 (6.7)
26th: 1953	6,186 (17.9)	Hatoyama Liberal 3,055 (8.8)	Yoshida Liberal 13,476 (39.0)		1,524 (4.4)

	Democratic	Liberal Democratic	Liberal	
27th: 1955	13,536 (36.6)		9,849 (26.6)	
28th: 1958		22,977 (57.8)		2,381 (6.0)
29th: 1960		22,740 (57.56)		1,119 (2.83)
30th: 1963		22,424 (54.67)		1,956 (4.77)
31st: 1967		22,448 (48.8)		2,554 (5.55)
32nd: 1969		22,382 (47.63)		2,493 (5.30)
33rd: 1972		24,563 (46.8)		2,646 (5.05)

POLITICS

Table 2-2. (cont.)

Election: year	Minor Parties	Socialist		Labor-Farmer	Communist	Total
22nd: 1946	6,473 (11.7%)	9,858 (17.8%)		→	2,136 (3.8%)	55,449
23rd: 1947	1,490 (5.4)	7,176 (26.2)			1,003 (3.7)	27,362
24th: 1949	1,602 (5.2)	4,130 (13.5)		607 (2.0)	2,985 (9.7)	30,593
		Right SPJ	Left SPJ			
25th: 1952	949 (2.7)	4,108 (11.6)	3,399 (9.6)	261 (0.7)	897 (2.6)	35,337
26th: 1953	152 (0.4)	4,678 (13.5)	4,517 (13.1)	359 (1.0)	656 (1.9)	34,602

Election		Kōmeitō	Democratic Socialist	Socialist			Total
27th: 1955	497 (1.3)		5,130 (13.9)	5,683 (15.3)	358 (1.0)	733 (2.0)	37,015
28th: 1958	288 (0.7)			Socialist 13,094 (32.9)		1,012 (2.6)	39,752
29th: 1960	142 (0.35)		3,464 (8.77)	10,887 (27.56)		1,157 (2.93)	39,509
30th: 1963	60 (0.15)		3,023 (7.37)	11,907 (29.03)		1,646 (4.01)	41,017
31st: 1967	101 (0.22)	2,472 (5.38)	3,404 (7.40)	12,826 (27.89)		2,791 (4.76)	45,997
32nd: 1969	81 (0.17)	5,125 (10.91)	3,637 (7.74)	10,074 (21.44)		3,199 (6.81)	46,990
33rd:* 1972	143 (0.27)	4,437 (8.5)	3,661 (7.0)	11,479 (21.9)		5,497 (10.49)	52,425

Source: Nishihira, *Nihon no Senkyo* [Japan's Elections] p. 265.
Asahi Shinbun, December 12, 1972.

white-collar workers and junior executives make up the core of the *kōenkai* ("supporters' societies") which provide the votes. The bureaucracy provides policy and legislative guidance, and also serves as an incubator for LDP candidates. Each leg of this tripod is important and serves a dual function; each is a prop, and the hollow interior of each serves as a pipe through which demands are sent up to the leadership. It must be understood that these demands, or signals, are often contradictory. Finance Ministry bureaucrats may promote trade liberalization as a means of coping with balance of trade surpluses, and thereby possibly offsetting the need for yen revaluation, while Ministry of International Trade and Industry bureaucrats may contend that such a cure is worse than the disease. What is important is that these groups with demands who serve as props and thus have access to the pipe-lines have more influence upon the councils of the LDP than those who do not.

The Socialist and Democratic Socialist parties have trade union federations as the bases of their organizational and voting strength. Sōhyō (General Council of Japanese Trade Unions) does for the SPJ what Dōmei Kaigi (Japan Confederation of Labor) does less successfully for the DSP. Endless debates take place in both parties and the union federations with which they are affiliated concerning the advantages and disadvantages of their dependence. While neither seems willing or able to cut the mutually beneficial umbilical cords, it goes without saying that these ties also impose constraints. For the political parties, it means that ideological orientations of the union leadership must be respected even if doing so might limit the pool of potential supporters. For the unions, it means that their influence over public policy remains relatively negligible so long as the parties with which they are affiliated are parts of a permanent Opposition. Most important, it means that the trade union movement has considerably less influence in the policy-making process than the size of the trade union electorate would appear to warrant.

Both the SPJ and DSP are finding themselves challenged with increasing vigor by the rejuvenated Communist Party (JCP). The gains posted by the JCP over the last three House of Representative elections (from 5 seats in 1967 to 14 in 1969 to 38 in 1972) have been impressive and somewhat unanticipated. The JCP has the advantage of relying on its own organizational capabilities and its own fund-raising efforts instead of the trade union federations. It also has expended far more energy than the SPJ in tackling the problems of daily life, and far less on ideological debate.

Last, but by no means least of the Opposition parties is the Kōmeitō, the only genuinely new party in postwar Japan, as all of the others can trace their roots back to the prewar period. Its basic appeal has been to that segment of the Japanese public which migrated into the major urban centers in the economic boom years of the 1950s and 1960s and could not cope with the new surroundings. Originally it was the political handmaiden of the neo-Buddhist Sōka-Gakkai (Value-Creation Society), but the Kōmeitō's current relationship with this body is ambiguous. Formally, the two organizations have severed the bonds which united them, but how complete the break is remains in question. The Kōmeitō's fortunes sagged in the December 1972 election for a number of reasons. Undoubtedly, the aftermath of the separation from the parent body played a role; so did a series of well-publicized, particularly by the JCP, scandals involving alleged interference with freedom of the press; also its fuzzy ideological image together with its seeming vacillation *vis-à-vis* the LDP contributed to voter disenchantment. Additionally, its candidates who were faced with Communist opponents did not fare well in several urban districts. It remains to be seen whether it is the Kōmeitō or the JCP which has been the proverbial flash in the pan.

Certain other aspects of the Japanese political party system require some elaboration to understand the behavior of their representatives in both chambers of the Diet. First, and possibly foremost, a deep and seemingly irreconcilable ideological chasm has persisted between the conservatives and progressive "houses" for the greater part of the postwar period. This chasm was particularly evident with respect to foreign policy problems such as the alliance with the United States — conservatives generally in favor of it, progressives generally opposed — or policy towards China — until the summer of 1972 the conservatives had generally supported the maintenance of official ties with Taiwan, whereas the progressives had tended to favor early establishment of official diplomatic relations with the People's Republic of China. There were also profound differences over perennial domestic issues such as constitutional revision, which was favored by a highly vocal segment of the conservatives and bitterly opposed by the progressives. In this context, the progressives perceive the Constitution — despite its fundamentally foreign parentage — as the embodiment of democratic ideals, a view which is not shared by certain leading conservatives, including former Prime Minister Kishi.

These profound differences over fundamental areas of national policy, to the degree that they reflect major fissures in the Japanese body politic, have complicated the traditional Japanese search for consensus and accomodation as it is conducted in the Diet. On a number of notable occasions, the best publicized of which was the 1960 imbroglio over the acceptance of the revised U.S.-Japan Security Treaty, these differences have led to a complete breakdown in the Diet's operations. Moreover, it is in-

34 POLITICS

Table 2-3. House of Representatives Election Results

Election		Liberal	Progr.	Coop.	Ind.	Minor Parties		Socialist	Labor-Farmer	JCP
22nd: 1946	A. B.	24.4 30.2	18.7 20.3	3.2 3.0	20.4 17.4	11.7 8.2		17.8 19.8		3.8 1.1
23rd: 1947	A. B.	26.9 28.1	Democ. 25.0 26.0	7.0 6.2	5.8 2.8	5.4 5.4		26.2 30.7		3.7 0.8
24th: 1949	A. B.	Democ-Liberal 43.9 56.7	15.7 14.8	3.4 3.0	6.6 2.6	5.2 3.6		13.5 10.3	2.0 1.5	9.7 7.5
25th: 1952	A. B.	Liberal 47.9 51.5	Progressive 18.2 18.2		6.7 4.1	2.7 1.5	Right SPJ 11.6 12.2	Left SPJ 9.6 11.6	0.7 0.9	2.6 0
26th: 1953	A. B.	Yoshida Lib. 39.0 42.7	Hatoyama Lib. 8.8 7.5	Progressive 17.9 16.3	4.4 2.4	0.4 0.2	13.5 14.2	13.1 15.4	1.0 1.1	1.9 0.2

		Liberal	Democratic					Socialist		
27th: 1955	A.	26.6	36.6	3.3	1.3		13.9	15.3	1.0	2.0
	B.	24.0	39.6	1.3	0.4		14.3	19.1	0.9	0.4
			Liberal Democratic					Socialist		
28th: 1958	A.		57.8	6.0	0.7			32.9		2.6
	B.		61.5	2.6	0.2			35.5		0.2
							Democ. Soc.			
29th: 1960	A.		57.6	2.8	0.4		8.8	27.6		2.9
	B.		63.4	1.1	0.2		3.7	31.0		0.6
30th: 1963	A.		54.7	4.8	0.15		7.4	29.0		4.0
	B.		60.6	2.6	—		4.9	30.8		1.1
						Komeitō				
31st: 1967	A.		48.8	5.6	0.22	5.4	7.4	27.9		4.8
	B.		57.0	1.9	—	5.1	6.2	28.8		1.0
32nd: 1969	A.		47.6	5.3	0.17	10.9	7.7	21.4		6.8
	B.		59.2	3.2	—	9.9	6.3	18.5		2.9
33rd: 1972	A.		46.8	5.0	0.3	8.5	7.0	21.9		10.5
	B.		55.2	2.8	0.4	5.9	3.9	24.0		7.7

Source: Based on Tables 2-1 and 2-2. A: % of popular vote. B: % of seats won.

correct to assume that the periodic breakdowns in decorum within the halls of the Diet are the only occasions when this lack of a national consensus has become manifest. It is and has been a constant factor. Only the degree of its intensity has varied.

Second, nearly all of the postwar Cabinets have been the exclusive preserve of the conservatives. Indeed, there was only one brief interregnum (1947-8) during which the Socialists shared in the exercise of executive power by participating in two coalition Cabinets. In the first of these (May 1947-March 1948) Katayama Tetsu, a Socialist, served as Prime Minister, a post he relinquished to Ashida Hitoshi, a Democrat (conservative), during the second (March-October 1948). With this limited exception — notable primarily for its brevity, although Socialist purists maintain that their comrades eternally compromised themselves by participating in these Cabinets and thus have adversely affected the party's capacity to gain the full support of the progressive voters — representatives drawn from the ranks of the "reformists" have not had administrative experience and therefore allegedly lack a sense of responsibility. It might be noted that while valid at the national level, this reproof is not well-founded with regard to the prefectural (provincial) level. Governor Minobe of Tokyo, a Socialist and former Tokyo University of Education professor of economics, is the best known of several leaders in this category. Nonetheless, in the exercise of executive power at the national level, it is the conservatives who have prevailed.

Third, party leaders demand — and in the overwhelming majority of instances receive — absolute obedience from their followers when there is a formal ballot in the Diet. One notable exception to this generalization was provided by Shiga Yoshio, a Communist, who decided to defy the wishes of the JCP's leadership by voting for the Partial Nuclear Test Ban Treaty in 1963. For his audacity he was expelled from the party, and he promptly formed the *Nihon no Koe* (Voice of Japan) Communist Party. In this instance, Shiga was responding to Moscow's rather than Peking's signals; the latter were stronger in the JCP at the time. Generally, however, resorting to a specific sanction — e.g. expulsion — is not necessary. Instead, party leaders can rely on the traditional Japanese virtue of loyalty and the extraordinarily strong sense of group identity that is to be found in all walks of Japanese life. Furthermore, all differences of viewpoint will have been thrashed out at an earlier, pre-parliamentary, stage of the legislative process. For many reasons, then, formal votes in the Diet are nearly always cast along the strictest of party lines.

Since its creation in 1955 the conservative Liberal Democratic Party has used each of these factors to its own advantage. When it has wanted to do so it has been willing to use the absolute majority that it has consistently won in both chambers of the Diet; it has demanded and received disciplined voting from its members; and it has tried to play the role of consensus-builder — in accord with hallowed tradition — when that has been deemed to be advantageous.

By contrast, the Opposition parties have been relatively impotent over the last quarter century, in large part because they have never come even close to controlling a majority of seats in either chamber. As a consequence, and most particularly when the LDP resorts to tactics of confrontation, the Opposition shouts "Foul!" (what else can they do?) and accuses the LDPers of using their majority in a tyrannical fashion. This indictment has peculiar potency in the context of Japanese society because of the high value that is placed on reaching the broadest conceivable consensus. When this search for consensus fails, as it must, given the ideological disparities that persist, the Diet's decorum is marred by scenes of near violence.

One overriding feature of Japanese political parties renders the foregoing description incomplete, accurate though it may be if attention is accorded only to the formal votes that are cast. Appearances of unity within each of the parties during formal decisions in the Diet are deceptive, for they hide the intense bargaining that has taken place inside the parliamentary parties at earlier stages of the policy-making and legislative processes. Especially in the cases of the LDP and SPJ, the facade of unity during Diet votes that each party seeks to project to the public obscures the considerable amount of strife that exists fairly constantly in each. It is the factions (*habatsu*) which are the real actors in intra-party politics in Japan. Their importance, especially in the LDP, cannot be overemphasized. It is the factions which have provided the most crucial leavening element in what might otherwise have become an LDP bulldozer and a relatively dull scene.

Factionalism can probably be traced back for many centuries, and is to be found in all segments of Japanese society. Indeed, one way of looking at Japan's modern political history is to view it as consisting of the rise and fall of various *batsu* (the generic root for "faction"), such as the *zaibatsu* (finance, business, and industry), *gunbatsu* (the military), *kanbatsu* (civilian bureaucracy), or a particular division of the *gakubatsu* (school or university), not to overlook *keibatsu* (family) *ad infinitum*. Factions have played so central a role in the recent evolution of Japan's political parties that any understanding of the legislative process must begin with a brief elaboration of the reasons for their existence in, and their effect upon, the parties, particularly the LDP and the SPJ.

That the LDP is a coalition of factions has become a cliche. Nonetheless it bears repetition if for no other reason than that America's most distinguished Ambassador to Japan, Dr. Edwin O. Reischauer, at his farewell press conference in Tokyo's Ōkura Hotel in effect scolded some of the American journalists (and others like myself who were present at the occasion) for being excessively concerned with factionalism in their analyses of Japanese politics. It seems to me that too little attention is accorded to factionalism by either foreign journalists and scholars in writing about or discussing that country's politics. Therefore I would like to invite the reader's attention to the question not of whether, but of why there are factions in the LDP and why they are influential.

First of all, the LDP is like a major river into which various tributaries have flowed. Even in terms of the simplest schematic representation, it is necessary to mention that each of the two major conservative parties that combined to form the LDP, that is, the "Liberal" and "Democratic" parties, brought with them their own internal divisions. Hence, the concept of the LDP as two parties brought together under one name is an oversimplification; the Liberal Party had been divided into the Hatoyama and Yoshida wings, and the Democratic Party had gone through a number of different incarnations in the immediate postwar years, each leaving its mark. Given the importance that is accorded to group loyalty in Japan, it is therefore not surprising that there are rivalries among those who trace their initial allegiance to various wings and incarnations. All of the LDPers may quite properly be labeled as conservatives, but the meaning of that label is imprecise and covers a broad spectrum of attitudes. Opposition to the "progressives" is the principal ingredient that holds them together, as is evidenced by the fact that the LDP came into existence in response to the — temporary — reunification of the Socialist Party.

A second factor, which is becoming considerably less important as the years go by and mortality takes its toll, is the conflict between those conservatives who were temporarily removed from active political life under the Occupation-induced purge of militarists and ultranationalists and those who had emerged as leaders during the years that their brethren were *persona non grata*. Hatoyama Ichirō, the unifier of the conservatives and first president of the LDP, had been declared "undesirable" by the Occupation on the eve of his election as Prime Minister in the spring of 1946. At the time, an agreement was ostensibly made between himself and his successor, Yoshida Shigeru, that when Hatoyama would be permitted to return to active political life, Yoshida would restore to him the reins of power. This well-publicized "secret" agreement was not honored by Prime Minister Yoshida. Earlier supporters of these gentlemen encountered some

Table 2-4. Actual Party Strengths in House of Representatives, 1961-73

Year	LDP	Ind.	Kōmeitō	DSP	SPJ	JCP	Total Opposition	Vacant	Total
1961	297	3		16	142	3	161	6	467
1962	295	3		15	142	3	160	9	467
1963	290	3		15	139	3	157	17	467
1964	289	1		23	144	4	171	6	467
1965	283	2		23	145	4	172	10	467
1966	279	3		23	142	4	169	16	467
1967	284	4	25	31	141	5	202		486[a]
1968	280	4	25	31	139	5	200	2	486
1969	275	2	25	31	137	4	197	12	486
1970	300	3	47	32	90	14	183		486
1971	301	2	47	30	91	14	182	6	491[b]
1972	296	3	47	29	87	14	177	15	491
1973	284	1[c]	29	20	118	39	207		491

[a]Subsequent to reapportionment adding 19 seats.
[b]Subsequent to reversion of Okinawa Prefecture adding 5 seats.
[c]Ind. elected with joint backing of JCP-SPJ, hence Opposition.

Sources: *Kokkai Binran* [Diet Handbook] (Tokyo: Nihon Seikei Shinbunsha, 1961, 1962, 1963, 1964, 1965, 1966, 1967, 1968, 1969, 1970, 1971, 1972, 1973).

difficulty, understandably enough, in becoming happy swimmers in the same LDP stream.

A third factor, also exemplified by the Hatoyama-Yoshida split, was and remains the substantial difference in orientation between those who entered political life through participation in local, prefectural or national legislatures as opposed to those who entered from the bureaucracy. In Japanese parlance, this is referred to as the division between *tōjin* (partymen) and the *kanryō* (bureaucrats). If Hatoyama epitomized the *tōjin* by having been re-elected thirteen times to the House of Representatives, Yoshida was the archetype of the ex-bureaucrat who came to dominate the LDP in the postwar period. Indeed, nearly all of the Prime Ministers have been drawn from the latter ranks: Shidehara Kijūrō (Foreign Ministry) 1945-6, Ashida Hitoshi (Foreign Ministry) 1948, Yoshida Shigeru (Foreign Ministry) 1946-7, 1948-54, Kishi Nobusuke (Commerce and Industry Ministry) 1957-60, Ikeda Hayato (Finance Ministry) 1960-4, Satō Eisaku (Transportation Ministry) 1964-72. In this context, the accession of Tanaka Kakuei to the presidency of the LDP and Prime Ministership in the summer of 1972 was a minor revolution. He was not an ex-bureaucrat — and his formal education had ended with elementary school.

Prime Minister Tanaka also reflects some of the ambiguities in the *tōjin* v. *kanryō* distinction. He was for many years a loyal retainer in former Prime Minister Satō's faction, and Satō had not only been a bureaucrat, but had been brought into parliamentary politics by Yoshida. In terms of lineage, Tanaka is another graduate of the so-called Yoshida school, which, in the persons of Ikeda and Satō, dominated the pinnacle of the LDP in the 1960s. Despite this kind of imprecision, the distinction between the *tōjin* and the *kanryō* is a reality that is felt and that is consequential in intra-LDP maneuvering.

Seiji shikin (political funds), or to put it less elegantly *o-kane* (money) provides the fourth factor contributing to factionalism in the LDP. While the party is generally conceded to be the wealthiest in Japan (technically, official reports indicate that the JCP — as a party — overtook the LDP in fiscal 1972; but that is misleading since the LDP factions also have their own sources of funds), its wealth is insufficient to support all of its endorsed candidates adequately. By the same token, few candidates can make up out of their own pockets the difference between what the party provides and what is required. Substantial sums are involved. Newspapermen estimated that many LDPers needed ¥100 million yen (*ichi-oku en*) each, or approximately $333,333.00 at the exchange rate then prevailing, to win and that might well lose if they had only 70 million yen (*nana-sen-man en*), or $233,333.00, in their campaign kitties. These estimates brought a new shorthand phrase, "*ittō-nanaraku*" ("win with one [hundred], lose with 70"), into the highly malleable Japanese language.[2]

This kind of money is not readily available, not even in certain of the increasingly affluent sectors of the Japanese economy. Hence, an aspiring candidate for a Diet seat, after receiving official party funds and contributions from his local supporters, usually finds it necessary to approach one of the faction leaders for about 25% of his campaign budget. Conversely, one of the principal prerequisites for becoming a faction leader (*oyabun*, literally translated "boss") is the ability to raise political funds. It is to be understood that the sums in Table 2-5 reflect only those that these major LDP factions have officially reported under the terms of the Political Contribution Control Law. How accurately they reflect actual income is a matter of considerable controversy. It would probably be fair to conclude that they reflect orders of magnitude, which are useful both for purposes

[2] Please see my "Ittō-Nanaraku: Japan's 1969 General Election," *Asian Survey*, March 1970.

of comparison and as indicators of which factions are in ascendancy and which in decline.

More importantly, even this level of available funding to each faction contributes to an understanding of why factions manage to survive as separate entities. On the basis of officially reported sums for the same periods in the above-mentioned report the income of the LDP, as a party, was ¥5,888 million and ¥1,898 million for 1971 and 1972 respectively. On that basis, the Ōhira and Tanaka factions each had incomes in excess of one-third of the total for the LDP, the Fukuda faction nearly 28%, the Miki faction 22.6%, and so forth for the first six months of 1972. It is no wonder that factionalism continues to thrive within the bosom of the LDP.

The amount of money a faction leader has access to obviously influences the number of LDPers, either as candidates or elected Dietmen, he can help to support, and who are therefore likely to become his followers. This factor becomes particularly salient at LDP conventions. Contests for the coveted post of party president, which automatically brings with it the Prime Ministership so long as the LDP retains its majority in the House of Representatives, are rarely charades. Alliances which are made, coalitions which are built, promises which are kept — and occasionally broken — during the course of these elections for LDP president provide the fifth reason for the persistence of factionalism.

A faction leader's power tends to be a reflection of the number of followers he has in the House of Representatives. Factionalism is less strong in the House of Councillors; and although LDP members of that House are also voting delegates to the party conventions, their votes are less crucial than those cast by the delegates who are members of the House of Representatives. It is the latter who predominate in the election of the Prime Minister. In this instance the formal allocation of power is mirrored in reality. If the leader has many followers, his ability to bargain with other faction bosses is enhanced, as is his ability to declare his own candidacy for the office of party president. However, the larger the number of his followers, the greater is the drain on his financial resources. Former LDP Vice-President Kawashima Shōjirō maintained that the optimum factional size was 25 Representatives. It was his contention that a faction boss could not provide adequate services to his followers if the faction's size exceeded that number. By "services," he was understood to mean financial support and assistance in securing for his followers Cabinet portfolios, Diet Committee chairmanships, parliamentary vice-ministerships, or important party posts. Less than 25 members would result in a loss of influence and bargaining power with the party president or the

POLITICS

Table 2-5. Liberal Democratic Party and Major LDP Factions' Political Funds (¥1,000)

		Jan.-June 1971	Income Jan.-June 1972	1971-1972 Increase or (−) decrease
	Liberal Democratic Party	5,880,000	1,890,000	−3,990,000
Ōhira Masayoshi	Shin Sangyō Seisaku Kenkyūkai [New Industries Policy Study Association]	112,240	355,700	243,460
	Shin Zaisei Kenkyūkai [New Financial Affairs Study Association]	137,710	330,370	192,660
	Total:	249,950	686,070	436,120
Tanaka Kakuei	Etsuzankai [Etsuzan Association]	151,892	199,240	47,348
	Zaisei Chōsakai [Financial Affairs Research Association]	64,442	143,854	79,412
	Shin Seikei Shinkōkai [New Politico-Economic Progress Association]	23,012	120,987	97,975
	Seiji Keizai Chōsakai [Politico-Economic Research Association]	50,266	107,171	56,905
	Keizai Shakai Kenkyūkai [Socio-Economic Research Association]	22,771	96,784	74,013
	Total:	312,383	668,036	355,653
Fukuda Takeo	Jikyoku Keizai Mondai Konwakai [Econ. Circumstances-Problems Conversation Society]	137,443	221,836	84,393
	Chiyoda Keizai Mondai Konwakai [Chiyoda Econ. Problems Conversation Society]	93,610	199,299	104,689
	Shin Seiji Keizai Kenkyūkai [New Politics-Economics Study Association]	55,567	106,914	51,347
	Total:	286,620	527,049	240,429

Miki Takeo	Seisaku Kondankai [Policy Consultation Society]	111,700	350,700	239,000
	Kindaika Kenkyūkai [Modernization Study Association]	17,170	78,000	60,830
	Total:	128,870	428,700	299,830
Nakasone Yasuhiro	Kindai Seiji Kenkyūkai [Modern Politics Study Association]	67,300	129,767	62,467
	Shin Seiji Chōsakai [New Politics Research Association]	99,860	121,560	21,700
	Sannō Keizai Kenkyūkai [Sannō Economics Study Association]	12,000	42,000	30,000
	Total:	179,160	293,327	114,167
Mizuta Mikio	Tatsumikai [Tatsumi Association]	0	104,550	104,550
	Rissuikai [Rissui Association]	54,900	83,690	28,790
	Total:	54,900	188,240	133,340
Satō Eisaku	Seikei Kenkyūkai [Politico-Economic Study Association]	124,066	101,659	−22,407
	Asia Kenkyo [Asia Study]	53,350	36,700	−16,650
	Ikuseikai [Political Education Society]	49,300	31,000	−18,300
	Total:	226,716	169,359	−57,357

Source: *Mainichi Shinbun*, January 12, 1973, p. 2. (Courtesy of George O. Totten.)

other faction bosses.[3] Yet, the record indicates that for a leader to have a reasonable chance for success in running to win for the party's presidency — contests for which were held every two years until 1972, but under the new party rules occur only every three years — the minimum number in his faction must be around 45 members in the House of Representatives. Thus, Ikeda had 53 personal factional followers in the House of Representatives when he became Premier, Satō had 49, and Tanaka 43. On the other hand, Kawashima undoubtedly had a point in that excessively large factions tend to develop sub-factions. For example, during the latter years of his Prime-Ministership, Satō's faction had become an unwieldy grouping of about 60 members; the faction really consisted of two separate entities, one pledged to Tanaka, who served Satō as Party Secretary-General for many years, and the other to Hori Shigeru, who served Satō as Chief Cabinet Secretary for much of the same period. Hori ultimately linked his fortunes to those of Fukuda Takeo, who in turn ran as the major rival candidate against Tanaka in the July 1972 LDP Convention. Regardless of how questions of money and factional size are dealt with, it is clear that contests for the party presidency serve to perpetuate whatever tendencies toward factionalism may already exist.

The unique medium-sized multiple-member district system under which candidates for Japan's House of Representatives are elected provides the sixth factor promoting factionalism. There are 124 districts, each returning three, four, or five members, depending upon the district's population. Voters write the name of one candidate on blank ballots, thus precluding multiple or weighted voting. It is a system which seems to have been peculiarly well-designed to drive campign managers and their candidates to distraction and despair, and which is exceptionally well-suited to exacerbating intra-party factional strife. Not all parties run more than one candidate per district, of course. For example, until the December 1972 election the JCP had always run only one, but broke with tradition by running two in Kyoto's 1st constituency. Both won.

The LDP, however, must run more than one candidate per district since the mathematics of winning a majority of seats in the House of Representatives requires it to do so. The House currently has 491 members; a bare majority would be 246; but there are only 124 districts. Hence, it is necessary to have two successful LDP candidates per constituency at the very least. Complicating these calculations is the declining strength of LDP

---

[3] Conversation with the late Kawashima Shōjirō, former Vice-President of the LDP in Hakone at a seminar-meeting of his faction to which he had been kind enough to invite me, August 8-10, 1963.

support in urban districts. For example, there was one urban district, Aichi's 6th (the city of Nagoya) in which no LDP member won in 1972. In effect, this means that the LDP must run more than two candidates in certain rural districts where "conservative" sentiment remains strong.

Thus the first task of the LDP's leadership is to determine the optimum number of candidates it should endorse. If too many aspirants receive the party's blessing there is the risk that available voting strength will be spread too thin. To endorse too few may embitter candidates who are not anointed and conceivably drive their supporters into the arms of one of the Opposition party candidates. In the 1972 contest, the LDP endorsed five candidates in Kumamoto's 1st district, a five-member constituency. Three were incumbents, each belonging to a different faction (Fukuda, Ōhira, and Miki). Of the two newcomers, one had pledged himself to Nakasone, and the other's affiliation was the very small Hayakawa grouping, an offshoot of the Miki faction. What made the whole matter of endorsement delicate was that the LDP had almost consistently won four of the five seats over the last five elections. By spreading itself to endorse the fifth candidate the LDP actually lost a seat, winning only 3 and allowing two Opposition party candidates (the incumbent Kōmeitōite and a new SPJer) to be elected. Furthermore, one of the LDP incumbents in the Miki faction was supplanted by a newcomer to the Nakasone faction, who had the good fortune of inheriting his deceased father's support organization.

In Kumamoto's 2nd district, the situation was even more complicated for the LDP. It too was a five-man constituency which had also consistently given four of its seats to the LDP. Endorsement was restricted to four (two Fukuda faction followers, an Ishii supporter, and a Tanaka man). So far so good, but additionally there were six "Independents" who were running, and all of them were "conservatives." What made the situation particularly poignant for Fukuda was not only that two of the incumbents were his followers, one of whom — Sonoda Sunao — was a recent convert who had previously been the leader of his own faction, but also that one of the "Independents" had been a private secretary or administrative assistant to Fukuda himself. In this instance, the LDP did retain its four seats — despite the district being the home of the infamous Minamata disease — but in the process one of the officially endorsed candidates, a follower of Prime Minister Tanaka, was defeated by one of the "Independents" who surfaced as a Nakasone supporter.[4]

Not all districts provide such difficulties for the LDP. There are some in which the election of their candidates is a foregone conclusion as soon as the formal party endorsements are made, providing — and the proviso is heavy with consequences — the party endorses the right number. One of these is Gunma's 3rd, a district justly famous by having two well-known candidates, Minister of State, and former Foreign Minister, Fukuda Takeo and Minister of International Trade and Industry Nakasone Yasuhiro. It is worth adding that both are also leaders of large factions in the LDP and that the former is a past and still potential LDP presidential candidate, and the latter a likely one for the near future.[5] Table 2-6 provides an overview of electoral results in this district over the last six elections.

After even a cursory glance at the results of the last three elections one could predict that the voters in Gunma's 3rd would send three LDPers to the House of Representatives, with the fourth seat reserved for a SPJer. Furthermore, given the weakness of the JCP in the district, the results to be obtained on December 10, 1972, were forecast with complete confidence as soon as the LDP and the SPJ had made their official endorsements and it was clear that no "Independent" would be foolish enough to declare his candidacy. What, then, could explain the intensely feverish campaigning that could be observed?[6]

Undoubtedly, the motivations of the campaign workers were varied. One overriding concern that goaded members of the Fukuda or Nakasone camps was the question of which of the two leaders would be returned as *saikō* or "number one." Fukuda had attained this coveted position regularly until the 1969 election, during which Nakasone's supporters had put forth a prodigious effort and enabled their leader to emerge triumphant. Fukuda's troops were not inclined to forget that "debacle" (obviously, merely to win a seat is poor solace), nor were they willing to forgive Nakasone for having supported Mr. Tanaka's bid for the LDP presidency at the party convention five months earlier. After all, no citizen of Gunma in Japanese history had ever come as close to becoming Prime Minister as Fukuda had on that occasion — only to have the prize plucked from

---

[4] Nishihira Shigeki, *Nihon no Senkyo*, pp. 414-15; *Shūgiin Giin Sōsenkyo Rikkōhosha* [Candidates for the House of Representatives General Election] (Tokyo: Jiyū Minshutō [LDP], November 23, 1972), p. 50; *Asahi Shinbun*, December 11, 1972, p. 2.

[5] It is also a district made famous in American analyses of Japanese politics in Nathaniel B. Thayer's *How the Conservatives Rule Japan* (Princeton University Press, 1969), pp. 98-102.

[6] Based on a personal tour of Gunma's 3rd district December 8, 1972. I am deeply indebted to Mr. Sam Jameson, Tokyo correspondent of the *Los Angeles Times*, who made all the arrangements, and to the campaign managers and workers in Mr. Fukuda's and Mr. Nakasone's camps who extended every possible courtesy.

Table 2-6. House of Representatives Election Results in Gunma's 3rd District

Candidate	Party	1958	1960	1963	1967	1969	1972
Fukuda Takeo	LDP	88,027	92,099[b]	95,378[b]	100,573[b]	99,466[a]	178,281[b]
Nakasone Yasuhiro	LDP	70,852[a]	76,274[a]	84,504[a]	72,731[a]	106,823[b]	93,879[a]
Kurihara Toshio	SPJ	53,237[a]	44,463[a]	44,496[a]	43,348	—	—
Obuchi Mitsuhira	LDP	49,762[a]	Obuchi Keizō (son)	47,350[a]	61,543[a]	50,185[a]	37,258[a]
Mutō Unjūrō	SPJ	35,457					
Yamaguchi Tsuruo	SPJ		39,398[a]	43,774	50,747[a]	59,659[a]	57,909[a]
Shōga Kenji	DSP	—	29,313	—	—	—	—
Niwayama Akira	Kōmeitō	—	—	—	—	35,942	—
Various Candidates	JCP	5,017	6,330	6,916	9,919	10,764	18,544

Adapted from Nishihara, *Nihon no Senkyo*, p. 326 (1958-69) and *Asahi Shinbun*, December 11, 1972, p. 2 (1972).

[a]Victor in the four-seat district.
[b]Top victor.

his grasp with the well-publicized assistance of that "terrible apostate" Nakasone. Thus on this occasion Fukuda not only came in first, but by a margin of nearly two to one, the largest ever. Mr. Nakasone, the third LDPer Obuchi, and the SPJer Yamaguchi were all also re-elected as predicted.

As has become amply clear by now, each district has its own characteristics. In nearly all of them, intra-party factional strife tends to be more important than the ostensible battle among the different parties. While these battles between presumed comrades-in-arms can be destructive of party unity (more on that later), they can also, as in Gunma's 3rd, serve to turn out the vote in contests which might otherwise induce voter apathy. Whatever the final balance of pluses and minuses one might wish to draw up, one point is clear: multiple-member constituencies do tend to promote factionalism within the LDP.

The seventh and final factor contributing to factionalism in the LDP is the most difficult to pin down because of its quicksilver properties. What is involved is the whole matter of public policy and the issue of tactics to be employed by the LDP towards the parties of the Opposition. LDPers tend to be highly pragmatic in their approach to politics, or to put it another way, are perfectly willing to permit others the privilege of being ideological or principled. (No implication is intended that ideology and principle are synonymous.) Yet, questions of policy do occasionally contribute to factional strife. Approval of the revised Security Treaty with the United States in the spring of 1960 was one such issue, as was the whole question of China policy. On the latter, for example, it was generally conceded that most of the so-called "Taiwan Lobby" supported Mr. Fukuda, whereas most of those favoring the re-establishment of relations with the People's Republic of China (PRC) were backers of Mr. Tanaka in the July 1972 Convention of the LDP. It would be totally misleading to conclude that this division over an issue of policy was the determining factor in trying to explain why Tanaka emerged victorious. At most it was marginal and quite possibly largely fictitious in that even if Fukuda had won he too would have undertaken a rapprochement with the PRC. There might have been a slightly different timetable involved, and there might also have been certain differences in nuance in the Japanese government's dealings with Taiwan. On elements of basic substance there would have been virtually no difference.

What creates perplexity in attempting to assess the influence of policy as an element in factional strife is its ambiguity. That is to say, one is never certain whether advocacy of an alternative policy contributes to factional strife or, conversely, that the requirements of factionalism demand the espousal of substitute ideas. It has not been uncommon for individuals to change their stands in accordance with whether they were moving into or out of the mainstream coalition in the party. If nothing else — and, on occasion this can be of more than passing consequence — factionalism does assist in the ventilation of alternative approaches to questions of public policy. Whether this process actually promotes factionalism cannot be conclusively answered.

In one respect there does appear to be a fairly constant division between two major groupings of factions in the LDP. On the surface it is a matter of style; at a deeper level it involves fundamental questions of parliamentarism, for at issue is the way in which the LDP as the majority party relates to the parties of the Opposition, especially the SPJ and the JCP. Some LDPers are eager to engage in tactics of confrontation, whereas others are far more interested in searching for areas of accommodation or agreement. Those of the former persuasion are generally labeled as belonging to the "Old Right" (that is more conservative), while the latter have been dubbed the "New Right" (that is more liberal). These disparate tendencies do exist, but they do not follow factional lines. In other words, a generally "Old Right" faction such as Fukuda's may well contain some "New Rightists," whereas such "New Right" factions as Miki's, Nakasone's and Ōhira's may also include some staunch conservatives in their ranks. Nonetheless, which style predominates in the coalition controlling a cabinet profoundly affects the Diet's operations. It, probably more than anything else, determines whether a particular session is going to be relatively stormy or comparatively placid.

While there are too many variables to encourage any absolute gauging of factional influence in the foregoing area, that influence can be measured with considerable accuracy in a related sphere, the making of personnel decisions. The selection of important LDP officials, Cabinet Ministers, Diet Committee chairmen, and parliamentary vice-ministers simply cannot be comprehended without considering the role of factions. This theme will recur in various contexts, but for the moment it will be illustrated by using Prime Minister Tanaka's Cabinet, established on December 22, 1972, as a case in point.

One noteworthy feature of this Cabinet is the rapidity with which it was formed. The House of Representatives election had been held on December 10. At its initial plenary session held during the afternoon of the 22nd, the first order of business was the election of the new Speaker and Vice-Speaker. It was a foregone conclusion that the candidates put forth by the LDP would win, and so they did. Nakamura Umekichi (Nakasone faction) was elected Speaker with 300 (of 485) votes and Akita

50 POLITICS

Table 2-7. The Second Tanaka Cabinet, formed December 22, 1972

Post, Ministry	Name	Age	No. of times elected	District	Faction
Prime Minister	TANAKA Kakuei	54	11	Niigata 3	Tanaka
Justice	TANAKA Isaji	66	12	Kyoto 1	Ishii
Foreign Affairs	ŌHIRA Masayoshi	62	9	Kagawa 2	Ōhira
Finance	AICHI Kiichi	65	7 + 1*	Miyagi 1	Tanaka
Education	OKUNO Seisuke	59	4	Nara	none
Welfare	SAITŌ Kunikichi	63	6	Fukushima 3	Ōhira
Agric. and Forestry	SAKURAUCHI Yoshio	60	9 + 1*	Shimane	Nakasone
Internal Trade and Industry	NAKASONE Yasuhiro	54	11	Gunma 3	Nakasone
Transportation	SHINTANI Torasaburō	70	5*	Nara	Ishii (Tanaka)
Posts and Telecomm.	KUNO Chūji	62	10	Aichi 2	Tanaka
Labor	KATŌ Tsunetarō	67	9 + 1*	Kagawa 2	Miki
Construction	KANEMARU Shin	58	6	Yamanashi	Tanaka
Autonomy (Home)	ESAKI Masumi	57	11	Aichi 3	Mizuta
Deputy Prime Min. Dir. Gen'l Envir. Agency	MIKI Takeo	65	14	Tokushima	Miki
Chief Cabinet Sec.	NIKAIDŌ Susumu	63	9	Kagoshima 3	Tanaka

Table 2-7. (cont.)

Education	Pre-Diet career	Selected prior important posts
Central Tech. Sch.	Business; construction	Min. of Post & Telecomm., Finance, Int. Trade & Ind.; LDP Policy Bd. Chr., Sec. Gen'l.
Ritsumeikan U.	Lawyer, local assembly	Min. of Justice, Autonomy (Home)
Tokyo U. of Commerce (Hitotsubashi)	Finance M. bureaucrat	Min. of Foreign Affairs, Int. Trade & Ind.; Chief Cabinet Sec.; LDP Policy Bd. Chr.
Tokyo U.–Law	Finance M. bureaucrat	Min. of Foreign Affairs, Justice, Autonomy (Home); Dir. Gen'l. Economic Planning Agency; Chief Cab. Sec.
Tokyo U.–Law	Home M. bureaucrat	Admin. Vice-Min. Autonomy (Home); Director LDP Gen'l. Affairs Bureau
Tokyo U.–Law	Labor M. bureaucrat	Admin. Vice-Min. Labor; Deputy Chief Cab. Sec.; LDP Deputy Sec. Gen'l.
Keiō U.–Econ.	Corp. exec.	Min. of Transp.; Min. of State, Science Bd. Deputy Chr.; LDP Deputy Sec. Gen'l.
Tokyo U.–Law	Writer; parliamentarian	Min. of Transp.; Min. of State, Science & Tech. Agency, Defense Agency
Tokyo U.–Law	Post. and Telecomm. Min. bureaucrat	Min. of Post & Telecommunications
Tōkai Middle School	Business; construction	LDP Policy Bd. Dep. Chr.; Chr. HR Committees: Constr., Cabinet, Educ, House Mgt.
Mukden For. Laws	Steamship co. exec.	Chr. HR Committees: Posts & Telecomm., Construction
Tokyo Agric. Coll.	Construc. co. exec.	LDP Diet Policy Comm. Chr.
Nihon U.–Econ.	Corp. exec.	Min. of State: Defense Agency (twice); LDP Diet Policy Comm. Chr.
Meiji U.–Law	Parliamentarian	Min. of Comm., Transp., Int'l Trade & Ind., Foreign Affairs; Min. of States Econ. Pl. Agency, Science & Tech. Agency; LDP Sec. Gen'l, Policy Bd. Chr.
U. of S. Calif.	Foreign & Navy Ministry bureaucrat	LDP Deputy Sec. Gen'l (twice); Chr. HR Comm.: Construc., Commerce & Ind.

52 POLITICS

Table 2-7. (cont.)

Post, Ministry	Name	Age	No. of times elected	District	Faction
Dir. Gen'l. P.M. Office and Okinawa Dev. Agency	TSUBOKAWA Shinzō	63	9	Fukui	Fukuda
Dir. Gen'l Admin. Mgt. Agency	FUKUDA Takeo	67	9	Gunma 3	Fukuda
Dir. Gen'l. Defense Agency	MASUHARA Keikichi	69	4*	Ehime	Fukuda
Dir. Gen'l. Econ. Planning Agency	KOSAKA Zentarō	60	12	Nagano 1	Ōhira
Dir. Gen'l Science Tech. Agency; Chr., AEC	MAEDA Kazuo	63	3*	Wakayama	Tanaka
Major Liberal Democratic Party officers					
President	TANAKA Kakuei	54	11	Niigata 3	Tanaka
Vice-Pres.	SHIINA Etsusaburō	74	7	Iwate 2	Shiina
Chr., Policy Bd.	KURAISHI Tadao	72	11	Nagano 1	Fukuda
Chr., Exec. Council	SUZUKI Zenkō	61	11	Iwate 1	Ōhira
Sec. Gen'l.	HASHIMOTO Tomisaburō	71	10	Ibaraki 1	Tanaka
House of Representatives presiding officers					
Speaker	NAKAMURA Umekichi	71	12	Tokyo 5	Nakasone
Vice-Speaker	AKITA Daisuke	66	10	Tokushima	Shiina

Note: * = House of Councillors (HC). All others House of Representatives (HR).

Table 2-7. (cont.)

Education	Pre-Diet career	Selected prior important posts
Fukui Mil. School	City Mayor	Min. of Construc.; Chr. HR Comm.; Commerce and Ind., House Mgt.
Tokyo U.–Law	Finance Min. bureaucrat	Min. of Agric. & For., Finance, Foreign Affairs; LDP Policy Bd. Chr., Sec. Gen'l.
Tokyo U.–Law	Home Min. bureaucrat	Min. of State: Dir. Gen'l. Defense Agency (twice); Governor, Kagawa Pref.
Tokyo U. of Commerce (Hitotsubashi)	Corp. exec.	Min. of Labor, Foreign Affairs; LDP Policy Bd. Deputy Chief.
Tokyo U.	Post & Telecomm. Min. bureaucrat	LDP Deputy Sec. Gen'l; Chr. HC Comm.: Transportation
Major Liberal Democratic Party officers		
Central Tech. Sch.	Business; construction	Min. of Post & Telecomm.; Finance, Int. Trade & Ind.; LDP Policy Bd. Chr., Sec. Gen'l.
Tokyo U.–Law	Commerce and Ind. Min. bureaucrat	Min. of Int. Trade and Ind., Foreign Affairs, Chief Cabinet Sec.; Chr. LDP Exec. Council.
Hōsei U.–Law London U.	Industrialist	Min. of Labor (twice), Agric. & For. (3 times); Chr. HR. Comm.: Agric. and For. (4 times)
Agric. & For. Res. Inst.	Adviser of Natl. Fed. of Fisheries co-op. assoc.	Min. of Welfare, Chief Cabinet Sec.; LDP Deputy Sec. Gen'l.
Waseda U.–Polit. Econ.	Newspaperman	Min. of Transp., Construc.; LDP Exec. Council Chr.
House of Representatives presiding officers		
Hōsei U.–Law	Lawyer	Min. of Justice, Construc., Educ.; LDP Policy Bd. Chr., Exec. Council Chr.
Tokyo U.–Econ.	Parliamentarian	LDP Foreign Affairs Research Council Dep. Chr.; HR Comm. Chr.; Educ., Soc. Lab., Foreign

Sources: *Sankei Shinbun*, December 23, 1972, p. 1; *Nihon Keizai Shinbun,* December 23, 1972, p. 2; *Shūgiin Yōran* (HR Directory), 1972; *Kokkai Binran* (Diet Handbook), July 1972.

Daisuke (Shiina faction) became Vice-Speaker with 280 votes (of 486).[7] It is noteworthy that both the Speaker and Vice-Speaker belong to factions which are classified as belonging to the *tōjin* (parliamentarians) wing of the LDP. Those decisions having been made, the next order of business was the formal election of the new Prime Minister. Each of the parties put forth its own candidates, and the resulting vote, conducted within minutes of each other in both chambers, was:

	House of Representatives	House of Councillors
Tanaka Kakuei (LDP)	280	128
Narita Tomomi (SPJ)	116	60
Nosaka Sanzō (JCP)	40	10
Takeiri Yoshikatsu (Kōmeitō)	29	23
Kasuga Ikkō (DSP)	20	12

Balloting in both chambers, for which not all members were present (which accounts for the totals not adding up to 491 and 252 respectively) was concluded shortly before three o'clock in the afternoon.[8] By 8:30 that same evening the entire Cabinet was ready to depart for the Imperial Palace for the formal attestation ceremony. Within two hours, everyone had returned to the Prime Minister's official residence for the first formal Cabinet meeting.

Several other points — aside from the unusual rapidity of the Cabinet's formation, reflective of the prior negotiations that had been conducted and the extraordinary degree to which Mr. Tanaka was in charge — require brief elaboration. First, and I believe foremost, Prime Minister Tanaka followed a pattern that has by now become traditional in creating cabinets: he constructed one which mirrored the current balance of factional forces in the LDP. Six portfolios went to important members of his own faction including himself, three to Ōhira's, three to Fukuda's, two each to Nakasone's, Miki's, and Ishii's, one to Mizuta's, and one (the thorny post of Education Minister) to Mr. Okuno, who is among the very few Representatives having no factional affiliation.

Second, the specific portfolios accorded to each faction once again reflected the comparative standing of each faction *vis-à-vis* the Prime Minister. Tanaka's faction not only had the Prime-Ministership, but also the crucial Finance Ministry portfolio as well as the post of LDP Secretary-General; Ōhira's the Foreign Ministry, the Economic Planning Agency, and the chairmanship of the LDP's Executive Council; Nakasone's, the two significant International Trade and Industry (MITI) and Agriculture and

---

[7]*Nihon Keizai Shinbun*, December 23, 1972, p. 2.   [8]*Loc. cit.*

Forestry Ministries plus the Speakership of the House of Representatives; Miki's the high-status Deputy Prime-Ministership; while Fukuda's was accorded three "Agencies," which, although headed by a Minister of State, are relatively low on the pecking order, with Defense being the only conceivable exception (and even its standing is higher in the eyes of foreigners than of the Japanese). These relatively low-ranking posts were partially offset by the selection of Mr. Kuraishi (Fukuda faction) to the important chairmanship of the LDP's Seichōkai, Policy Affairs Research Council.

In Mr. Fukuda's case there were problems for all concerned. He had been Tanaka's principal opponent for the LDP presidency five months earlier. No one had forgotten that contest. Moreover, Fukuda had powerful enemies inside the party, not the least of whom were Nakasone (viz. Gunma's 3rd) and important members of Mr. Miki's faction, as well as those of Mr. Ōhira and Mr. Shiina. Should Prime Minister Tanaka invite his archrival to join and thus guarantee himself a burr in the saddle; and, conversely, should Fukuda allow himself to accept an invitation if it came, thereby limiting his capacity to act as a critic? As noted, he was asked to join, and he did so. Out of the welter of motives, two related ones are conceded to have been crucial. Gains made by the Opposition parties, especially the JCP and the SPJ, and the relative decline of the LDP provided one powerful goad. The other was the resultant need for unity among the Liberal Democrats; and what kind of party unity could there be if the leader of the largest faction (Fukuda) were not in the Cabinet? In the end, the circumstances required that Prime Minister Tanaka bring all major faction leaders into the Cabinet.

Finally, two ancillary factors provided proof of the weight of tradition in Premier Tanaka's personnel decisions at the apex of Japanese politics. As before, eight of the twenty Cabinet Ministers were Tokyo (Imperial) University graduates. Second, nine of these gentlemen had begun their careers as bureaucrats. Tanaka himself might be a plebeian, but as yet there were no fundamental changes in the continuity of prerequisites providing access to the top. It was, by and large, a Cabinet of tested and experienced veterans. Factionalism had triumphed again.

Factionalism is also a fact of life for the Socialists, who are still the largest party in the "progressive" house in Japanese politics. In certain respects the SPJ is even more badly split than the LDP. In the early 1950s there were two Socialist parties, the "Right" and the "Left." Since January 1960, there has existed an unrepaired fission between the major SPJ and the increasingly minor DSP. Many SPJers would reject the notion that the DSP is still in fact a "socialist" party. Viewed from the perspective of the Second Internationale, the DSP is akin to the British Labour Party or

Table 2-8. LDP Factions 1962-73

	1962[c] HR[a] HC[b]	1963[c] HR HC	1964 HR HC	1965 HR HC	1966 HR HC
Ikeda Yoshida	53	50	48 11	Maeo 47 15	47 15
Satō	53	49	45 49	44 52	44 52
Kaya	5	3			
	Fukuda 25	17		20 1	20
Kishi	42 ──→ 4	5			
	Kawashima 25	18		18	18
					Nanjō
Fujiyama	40	24	21 12	18 11	18 11
Ishii	23	14	15 19	14 10	14 10
Ōno	32	29	29 12	16 ⎾ 9	3 9
				→Murakami	11
				→Funada	12
Matsumura-Miki	33	32	37 12	37 10	36 10
Ishida	6	4			
					↑Mori-Sonoda
Kōno Hatoyama	34	31	47 18	46 14	├─44 14
					↓Nakasone
Ishibashi	4	4			
Unaffiliated	2	2	8 8	16 16	15 15

[a]HR = House of Representatives; [b]HC = House of Councillors.
[c]Many double entries in HR; factions not yet formalized in HC.

Sources:
Watanabe Tsuneo, *Habatsu* [Factions] (Tokyo: Kōbundō, 1964), pp. 181-91.
Kokkai Binran [Diet Handbook] (Tokyo: Nihon Seikei Shinbunsha, 1962, 1963, 1965, 1966, 1967, 1968, 1969, 1970, 1971, 1972).
Yomiuri (Shinbun, mimeo., n.d., but December 13, 1972) and private inquiry February 1, 1973.

the SPD in West Germany. Its leadership is moderate in its policies and more fully dedicated to parliamentarism than any other party in Japanese politics. An influential segment of Japan's academic and intellectual communities finds in the DSP a respectable haven, while at the same time allowing it to be critical of the LDP. Yet, as a party, it is no more than the smallest of the Opposition groupings.

Of the three major factions in the SPJ itself, the Eda and Katsumata

Table 2-8. (cont.)

1967 HR	1967 HC	1968 HR	1968 HC	1969 HR	1969 HC	1970 HR	1970 HC	1971 HR	1971 HC	1972 HR	1972 HC	1973 HR	
42	11	43	18	43	18	44	19 Ōhira	43	18	43	19	44	Ōhira
57	52	54	46	45	46	59	46	60 ┃ 44 →Tanaka →Hori		42	39	47	Tanaka
23		28	8	28	8 ┌	38	18	39	20	"new" 65	28	53	Fukuda
17		17	6 ──	17	── 6		20 Shiina	18	4	17	4	18	Shiina
17	9	7	10	7	10	6	2	6		3			
14	10	13	9	13	9	12	9	13		13	5	9	(Ishii)
10	3						Mizuta	4		→16	2	14	Mizuta
10	3	10	3	10	3	10	3	10	2 ┘				
15	6	13	5	13	5	14	5	12	4	10	4	9	Funada
4		4		4		3	Kawasaki	3		3			
35	10	37	10	37	10	42	9	42	12	┌→39	11	39	Miki
										→Hayakawa 3			
						6		6 ──					
4	5	11		11		14		14 ──					
	15				12				7		7		
			25		25		36	16	35		33		39 Nakasone
	24												
11	4	8	18	8	18	5	12	5	25	14	17	9	Unaffiliated

factions are comparatively moderate in their ideology, while the Sasaki faction perceives itself as militantly Marxist, or rather, Marxist in a Maoist way. Indeed, if there is a significant difference which distinguishes factionalism in the SPJ from that in the LDP, it is that the Socialists take their ideological commitments considerably more seriously. Moderates may — and do — accuse the hard-liners of being excessively concerned with "ideological purity," especially with regard to insisting that the SPJ be a "class party," which the moderates believe to be counter-productive to prospects for enlarging the potentially available popular support for the SPJ. In turn, the militants accuse their comrades of not being "sincere," an attribute of profound significance, in their commitment to socialism, and worse of being ready to sell out to the conservatives who rule Japan. One of the reasons for the emotion-laden quality of these debates is the unpleasant memory from the 1930s of many of the party elders diluting their principles by becoming staunch nationalists and thereby supporters of Japan's militarist policies.

Table 2-9. Socialist Factions in the Diet

	1961[c] HR[a] HC[b]	1963[c] HR HC	1965 HR HC	1966 HR HC	1967 HR HC
Nishio-DSP	16	15	23 7	23 7	
Kawakami	27	25	25 7	22 7	Kōno Mitsu 18 7
Eda			10 24	19 24	26 23
Wada	35	35	34 12	37 12	Katsumata 29 12
Unaffiliated-neutral		3	18 6	15 10	10 6
Suzuki-Sasaki	45	9 ⌐ 14	41 24	36 24	14 26
Nōmin (Agric.) Dōshikai (friends)		5 1	4 1	3	3 1
Kuroda	4 →				
Leftists	8 →				
Heiwa (Peace) Dōshikai (friends)	18 ⌐	→15	11	10	

[a]HR = House of Representatives.
[b]HC = House of Councillors.
[c]Factions not yet organized in House of Councillors.
Based on: *Kokkai Binran*, 1961, 1963, 1965, 1966, 1968, 1970, 1971, 1972, 1973.

Another difference between the LDP and the SPJ is that if the LDP's conventions tend to be models of propriety on the surface (infighting takes place behind the scenes) and thus rather lackluster affairs, the SPJ's conventions are raucous and filled with sound and fury. Its 33rd Convention, held April 20-1, 1970, almost could not take place because the Hansen Seinen Iinkai (Anti-war Youth Committee), an important SPJ support organization made up of students and young blue-collar workers, was almost successful in barricading the doors leading into the Kudan Public Hall. They made the attempt because they feared that the delegates would adopt a "moderate" platform and elect a "moderate" central committee, "moderate" from the perspective of the Han-sen Seinen Iinkai, of course.

Table 2-9. (cont.)

1968		1969		1970		1971		1972		1973		
HR	HC	HR	HC	HR	HC	HR	HC	HR	HC	HR	HC	
31	10			32	10	30	13	29	13	20	13	
16	2		2	14 ⎡ New Eda		30 ⎤		29 ⎤		4 29 ⎤		Eda
23	7	23	7	15 ↓→ 33			33		31		29	
29	7	29	7	22 ⎣		21 ⎦		20 ⎦		25 ⎦		Katsumata
14	29	14	29	15	10	21	18	21	20	27	19	Neutral
→Yamamoto				4								
44	19	44	19	16	20	16	14	16	14	38	14	Sasaki
			3		3		2		2		2	
											3	Shakai Shugi Kyōkai [Socialism Assoc.]
8				4		1		1		2		Anpo-Funsai Dōshikai [Crush Security Treaty Friends]

Not until the arrival of the *kidō-tai* (riot police), whose activities the Socialists tend to deplore, and some physically robust mine-workers, who joined in shoving the obstructionists from the massive doors, could the delegates enter and begin their deliberations.[9] The balance of the convention was held behind closed doors.

In other respects, SPJ factionalism has many of the same attributes as that in the LDP. The SPJ also is a party that was created out of a diversity of prewar parties. It too has its quota of purgees and non-purgees. "Parliamentarians" vie for positions of leadership with trade union bureaucrats. In turn, different unions tend to support different factions with campaign contributions, though this is hard to prove with exactitude. Contests for positions of leadership in the party at its conventions also contribute their

---

[9] For details, please see *Nihon Shakaitō Dai Sanjū-san-kai Rinji Zenkoku Taikai Sokkiroku* [Proceedings of the Thirty-third SPJ National Convention] (Tokyo: SPJ, n.d., but 1970). It should be added that I was among the observers of the proceedings and was given special dispensation to depart and return by way of subterranean passages leading to back doors which were not barricaded.

share to the longevity of factionalism in the SPJ. Finally, the SPJ too is faced with the need to run more than one candidate in the multiple-member constituencies. It is only with respect to the intensity with which matters of ideology are felt and debated that the SPJ differs from the LDP. It is generally conceded that the LDP — by being more successful — has managed to cope with factionalism better than the SPJ. It is a conclusion with which I agree.

Japanese Communist Party (JCP) has not been immune from factional strife, despite its disciplined organizational structure. Ideological disputes plagued the party even during the prewar period when it was illegal. Unlike other Japanese parties the JCP suffered from an excess of foreign control which was often heavy-handed and all too often was more reflective of the Kremlin's politics than a response to Japanese circumstances. After a short period of relative freedom in the initial years of the Occupation era, during which the party flourished and succeeded in creating a "lovable" image, it suffered, in 1950, two nearly fatal blows. It was badly shaken by the Cominform's stern criticism, and while responding to that by adopting a more militant posture fell foul of the Occupation authorities, who proceeded to declare most of the party's leadership ineligible to hold public office. Many of the party's younger leaders fled into exile in Peking, and upon their return to their homeland established themselves as a "China Lobby" in the late 1950s and early 1960s. By then, the party was faced with trying to cope with the Sino-Soviet dispute, a reality that the leadership had tried to avoid. In effect, three groupings emerged: the "China Lobby," which was also sometimes referred to as the "young officers," the older Kremlin-oriented group, and — for want of a better descriptive term — the "nationalists."[10]

Since 1966, however, factionalism in the JCP has been kept to a minimum under the astute leadership of Praesidium Chairman Miyamoto Kenji, who gives every indication of having succeeded in emphasizing the "Japan" in the party's name. As noted, the party's fortunes are in the ascendant under Miyamoto's *jishu-dokuritsu rosen* ("autonomous independent line"). Some remnants of the "China Lobby" still exist, as — to a lesser extent — do the older Kremlin crowd. Power is in the hands of Miyamoto and his younger followers such as Fuwa Tetsuzō, Ueda Kōichirō, and Matsumoto Zenmei. Under their leadership, the JCP has regained respectability — almost too much for some of the younger stu-

---

[10] Please see my "Yoyogi and Its Rivals" in Robert A. Scalapino, ed., *The Communist Revolution in Asia*, 2nd. ed. (Englewood Cliffs, N.J.: Prentice-Hall, 1969), pp. 212-33.

dent radicals in the hard-left anti-JCP wing of the Zengakuren (National Student Federation) who talk as if the JCP has become one more segment of Japan's establishment. With these minor caveats, the party for the moment is relatively free of factionalism. To the degree that it exists at all it is under the strictest kind of control, as is evidenced by its ability to successfully run two candidates in one district. In Kyoto's first district Taniguchi Zentarō and Umeda Masaru came in first and third respectively in a five-man district, a feat which required iron discipline in the distribution of votes between them. In all of the other districts the party continued to run only one candidate, so that the tendency towards factionalism that sets in under the pressures of multiple candidacies in the same constituency was not present.

Little factional strife is as yet to be noted in the Kōmeitō (Clean Government Party). Its extremely rapid growth in the 1960s (see Table 2-1) very possibly assisted in preventing its members from engaging in internal infighting. Everyone was far too busy "making it," so to speak. Furthermore, as in the case of the JCP, the Kōmeitō has only run one candidate per district. It has even gone one step further by importing potential Kōmeitō supporters (that is members of Sōka-Gakkai) from neighboring constituencies in order to ensure — insofar as possible — that one of its candidates would be assured of having enough votes to win. This was possible under the election law so long as the voters transferred their place of residence and officially registered three months prior to the election. One of the reasons for the decline of the Kōmeitō in the 1972 election was allegedly that it had not expected the election to take place until the spring of 1973, and thus had not had time to move its supporters around in advance of December 10.

Until that election for the House of Representatives the Kōmeitō had never really confronted the whole range of emotions associated with a decline in political strength. It is too early to assess whether doing so will bring forth the bitter internecine struggles that, for example, have wrought havoc inside the SPJ when it has had to sort out the reasons for a "defeat." It is of course possible that the doctrines of Nichiren Shōshū* will provide sufficient unity to prevent factionalism from appearing in the Kōmeitō. However, it would be surprising if that should prove to be the case in the long run.

---

*Nichiren Shōshū is a sub-sect of Nichirenshū, a Japanese Buddhist sect founded by Nichiren, a thirteenth century priest. Sōka-Gakkai (literally, Value-Creation Society) is a secular arm of this sub-sect and was established in 1930. Since 1956 Sōka-Gakkai has successfully returned its members to the Diet. It organized the Kōmeitō, a political party in 1964.

There can be little doubt that factionalism exists as a fact of life — probably the basic fact of life — in Japanese politics. Disagreements arise, however, over the worth of its continued existence in the conduct of that country's politics. Many members of the academic and intellectual communities criticize factionalism because, for them, the *batsu* are an atavistic remnant of Japan's feudal past. Furthermore, they contend that Japan's political party system cannot become modern or truly rational so long as these factions — which by their very nature tend to emphasize the role of personality in politics and the bonds of loyalty between a leader and his followers (the *oyabun-kobun* relationship) — interfere with the goal of doing what is best for Japan. Policies cannot be developed and decisions cannot be made on the basis of some abstract notion of rationality, it is averred, so long as factionalism interferes by introducing the presumably non-rational personal element into the political process.

I disagree, and for several reasons. The structure of the Japanese political party system is the basic element. There is every likelihood that the Liberal Democratic Party will continue to be the majority — and hence governing — party for the foreseeable future, given the relative weakness and disunity of the Opposition parties, i.e. the SPJ, DSP, Kōmeitō and JCP. For the time being, they have extremely limited prospects of becoming a majority if for no other reason than that they are divided.

Second, if the foregoing is a reasonably accurate forecast of trends of Japanese politics, then the LDP — if it were an absolutely united party — might become authoritarian or its president (in his capacity as Prime Minister) might become dictatorial. While this latter contingency is unlikely, given the submergence of the individual in the group which in itself has provided a barrier against dictatorship in Japan, oligarchical authoritarianism is a danger against which factionalism has been, and has every prospect of continuing to be, an important protective shield.

Third, factions allow different segments of the Japanese public to have influence, and thereby allow alternative ideas, policies and legislative proposals to have supporters and opponents inside the party which governs Japan. It is inside the majority party, in the pre-parliamentary negotiations, that the fundamental decisions are made, and it is therefore vital that alternative proposals be ventilated at that stage of the policy-making process. One can of course argue that even with the existence of factions in the LDP the spectrum of views which have their spokesmen in the highest policy-making councils of the Japanese government is insufficiently broad. That may be true in ideal terms. Relatively speaking, however, so long as factions exist there will certainly be a broader spectrum of views which must be taken into account than if they were abolished.

In conclusion therefore, factions and factionalism contribute their share to making Japanese politics more open and competitive. In the context of Japan's political party system, factionalism is not only advantageous, but also eminently rational. Furthermore, only by coming to terms with the intra-mural disputes that take place within the political parties themselves can one come to grips with the realities of Japanese politics.

Editor's Note

This chapter covers the years up to 1973. Some changes have occurred in Japan's political world, but nothing so radical as to warrant reassessment of the chapter's main thesis. A few supplementary notes, however, are in order.

After the December 1976 general election, the seats in the House of Representatives were distributed as follows:

LDP	249	SPJ	123	Kōmeitō	55
DSP	29	JCP	17	NLC	17
Independents	21				
				Total	511

The most notable result of this election was the acquision of 17 seats by the newly organized Shin Jiyū Kurabu (New Liberal Club). The new party was founded by five young Diet members, headed by Kōno Yōhei (b. 1937), who rebelled against the LDP's aging leadership and factionalism. Though conservative in their outlook, NLC members act as part of the Opposition.

After the general election in July 1980, the seats in the House of Representatives were distributed as follows:

LDP	284	SPJ	107	Kōmeitō	33
DSP	32	JCP	29	NLC	17
USDP	3	Independents	11		
				Total	511

Shaminren (United Social Democratic Party) was founded in 1978 by those who split from the SPJ. In this election, the LDP gained a large number of seats and at present still boasts a majority in the Diet. No major change seems likely in the near future.

The World of the *Zaikai*

TANAKA YŌNOSUKE

The term *zaikai* is one of the staples in newsreporting and discussions on national or current affairs, just as the comments of *zaikai-jin* ("*zaikai* people") are invariably solicited whenever anything important happens in the economy or in politics. *Zaikai* is often rendered in English as "financial circles," or "business world," but neither phrase is really adequate. *Zaikai* is probably better described as that group of people who, apart from their identification with specific companies or industries, speak from the capitalist position and exert a strong influence on politics.

The Japanese public generally believes the *zaikai* to be the nation's largest and most powerful pressure group and that the government is covertly, if not overtly, dominated by the wishes of the *zaikai-jin*. Since the ruling conservative party depends so greatly on the *zaikai* for its political funding, the public also believes that party politicians are at the *zaikai*'s constant bid and call.

Although the conservatives have been in power almost continuously since the end of World War II, party organization and finances are relatively weak, especially when one compares them to their Western counterparts. Membership dues cover only a fraction of the party's outlay, and the result has been nearly exclusive dependence on big business to finance party activities. The channels for funds have become so institutionalized that not even the recently enacted legal restrictions on corporate political donations have had much effect.

The popular image of the conservative party as the indebted servant of the *zaikai* would thus seem to have ample justification. Just how accurately this image reflects reality, however, is another question. Of course there are elements of both truth and fiction in the popular conception, which stem from the complex party-*zaikai* relationship and the considerable changes that have occurred in it over the years.

In the decades before World War II, the activities of Japan's two leading political parties (both conservative) were financed almost entirely by the two dominant *zaibatsu*, Mitsui and Mitsubishi, and as a consequence, the positions and actions of both parties reflected their patrons' wishes fairly faithfully. Mitsui supported the Seiyūkai (Political Friends' Society) and Mitsubishi the Minseitō (Democratic Party) in the competition for political hegemony. The term *zaikai* at that time was literally synonymous with Mitsui and Mitsubishi. By the 1930s, however, several new *zaibatsu* had emerged, capitalizing on the burgeoning military procurement that accompanied Japan's advance into Korea and China. These new *zaibatsu* eventually teamed up with the military and the bureaucracy, forming a coalition dominated by radical military leaders which plunged Japan into World War II.

The postwar *zaikai*, whose roots lie partly in the prewar *zaibatsu*, may be analyzed from the two aspects of organization and personal political connections. Looking first at organization, there are four main national economic organizations in Japan: Keidanren (Federation of Economic Organizations), JCCI (Japan Chamber of Commerce and Industry), Nikkeiren (Japan Federation of Employers' Associations), and Keizai Dōyūkai (Japan Committee for Economic Development). The leaders of these organizations comprise the core of the *zaikai*. They are often seen together, not only at formal conferences, but also at informal gatherings, on the golf course, and at wedding receptions. The *zaikai*, of course, has no official roster, but the leaders of these important organizations can be considered as a formal group. In addition to this group, however, is a more amorphous one comprising businessmen who are particularly close to the incumbent prime minister. In actual practice, these two groups overlap considerably.

Immediately after the War, SCAP disbanded the *zaibatsu* and purged many of the country's political and economic leaders. It was not long, however, before there emerged two groups of businessmen who addressed themselves to the nation's future economic development. One such group, the "Miyajima group," led by Miyajima Seijirō, then president of Nisshin Spinning, included the presidents of some of the nation's major banks and firms. Another group, called the Keizai Dōyūkai, was composed of junior executives who met regularly in a salon-type atmosphere which still distinguishes the organization. (It continues to offer only individual, not corporate, memberships.) They discussed ways of making the economic system more democratic and less prone to *zaibatsu* domination, and appealed for more coordinated action by management. I should point out that there was a considerable overlap in membership from the very beginning.

These men recognized the need for close ties with the government if they were to have any impact on economic policy, and they worked to strengthen both institutional bonds with the bureaucracy and personal bonds with leading politicians. The first government leader to show a strong interest in developing truly strong ties with the emerging business groups was Prime Minister Yoshida Shigeru. Yoshida and Miyajima were classmates at Tokyo University law school, and remained close after graduation. Miyajima advised Yoshida to concentrate on the nation's problems and not to worry about finances. Miyajima himself kept a low posture as well, entrusting the task of political fund raising to other "Miyajima group" colleagues.

Miyajima's relationship with Yoshida of course did not stop at fundraising. The two men engaged in continual dialogue concerning Japan's postwar reconstruction. They agreed that the nation would fare best as a peaceful trader under the wing of American defense.

Not only the Miyajima group but the entire business world endorsed Yoshida, and this tradition of business support for conservative leadership remains to this day, though the degree of support varies from prime minister to prime minister. Business was relatively cool, for example, toward Hatoyama Ichirō, who became Prime Minister after Yoshida from 1954 to 1956. Hatoyama did have some important friends in business, however, including Fujiyama Aiichirō, then president of the Japan Chamber of Commerce and Industry. When Hatoyama announced his plan to conclude a peace agreement with the Soviet Union, the *zaikai* split into two factions — one endorsing Hatoyama's position and one opposing it. Hatoyama's hands were tied by the lack of *zaikai* consensus. Near the end of Hatoyama's term the *zaikai* ultimately withdraw effective support and called for his resignation.

The *zaikai* was also rather cool toward Prime Minister Kishi Nobusuke (1957-60), who succeeded Hatoyama, but it gave its full support to the next two prime ministers, Ikeda Hayato (1960-64) and Satō Eisaku (1964-72), who were both formerly associated with Yoshida's political camp.

When Satō stepped down as prime minister, *zaikai* support was divided between Fukuda Takeo's staid conservatism and Tanaka Kakuei's dynamism. Tanaka ended up as Prime Minister (1972-74), but his support quickly eroded when his name surfaced in numerous scandals which also damaged the *zaikai*'s own reputation. The *zaikai* remained generally aloof when Prime Minister Miki Takeo took office (1974-76), but returned to prominence when Fukuda (1976-78) succeeded Miki. The Ikeda and Satō administrations are still regarded as the "mainstream" of Japanese conservatism, and the group of powerful businessmen who were close to these two men and shared their views is regarded as the *zaikai* mainstream. To understand this institution more fully, it may be useful to look at the four main *zaikai* groups in closer detail.

Keidanren (Federation of Economic Organizations)

Keidanren is a federation of powerful industrial organizations, including the Japan Iron and Steel Federation, the Petroleum Association of Japan, the Federation of Electric Power Companies, the Japan Automobile Manufacturers' Association, the Shipbuilders' Association of Japan, and the Japan Chemical Industry Association. Its membership also includes wholesale and retail businesses, trading houses, banks, insurance companies, and securities houses. In short, Keidanren encompasses all sectors of private business and wields by far the strongest influence of any economic organization in Japan. The president of Keidanren is commonly referred to as "the prime minister of the *zaikai*." It is an appropriate appellation.

Keidanren was inaugurated in 1946, but the extensive postwar purge of businessmen left such gaping holes in *zaikai* leadership that the organization was at first at a loss to find a president. The corporate executives who were left were too busy rebuilding their own shattered companies and coping with inflation, material shortages, surplus labor, etc. to worry about the Japanese economy as a whole. Many viewed Keidanren as a needless luxury. It was significant that Ishikawa Ichirō, who assumed leadership of Keidanren in 1948, had a background in engineering, not management, and his disinterested stance suited the mood of the times.

Ishikawa was succeeded in 1956 by Ishizaka Taizō, who presided over the organization for twelve years. He took office at about the time when the economy had reached prewar levels and was about to enter a phase of rapid industrialization. Born in 1888, Ishizaka joined the Ministry of Communications after graduating from Tokyo University. He later joined Dai-Ichi Life Insurance and eventually became its president. After World War II, he was asked to head Tokyo Shibaura Electric Co., Ltd. (Toshiba), which had been plagued by a fierce labor dispute. Under Ishizaka's strong leadership, the company revived and developed into the major corporation it is today. Not only was Ishizaka a competent manager, he was supremely confident in the market economy and in Japan's ability to compete internationally. His integrity was unquestioned, and he was uncompromising in his disapproval of special ties between businessmen and politicians. He held fast to his public stance concerning economic issues, not once involving himself in a political dispute. His personal stature did much to enhance

Keidanren's prestige. During Ishizaka's term of office, Keidanren's stature and influence rose conspicuously, bolstered by the phenomenal growth of big business. Meanwhile, the Miyajima group entered into a period of decline, although it retained some influence through its ties with the Ikeda and Satō administrations.

That intimate association between business and government known as "Japan, Inc." presumably had its heyday during the decade or so of Ishizaka's leadership, although Ishizaka himself was known for his dislike of the bureaucracy. A believer in the classical free-market philosophy, he encouraged businesses to develop on their own, with only a minimum of government assistance. At the same time, he strongly favored a program of rapid economic growth. When Keizai Dōyūkai sounded a warning about the government's proposed National Income Doubling Plan in 1961, Keidanren urged the government to continue its stimulation of the economy. Ishizaka's famous remark that the Japanese economy should not be likened to a speeding car with defective brakes is a vivid expression of his confidence in Japan's economic potential.

Another example of Keidanren's free-market philosophy was its successful attempt in the early 1960s to frustrate enactment of the Tokushin-hō (Law on Extraordinary Measures for Specific Depressed Industries) by the Ministry of International Trade and Industry. The bill provided tax and monetary incentives for certain industries to rationalize and consolidate in an effort to prepare them for more open competition with foreign goods introduced into Japan. But Ishizaka torpedoed the bill out of his aversion to bureaucratic controls. Thus, while Japan's booming industrial growth is commonly attributed to the collusion of politicians, bureaucrats, and *zaikai* known as "Japan, Inc." most credit must go to those private enterprises which strove to develop on their own, without bureaucratic intervention.

In 1968, Ishizaka retired and was succeeded by Uemura Kōgorō. Uemura's leadership wrought a change in the organization's character, in that he was a former career bureaucrat, not a corporate executive. His role in the *zaikai* was mainly that of a mediator and caretaker. Upon assuming the Keidanren presidency, he established a collective leadership within the organization and encouraged cooperation between government and business.

This policy marked a sharp departure from Ishizaka's, but it was in a way indicative of the changing times. Externally, Japan was faced with growing pressure to liberalize restrictions on the introduction of foreign capital; and internally the nation was experiencing serious economic dislocations in the form of environmental pollution and inflation. These problems could not be resolved without the coordinated efforts of business and government. Cooperation was vital if Japan was successfully to restructure her industries and to compete in the world market. Business needed the government's help in developing export markets, insuring stable supplies of raw materials and energy resources, and improving the living environment. Even as Keidanren changed its tune to meet the needs of a new age, however, some business leaders continued to support the old Ishizaka philosophy of a free market economy and regarded Uemura as a weak leader. Meanwhile, Keidanren acquired a reputation as a government subsidiary. Whether that reputation was deserved or not, Uemura's warm personality and diplomatic skills made him the ideal link between business and government.

In 1954 a scandal broke out in Japan's shipbuilding industry. The Minister of Justice invoked his authority over public prosecutors and managed to keep a lid on the investigation, but the incident generated widespread public criticism, especially of ties between government and business. In the face of this criticism, business leaders instituted a system of political contributions to prevent government interference with the free market. Political funding would be completely separated from the specific interests of the companies and industries which provide the money. Uemura, already an executive officer within the Keidanren organization, played the central part in creating the new system. Because of such activities he was a well-known figure in business and politics when he assumed the Keidanren presidency, and little friction arose between the *zaikai* and the political world during his presidency, in contrast to the Ishizaka years.

In 1974, Dokō Toshio, then Chairman of the Board of Toshiba, was elected fourth president of Keidanren. He assumed the post at a time when the nation was facing some of its most serious difficulties since the postwar period. The economy was in the grip of soaring inflation following the 1973 oil crisis, and the public was in an outrage over a string of malpractices. The big trading houses had been engaging in massive land and commodity speculation, and the Lockheed scandal, which was eventually to bring down the Tanaka Kakuei government, was just beginning to surface. Public opinion against big business had reached a new height.

Dokō startled the public, therefore, when he announced that Keidanren would wash its hands of political donations. Yet little has come of this declaration, and the financial channels from the *zaikai* to the political world remain more or less intact. The Political Contributions Control Law, enacted in 1976, has placed some limitations on contributions, but realistically speaking no great change will take place until the conservatives firmly establish an independent financial base. The Japanese Communist

Party and the Kōmeitō (Clean Government Party) have sound financial backing from individual supporters, and the Japan Democratic Socialist Party and the Socialist Party of Japan rely on financial support from the trade unions. The Liberal Democratic Party (LDP), however, has no such clearly defined source of funds. At the same time, since the LDP is the mainstay of the conservative forces dedicated to preserving the economic status quo, the *zaikai* cannot afford to withdraw its support.

A man of personal integrity, Dokō favors keeping business aloof from politics. Under his leadership, it is hardly likely that Keidanren will abandon its concern for the general welfare of the nation's economy for the sake of financial gain through petty political maneuvering. Nevertheless, Keidanren is in an unenviable position, committed to supporting the LDP at a time when public skepticism of such support has reached unprecedented heights.

Nikkeiren (Japan Federation of Employers' Associations)

In the early postwar years the spectre of socialism haunted business leaders. When SCAP issued orders increasing the rights of workers, labor unions, controlled in large part by communist leaders sprang up in rapid succession throughout the country. Employers were not prepared for this sudden labor offensive, and out of their dilemma Nikkeiren was born in 1948.

Nikkeiren is an organization of employers. Many of its leaders were also members of the Miyajima group, which, as we have seen, had numerous ties with the Yoshida government. By placing its members in Nikkeiren, the group sought to make the organization a principal forum for its political activities.

Nikkeiren first became involved in a labor dispute at the Tōhō Movie Company, throwing its full support behind the Tōhō management. The dispute began when management fired 270 employees, and escalated steadily until the labor union occupied the movie studios in a show of protest against the mass firings. SCAP, in a sudden reversal of its sympathetic stance toward the labor movement, promptly moved to quell the unionists, dispatching a parade of tanks to Tōhō's strike-bound facilities. The strike turned into a test of strength between the forces of labor and the forces of management, and management's ultimate victory became a milestone of immense significance.

Nikkeiren then threw its support to management in labor disputes that followed at Toshiba, Hitachi, and Nissan Motors, all of which seriously threatened the very foundations of Japan's political and economic system. During this turbulent decade or so of serious labor-management strife, which ended with the settlement of Mitsui Mining's Miike Coal Mine dispute in 1960, Nikkeiren served as headquarters for anti-revolutionary forces in Japan, and it earned the nickname "fighting Nikkeiren."

Nikkeiren has also been nicknamed the *zaikai*'s "anti-labor headquarters." When Sōhyō (General Council of Trade Unions of Japan) began its annual, nationwide "spring offensive" (*shuntō*) to press for wage hikes in the 1950s, Nikkeiren confronted Sōhyō with counter-offers considered appropriate by management. Corporate management typically relied on Nikkeiren's wage guidelines in its effort to counter pressure from labor. Labor came out the worse for it, but the surplus funds which did not go into wage increases were channeled instead into capital investment, which in turn sped the economy to a period of phenomenal growth in the 1960s. Nikkeiren was now at the height of its influence. By the 1960s, however, industry as a whole had become noticeably more prosperous and far more amenable to granting large wage increases, and much of the sting was removed from labor-management disputes. Labor was now in short supply, moreover, and management was much more interested in increasing production than in exacerbating labor relations by following Nikkeiren guidelines. Nikkeiren's directives fell on increasingly deaf ears, and its influence suffered a decline.

In 1970, Nikkeiren argued that wage hikes should be kept within the limits of real productivity growth and set up its guidelines accordingly; but they were largely ignored by prospering firms that were all too willing to grant large pay increases. The situation changed after the 1973 oil crisis, however, and wages have been generally brought into line with productivity.

Nikkeiren's other main function has been public relations. Particularly in the first couple of decades after the War, the Japanese press had maintained an anti-government, anti-establishment stance. Unlike the Western press, it had a distinct leftist leaning and a conspicuous lack of concern for the free-market society. This tendency caused understandable apprehension among the conservative economic leaders and roused start propagating their own views. In 1955, Nikkeiren began a campaign to exert its influence on the media, but with little success. Mizuno Shigeo of the Miyajima group managed to gain a foothold in the Fuji-group radio, television, and newspaper venture, but his efforts were only moderately successful. As it turned out, the press grew more and more disenchanted with the Marxist philosophy, but the change in attitude stemmed less from Nikkeiren's efforts than from the general rise in living standards, steady economic growth, and the spread of knowledge about living conditions within the Communist bloc.

Nikkeiren is no longer the "fighting Nikkeiren" of old. Sakurada Takeshi, who has led the organization since its founding, is a capable leader. In 1945 he was chosen by Miyajima to take over the presidency of Nisshin Spinning at the age of forty-one. The topics of his speeches at Nikkeiren conventions range from labor and education to defense and law and order, and they are invariably given extensive coverage by the mass media as representing *zaikai* opinion on those issues. Sakurada now sees his organization's main function as educational. Not only does it train junior executives at its own institute, it also emphasizes on-the-job "foreman education." The transformation from a "fighting Nikkeiren" to "teaching Nikkeiren" reflects some very fundamental changes in the economic realities which now face the country.

Japan Chamber of Commerce and Industry

The Japan Chamber of Commerce and Industry (JCCI) is the oldest of Japan's economic organizations. It had its origins in the Tokyo Shōhō Kaigisho (Tokyo Chamber of Commerce), founded by Shibusawa Eiichi, the famous entrepreneur, in 1878. JCCI is essentially a forum for smaller enterprises, which form the overwhelming majority of its membership. It has branches nationwide.

After World War II, the Chambers of Commerce and Industry Law was revoked and JCCI lost the services of its president, Fujiyama Aiichirō, who fell victim to the Occupation purge. In 1950, however, the Chambers of Commerce and Industry Law was reinstated, and in the following year Fujiyama was cleared and allowed to reassume the JCCI presidency. In an attempt to revive JCCI authority, he proposed a reorganization of economic organizations which would restore the Chambers of Commerce and Industry to leadership. His ideas were coldly received by the others at that time and soon forgotten.

Until recently the least influential of Japan's major economic organizations, JCCI has become very active since Nippon Steel Board Chairman Nagano Shigeo assumed its presidency in 1970. While it may seem somewhat inappropriate for the leader of the world's largest steel manufacturer to take over the leadership of a group representing small-business interests, Nagano took a different view. On taking office, he declared: "Individual farmers are weak, but their livelihood is protected and supported by a system of agricultural cooperatives. Small businesses, by contrast, lack this organizational strength, and they have no say in politics and have difficulty borrowing money. This is unfair. The *zaikai* should consider it its task to join small businessmen together and thus to correct this inequality in the system."

Nagano promptly announced plans to bring some eleven million small businesses into the JCCI fold. Another group, Minshu Shōkōkai (Democratic Association of Merchants and Industrialists), controlled by the Japanese Communist Party, was steadily gaining influence with these smaller businesses by virtue of an "anti-taxation" drive.

Nagano also reformed JCCI's organizational structure to give greater voice to regional businesses. Up until then, JCCI presidency had been automatically filled by the president of the Tokyo Chamber of Commerce and Industry; similarly, five vice-presidencies had been filled by the local chamber presidents in Osaka, Yokohama, Nagoya, Kyoto, and Kobe. Nagano's reform involved dividing the nation into nine regional blocs and made room in the executive council for chamber presidents from Sapporo, Fukuoka, Hiroshima, Sendai, Niigata and Takamatsu (Tokyo, Osaka and Nagoya represented both their cities and their regional blocs). Nagano also invited key cabinet ministers to JCCI's monthly Executive Board meetings. Government leaders could not ignore the meetings, and their presence lent prestige to the JCCI. The success of this initiative stemmed largely from Nagano's long career as a powerful *zaikai-jin*.

In 1972 Nagano proposed the creation of a one trillion-yen fund within the government's Small Business Finance Corporation to assist small, specialist industries by furnishing unsecured loans of up to one million yen to small businessmen, when such loans were deemed appropriate by the local chamber of commerce and industry. Thanks to Nagano's political influence, the system was inaugurated the following year and proved extremely helpful to small businesses which had had difficulty in obtaining bank loans.

In 1978, the value of the yen soared to unprecedented heights on international currency markets, generating huge windfall profits for the gas, electricity and petroleum industries from their imports of fuels and raw materials. Distribution of the profits subsequently developed into a major political issue, dividing opinion between those who wanted directly to reimburse the consumer public through rate reductions, and those who urged that profits be invested in plant and equipment to stabilize utility rates over the long run. Quickly seizing upon the issue, the Socialist Party of Japan advocated direct reimbursement, but the government, especially the Ministry of International Trade and Industry, took the side of expanded plant investment. Then Nagano declared himself in favor of direct reimbursement. Others rushed to join him and the opposition capitulated. This episode attested eloquently to Nagano's acumen and insight. Asked about the future, he says he hopes to change the JCCI from a "dormant" to an "activist" organization.

Keizai Dōyūkai (Japan Committee for Economic Development)

Keizai Dōyūkai was founded in 1946. Moroi Kanichi, who served as chairman as its inaugural meeting, said, "Keizai Dōyūkai is an organization of progressive, middle-rank businessmen. As professional businessmen realizing the basic importance of production, we intend to study the problems of economic reconstruction and wish to develop our studies into recommendations to the government."

Ōtsuka Banjō (President of Japan Specialty Steel Pipe Co.), one of the founders of Keizai Dōyūkai, attracted attention by advocating what he called "amended capitalism." Convinced that pursuing profits through the virtual exploitation of labor would no longer be effective in the face of the rising labor movement, he came up with a plan for industrial democratization. He defined an enterprise as an organization jointly operated by representatives of management, capital, and labor, and stressed that a corporate council including representatives of all three parties should be the supreme decision-making organ. This concept became the target of scathing criticism and was, in the end, shelved. Nevertheless, it was characteristic of Keizai Dōyūkai that such a radical idea had come from one of its officers.

From the outset, Keizai Dōyūkai represented the progressive side of the business world. In marked contrast with "fighting Nikkeiren," its proposals emphasized harmony between management and labor. While Ishizaka's Keidanren pursued classic capitalism and committed itself to the development of individual enterprises, Keizai Dōyūkai stressed cooperation between the government and the private sector. Always mindful of the economy as a whole, Keizai Dōyūkai has stressed business's social responsibilities.

As already noted, Keizai Dōyūkai does not represent any particular economic organization or business. Composed of individual businessmen, it is closer to a fraternity of like-minded businessmen. Many of its members have come to assume concurrent posts in Keidanren and JCCI, and Keizai Dōyūkai has come to be regarded as a school for training elite *zaikai-jin*.

In 1966, the three Keizai Dōyūkai leaders, Tokyo Electric President Kikawada Kazutaka, Industrial Bank of Japan Chairman Nakayama Sohei, and Fuji Bank President Iwasa Yoshizane, organized the ten-member Sangyō Mondai Kenkyūkai, or "Sanken" (Industrial Issues Study Council), in which Dokō Toshio and Nagano Shigeo were also members. A private group for studying Japan's industrial system in the age of internationalization, Sanken included Keizai Dōyūkai *zaikai-jin* and leaders of all the major corporate groups except Mitsui and Mitsubishi. When Mitsui and Mitsubishi executives later joined, Sanken became an all-inclusive body of influential *zaikai* figures. This group of leaders engineered the 1970 Yawata-Fuji merger to form Nippon Steel, the world's largest steel firm. Sanken also took the leadership in formulating international economic policies, including the policy for capital liberalization.

In the early 1970s, Kikawada became virtually the sole voice of Keizai Dōyūkai. Partly because he was from the public-utility sector, he placed particular emphasis on the social responsibility of business. He stressed the need for orderly management of the economy and harmony between the individual and the whole, and warned against corporate strife over ever-bigger market shares.

Kikawada perhaps acted more as a conscience than a leader, but he exerted considerable influence over the *zaikai*, and he had a feeling for the direction of international economic currents, foreseeing such developments as the appreciation of the yen. Since he passed away in 1978, Keizai Dōyūkai has lost influence rapidly.

Zaikai Today and Tomorrow

There seem to be three major problem areas facing the *zaikai* as it heads into the 1980s. First, many of the *zaikai* leaders have grown old. While the aging of leadership is not limited to the *zaikai*, it is especially conspicuous there. President Dokō of Keidanren, President Nagano of JCCI, and Representative Executive Director Sakurada of Nikkeiren are all in their late seventies and early eighties. The average age of the chairmen and presidents of all the large corporations is already over sixty-five. When Keizai Dōyūkai was inaugurated, its members were in their forties. Filling executive posts vacated by older men who had been purged, they led Japan's economic recovery and growth for three decades. Now they are old.

Japanese business today has a strong and growing "chairman" class. Unlike U.S. companies, almost all Japanese corporate chairmen were once employees of their firms and served as president before assuming the chairmanship. Many stay on as chairman after serving two or three terms as president, and so retain personal authority and considerable supervisory power in the company's management even after turning the presidency over to younger men. Indeed, given Japan's traditional respect accorded age, many of them have more influence than the company president.

Asked why they gave up the presidency for the chairmanship, these men explain that they need the chairmanship for their *zaikai* activities — not because the chairmanship entails greater prestige but because they are too busy as president to devote adequate time to *zaikai* activities. By stepping up to the chairmanship, they free themselves from the internal workings of their companies and have more time for outside activities. In Japanese society, it is a mark of status to have an important title in a big company. Powerful presidents therefore want to serve as many terms as possible and then stay on in the post of chairman. This has delayed succession by younger leaders and generated a gerontocracy within the *zaikai*.

A second set of problems results from the fact that as businesses have become bigger and more highly structured, bureaucratic trends have also become more pronounced than ever. As already noted, Japan's top executives have generally worked their way up through the ranks. Very few of them have gone directly into management. Accordingly, they are not as strongly profit-conscious as are U.S. executives, and they seem primarily interested in serving out their terms of office without any serious blunders. Since their companies' balance sheets do not directly affect their salaries or dividends, they do not have the dedication and single-minded devotion to profits that company founders and owner-managers do.

In a way, such attitudes are also one of Japanese management's strengths. The social climate has fostered the idea that a company is not private property but a public entity operating with the public blessing, which helps to explain the particular sense of values of Japanese business executives. Differences in values of Japanese and American businessmen were highlighted in two surveys in which Japanese and American executives were asked to choose between two sets of values.* Set A posited that the government governs best which governs least, that private property rights are sacred, that society is made up of its individual members, and that survival of the fittest and competitive principles are important. Value-Set B postulated that the government is expected to set social goals

*This comparison was compiled from the results of two surveys conducted in generally the same way: William F. Martin and George Cabot Lodge, "Our Society in 1985 — Business May Not Like It," *Harvard Business Review*, 53:6 (Nov.-Dec. 1975), 143-152; and "Dai-Kigyō Shachō 200 nin ni Kiku: 10 nengo no Kachikan"(Business Values 10 Years from Now: The Opinions of 200 Corporation Presidents), *Shūkan Daiyamondo*, 63:27 (June 28, 1975), 36-44.

and to serve as a mediator, that property rights are secondary to the needs of society, that individuals are integral parts of the social whole, and that harmony is more important than competition. Whereas about three-fourths of the American executives favored Set A, approximately two-thirds of the Japanese executives respondents expressed preference for Set B. Since the Japanese economy is largely governed by free-market principles, most Japanese executives naturally conduct themselves in accord with Value-Set A in their day-to-day business, but they turn to Set B to express their basic philosophy. Indeed, Set B crystallizes the Keizai Dōyūkai philosophy.

Third is the question of the *zaikai's* influence upon government and society. The general public is interested in the *zaikai* not simply for its occasional opinions and recommendations but because of the suspicion that the *zaikai* has close, strong ties with politics. Some believe that nothing happens in politics – from selection of a prime minister to the determination of basic policies – without *zaikai* consent. That idea is probably for the most part inaccurate. Any special relationship between the *zaikai* and the politicians seems, in fact, to be growing weaker. As mentioned above, the Miyajima group formed very close ties with the Yoshida administration shortly after the War, but the *zaikai* even then did not dictate policy to the government. Rather, the Yoshida and Miyajima groups were in broad agreement on basic national goals.

The Ikeda and Satō administrations also had close relations with the *zaikai*, to the extent that some say the *zaikai* was responsible for their very existence. While it is true that the mainstream *zaikai* supported both Ikeda and Satō in their bids for the prime ministership, these two men rose to leadership through their own political skills. The *zaikai* is all too aware that excessive intervention in politics can be counterproductive. In 1956, for example, the *zaikai* openly urged early retirement for Prime Minister Hatoyama, provoking a strong backlash from politicians. The public did not back the *zaikai*. Since then, the *zaikai* has been careful not to meddle too openly in politics, especially in intra-party affairs. The most it will do is express tacit support for certain leaders. Thus, no direct *zaikai* influence was seen in the selection of Ishibashi Tanzan, Kishi Nobusuke, and Miki Takeo as prime minister. When Prime Minister Satō stepped down in 1972, the *zaikai* leaned to Fukuda Takeo as his successor. Yet Tanaka Kakuei was chosen. While *zaikai* support can help a particular politician, the final choice hinges upon his standing and leverage with other politicians. Although *zaikai-jin* may have had their reservations about Tanaka, few openly opposed him. *Zaikai-jin* generally refrain from expressing any clear opinions in such an election in order to retain a free hand no matter who reaches the office of Prime Minister.

The relationship between the *zaikai* and government policies has been characterized by an extensive commonality of views between the *zaikai-jin* and the conservative party, in office almost without interruption since 1946. Beginning with the agreement in the immediate postwar years that Japan should concentrate on economic reconstruction with a minimum expenditure on defense under United States protection, this basic concurrence has continued to the present. But Japan's increasing economic power has been accompanied by rising discord between government and business, and even within the business community itself, over specific policy objectives. The discord is likely to grow in the years ahead.

During the years of rapid growth, policies weighted heavily in favor of economic priorities were supported not only by politicians and businessmen but by most of the population. However, now that the Japanese economy has slowed down somewhat and demands for environmental protection, improved social services and expanded infrastructure investment are increasing, government and business are bound to agree less on policy priorities. Accordingly, *zaikai* influence on the government will continue to decline.

This growing divergence of views compounds the problems caused by an aging *zaikai* leadership and seriously affects the authority of the *zaikai*. Important *zaikai-jin* are losing influence even within their own companies in a trend which will only grow stronger as the scale of corporate activities expands, as companies become more independent, and as the business world splinters. Some observers even claim that the *zaikai* as such no longer even exists.

So long as big business exists in Japan, however, the *zaikai* will remain, with a collective group of *zaikai-jin* at its head and its position as a powerful political pressure group is not likely to change. Moreover, so long as the conservative party continues to rely upon the *zaikai* for political funding (there seems little chance of change in these patterns), it is inconceivable that the *zaikai* will lose all political influence. At the same time, there is no doubt that the political and social influence of the *zaikai* is waning. Under these conditions, the word "*zaikai*" will gradually lose its connotations of secret power and become merely a synonym for "business representatives."

The Bureaucracy:
Japan's Pool of Leadership

JAPAN CULTURE INSTITUTE

In his first year with the ministry, a newly appointed employee is assigned to the planning staff of one of its key divisions to gain a general orientation. In his second year, he is sent to a district branch for further grooming. His third and fourth years are spent at some prestigious university overseas at the ministry's expense. Advanced degree in hand, he returns to the head office to manage for a year one of the smaller administrative sections. In his sixth year he assumes management of a branch office. Then, fully accustomed to the responsibilities and prerogatives of power, he returns to take his hard-earned place within the ministry hierarchy in Tokyo.

This carefully-groomed young man is actually not *one* man at all, but a composite portrait of the score or so of fledgling career-bureaucrats hired by Japan's Ministry of Finance every year. Minor differences notwithstanding, each member of this elite group receives basically the same training. The Ministry of Finance itself is conspicuous within the Japanese bureaucracy only for the lavishness of its attention; all ministries give new career-bureaucrats the same broad exposure to the obligations — and privileges — of membership.

Membership is attained through what is perhaps the most rigorous process of selection anywhere in the world. The process consists of a series of ruthlessly competitive examinations, which may begin, indirectly, as early as kindergarten. For though parents may not consciously plan a bureaucratic career for their sons (it is still largely a male-dominated profession) when they queue up to enroll them in "good" kindergartens, their hope is nonetheless to give them as much of a headstart as possible in the race for the best jobs when they have grown up. Admission to a good school insures that the student is that much better prepared for the entrance examinations to the next school up on the educational ladder. From the simple counting tests and parent interviews, which are part of the admission process to a prestigious kindergarten, to the nerve-wracking examinations for university entrance, academic performance is the criterion for advancement at every step. After graduating from a university, a would-be bureaucrat must once again score highly—this time on the ministry's own qualifying examination. Those who succeed are surely the cream of the crop, and it is no wonder that the ministries take such pains in preparing their newly appointed employees for their future leadership role.

The Ruling Triad

It is above all the unique leadership role of the bureaucracy as a whole in Japanese society, rather than leadership provided by any individual within a ministry or agency, which warrants our attention. Those familiar with Japan are aware that the country's power elite is a triad of conservative politicians, leading businessmen, and high-ranking bureaucrats. Virtually all throughout the postwar years, the conservatives have maintained a solid majority in the Diet and, except for a brief period in the late 1940s, it was they who formed the cabinet. Thus, they have in effect controlled both the legislative and administrative branches of government. Meanwhile, business has maintained close ties with the Liberal Democratic Party (LDP, formed in 1955) and its conservative predecessors. Business has both buttressed conservative rule and benefited from it. Not only has the business community cooperated with the LDP on major policy issues, it has been the party's primary source of campaign funds.

The third member of the ruling triad, the bureaucracy, works closely with both politicians and businessmen. It serves Diet members in general but particularly those members who head the administrative branch (as cabinet ministers) by helping to formulate policy. While the bureaucracy's principal task is executing administrative policy, it traditionally collects, processes, and analyzes the data needed for policy formulation as well. And because the bulk of government policy is designed to insure the nation's economic health, its drafting and implementation necessitates close cooperation with business. The bureaucracy is also a major supplier of the nation's ruling elite and a proving ground for future politicians and business leaders. It is not uncommon for a bureaucrat to retire early to run for public office or to assume an important position in a major corporation. Many of the nation's prime ministers have been bureaucrats-turned-politicians. If we take their terms of office all together, they comprise the better part of postwar Japanese history. The presence of these ex-bureaucrats in both business and political circles further enhances the bureaucracy's influence and cements the bonds among the nation's ruling elite.

The Sources of Power

The sources of the nation's bureaucratic power are threefold: regulatory authority, budgetary discretion, and public esteem.

1. At the base of its regulatory authority is the bureaucracy's legal prerogative to grant official sanctions and licenses. The Ministry of Transport, for example, holds complete jurisdiction over the nation's air, rail, and bus services, right down to the number of vehicles which may operate within any given area. The Ministry of Posts and Telecommunications issues licenses to radio and television stations. And the Ministry of Health and Welfare approves new drugs and medicines. Such regulatory powers are by no means unique to the Japanese bureaucracy, but one cannot overlook their importance as the cornerstone of the bureaucracy's authority and prestige.

2. The bureaucracy drafts the national budget, as well as legislation for budgetary appropriations, in accordance with policy objectives. Faced with a critical food shortage after World War II, the Ministry of Agriculture and Forestry used its financial resources to encourage farmers and stimulate rice production, a policy so successful that in recent years farmers have produced too much rice. Now the Ministry provides enormous subsidies to help farmers convert from rice to fruit, vegetables and livestock.

The Ministry of Finance plays the pivotal role in the bureaucracy by drafting and implementing the national budget and the annual Fiscal Investment and Loan Plan. Naturally, no policy can succeed without sufficient financial support, and the enormity of the ministry's power becomes evident each December, when work on drafting the budget for the coming fiscal year (April 1-March 31) is in full swing. Lobbyists throng the ministry's corridors awaiting their turn to meet with officials and file their petitions, often with covering letters from friendly Diet members.

The Ministry of Finance also supervises tax collection administration, including the National Tax Administration Agency. Together with the Bank of Japan, the Ministry also wields enormous authority through the issuance of official sanctions and licenses, and through the Foreign Exchange and Foreign Trade Control Law over bank operations, insurance policies, and overseas banking transactions. This authority is one of the foundations of the ministry's power, and is symbolic of the highly centralized mechanisms that control the Japanese economy.

3. The power of the bureaucracy also derives from public trust, and

individual bureaucrats must be well-suited to their jobs, both by temperament and ability. Without ability commensurate with the great authority accorded it, bureaucrats in the Ministry of Finance, for example, could not command the confidence of businesses and other groups under its jurisdiction, and its guiding role could not be maintained. But the Japanese bureaucracy functions smoothly, and is backed by a high level of public confidence in its policy-making abilities.

By contrast, political parties traditionally lack this power to formulate policy. Diet members tend to work not as legislators concerned with the national interest but as lobbyists concerned primarily with their local constituencies and supporters. Diet members rely heavily on the bureaucracy's assistance in researching and formulating policy measures; the few politicians with lofty ideals rarely have the staff or the time to draw up legislation on their own. Japanese political parties do little more than insure that the bureaucracy does not wander too far astray of the public interest. In recent years, however, politicians themselves have become targets of considerable criticism. The public has become increasingly cynical about politics, and many believe that the bureaucracy has provided a valuable check against the excesses of political parties.

Business also became the butt of considerable criticism as the public began to realize that economic growth was a mixed blessing and that the imbalance invariably made big business the winner. The bureaucracy, however, has remained largely unscathed by the general public cynicism. The Lockheed Aircraft scandal is a case in point. Investigations in 1975 into questionable payments in a trade deal developed into one of the most serious scandals of the century. More details were unearthed and the web of involvement widened until the list of plaintiffs charged with bribery and other offenses included the top executives of a major trading company and a major domestic airline, many government officials, and a former prime minister. A scandal of this scope would not have occurred had the transaction been carried out in an atmosphere of completely open and free competition. The system of bureaucratic control over private business provides openings for political intervention and abuse which in this case actually magnified the scandal.

Curiously, no bureaucrat was arrested or implicated in the Lockheed affair. The bureaucrats are aware of such scandals, but rarely attempt to use them for personal gain. In general individual bureaucrats are honest people, and the bureaucracy as a whole maintains its freedom from political entanglement, especially with individual politicians or party factions.

An image of detached, competent neutrality has contributed considerably to the public trust that the bureaucracy enjoys. High-ranking bureaucrats are continually surrounded by politicians and lobbyists seeking special favors and consideration, but they are generally successful in maintaining a posture of neutrality and remaining faithful to the national interest. While not completely immune from corruption, bureaucrats rarely succumb to temptation. A few incidents have occurred on the lower levels of officialdom but involvement by high-ranking officials is virtually unheard-of.

Disinterested Competence

Professional satisfaction and knowledge of a secure future firmly bolsters up bureaucratic integrity. The high-ranking bureaucrat prides himself on selfless dedication to the general welfare and commitment to furthering national objectives. In return he commands great respect and the assurance of security. In the long tradition of the Japanese bureaucracy, a public official is virtually guaranteed tenure during his active years and generous pension benefits after he retires. Although his relative financial standing has been somewhat eroded by inflation and by improved working conditions for employees in large corporations, he nonetheless retains his enviable position in society. A capable, high-ranking bureaucrat who normally retires at the age of 55, can look forward to lucrative offers from political parties, prestigious firms or public corporations to join their ranks. The retiring bureaucrat is thus considered not a gentleman of leisure but a "gentleman of potential."

A bureaucrat can easily afford detachment and neutrality precisely because his future is guaranteed. In the long run it is clearly more to his advantage to maintain his distance than to take sides in hopes of immediate personal gain. Accordingly, allegations of collusion between individual bureaucrats and politicians are the exception, not the rule. Although they are by no means political lackeys, bureaucrats will not openly defy a political leader. Some bureaucrats do occasionally identify themselves with specific political factions. When Kōno Ichirō was Minister of Agriculture and Forestry in the mid-1950s, for example, he reshuffled the personnel of the whole ministry, placing trusted followers in key posts. Aside from such exceptional cases, however, personal links with politicians are usually not in the bureaucrat's best interests. There are, nevertheless, many friendships since incumbent and former bureaucrats identify strongly with other members of the ministry "family"; and it is common for bureaucrats to be on very good terms with former colleagues from the same ministry who have become politicians. Such bonds are not so much a matter of politics as they are of camaraderie, and amicable personal relations among a ministry's colleagues are among an individual bureaucrat's most precious possession. The bureaucrat is much more likely to rely upon "family" cooperation and assistance than to ally himself with an outside politician in hopes of personal gain. Good "family" relations are crucial not only during his years as a ministry official, but also for his future in business or politics after he retires.

The bureaucracy is subject to political pressure, but it will put up all rational resistance against it. By "rational" is meant logically sound and consistent with overall policy. Rationality is the byword of the bureaucracy. Fairly low-level officials at the Ministry of Finance, for example, rough draft the national budget in consideration of the requests of other ministries. This completed, they must present and defend it to their ministry superiors. It is then studied from every conceivable angle and worked into more concrete shape. Other ministries formulate policy in much the same way: the low-ranking bureaucrat presents his arguments on specific matters, and the high-ranking bureaucrat views overall policy from a balanced perspective.

The emphasis on harmonious "family" relations within a ministry and on rational policy formulation not only keeps close ties between bureaucrats and politicians in check, but also keeps the bureaucracy as a whole relatively free of scandal. The bureaucracy's tradition of integrity goes back more than a century and if, as is often said, graft and pay-offs impede economic progress, then the integrity of Japan's bureaucracy has certainly been a major factor in the nation's successful modernization. Over two and a half centuries of peace under the Tokugawa shogunate rule over peasants, artisans, and merchants was administered by a bureaucratic elite dominated by the samurai class. These samurai officials were not always honest, but when the Meiji government was formed, many of its leaders were the sons of lower-ranking samurai, under whose rejuvenated leadership a new, uncorrupted bureaucracy was forged in pursuit of the common goal.

After the Meiji Restoration, Japan's leaders committed themselves to modernization in order to bring their nation up to an equal footing with the industrialized West. The first step was the creation of a centralized government consolidating the authority theretofore dispersed among the semi-independent *han* (fiefdoms) which formed the system of provincial rule. Next, measures were taken to build modern industries, and ex-samurai and their sons, who exchanged their swords for the power of the bureaucratic pen, stayed on at the helm of government. The people responded favorably to these changes and generally acquiesced to their authority. The traditional obedience of the populace was reinforced by the devotion to duty and aversion to corruption shown by the new bureaucracy.

Until the Second World War, the real power in Japan was shared by the military and the bureaucracy, particularly the Ministry of the Interior. The Prime Minister appointed prefectural governors from among the officials of that ministry. As a result, the ministry controlled local government as well as the nation's police force, giving it almost absolute control over the people's lives. After the War, the ministry was disbanded and replaced with the Ministry of Home Affairs, which holds far less power than its predecessor.

In postwar Japan, the ministries directly involved in regulating the nation's economy have enjoyed the most power. Politicians, businessmen, and the public turned from illusions of military might to reconstruction and industrial development, and the bureaucracy devoted itself to planning, controlling, and guiding the nation's economic growth.

We should note that of the nation's prewar power groups, only the bureaucracy survived the defeat almost unscathed. The military was abolished by the Occupation authorities and many prominent politicians and businessmen were purged. Yet the bureaucracy experienced only minor renovations, such as the reorganization of the Ministry of the Interior mentioned above and the reduction of police power. Having remained virtually intact, it eventually became synonymous with government.

The bureaucracy undertook the task of formulating policy, setting up priorities for industrial rehabilitation and preferential financing, and granting loans and subsidies to stimulate national reconstruction. Its guidance was of two types, legal and extra-legal; and as each form of official intervention became institutionalized, the bureaucracy's authority expanded.

The Ministry of International Trade and Industry became notorious outside of Japan as it attempted to create a strong domestic economy either by closing the Japanese market to foreign goods or by placing foreign industries at a disadvantage until domestic industries were strong enough to compete internationally. Such solicitousness of the bureaucracy on behalf of domestic industry gave the bureaucracy all that much more leverage in controlling economic policy.

The bureaucracy gradually augmented its power through a policy of staunch fairness until it became the bulwark of the establishment. Individual politicians, businessmen, and intellectual leaders have some influence, but they wield it largely at the pleasure of the bureaucracy. Since the Meiji Restoration, the bureaucracy has possessed some of Japan's greatest talent and has consistently attracted the best and brightest of the nation's youth.

Education: The Key

Just as Tokyo University remains undisputedly Japan's most prestigious university, a career as a high-ranking bureaucrat continues to be the nation's most prestigious occupation. Admission to both is gained solely through scholastic achievement. Insofar at least as education is the sole criterion for advancement, Japan is today perhaps the world's most egalitarian society. The young men who enter the ministries as career bureaucrats are intellectually the cream of the university crop, and most of them are graduates of Tokyo University. This university has outstanding departments in all fields, and attracts the nation's most promising students. Their training there in turn gives them an advantage in the impartially administered Principal Senior A-Class Examination for entrance into the bureaucracy, a final test designed to screen out all but the very best.

Even more important than their university education, however, is the training these young public servants are given *after* they are hired. In a lecture delivered in Tokyo in 1977, Ezra Vogel, Harvard Professor of Sociology, noted the advantages of the Japanese bureaucratic system and cited the careful grooming program for young officers as one of the principal factors in its success. This program, referred to above, deserves to be reviewed in greater detail, again using the Ministry of Finance as an example.

The bureaucracy consists of a select corps of high-echelon "career" officials and candidates and numerous lower-ranking "non-careerists." Like all the ministries, the Ministry of Finance holds a public examination each year; the 20 or 30 top-scoring applicants are hired as "apprentices," who, as mentioned earlier, receive approximately six years of special academic and practical training. They are given constant personal attention in an effort to integrate them fully into the Ministry of Finance "family."

The candidate spends his first year of apprenticeship in a planning and research section of one of the various bureaus, such as the minister's secretariat, the document section, or the general affairs section. These sections are responsible for coordinating information and activities within the ministry, formulating policy vis-à-vis Diet procedures, and conducting overall planning, and the work load frequently keeps them working long after hours. Through his duties of copying the documents drafted by his seniors and assisting in their research, the trainee learns the ministry's work patterns and strives to mold himself into an integral part of the ministry family.

At the end of their first year of service, most young ministry officials are assigned to an outlying bureau as an investigator to continue their on-the-job training in taxation and finance. The senior officials of the local Tax Administration Bureau where they are assigned take special care of "these young men from Tokyo," not only training them in official functions but also helping them to develop sound interpersonal relations.

These two years of experience behind him, the young candidate is often sent to the United States or Europe, all expenses paid, for postgraduate university study. While overseas postgraduate work usually lasts two years, but may be prolonged to three years or longer if the individual decides to continue for a Ph.D. Even those candidates who are not selected for overseas study are encouraged to devote their third-year as much as possible to academic pursuits. Priority during this year is on individual study, and they are under no obligation to help their colleagues with routine work, no matter how busy the ministry may be.

Next, a candidate is appointed to the post of sub-section chief, and in the following year, section chief. In his sixth year, he is appointed chief of a local tax office, with a staff of 40-50 officials under him and a chauffeured car at his disposal. At the age of about twenty-eight, he may command one of the highest positions in local power. While carrying out his duties at the office (an office specifically selected for its relative freedom from serious problems), the young tax chief has ample opportunity to grow accustomed to the prerogatives and obligations of power. Aside from the danger of being spoiled, this period at the local tax office is an excellent opportunity for an aspiring careerist to gain practical experience in all the skills he will need. When his term of office is up, usually after one year, he is called back to the ministry in Tokyo.

While Japanese companies also customarily provide new employees with good vocational training based upon the assumption of life-long employment, training in the private sector is generally no match for that offered in the bureaucracy, particularly the Ministry of Finance. In many ways, the Ministry of Finance may be considered a special case, but it is typical of the serious investment the bureaucracy makes in the training of its new members. The principle behind this practice is that new people are employed not necessarily for their immediately available abilities but as "human resources" to be refined and developed over the years until the time comes when their talents can blossom fully within the organization.

Even after this extensive training, a public official continues his career by serving several years in a wide variety of posts which broadens his proficiencies and deepens his experience.

Today the increasing specialization and complexity of the economy necessitates sophisticated technical knowledge in specific areas, and high-echelon officials have been given special training: specialists in the Budget Bureau to draft the budget, in the Tax Bureau to be in charge of tax administration, in the Banking Bureau to execute financial administration, and in the International Finance Bureau to deal with global economic affairs. The Budget Bureau was once regarded the core of the ministry's work while other bureaus and departments were considered merely peripheral. Progressive economic internationalization, however, has meant that today those responsible for international economic affairs enjoy the most power and prestige.

A Comparison with the British Bureaucracy

In Britain, high-level public officials are largely the children of the establishment who attended "public" schools, graduated from Oxford and Cambridge and entered the bureaucracy through the competitive civil service examinations. From fifty to ninety percent of those who pass the civil service exam are Oxford and Cambridge graduates and products of the elite public schools, indicating the degree to which the upper class dominates in the bureaucracy.* Likewise in Japan, high-ranking bureaucrats are part of the establishment. They may be graduates of Tokyo University; but unlike their British counterparts, this does not necessarily mean they are children of the upper-class establishment. In Japan, being the son of a bureaucrat is of no particular advantage. While there have been many second generation leaders in the political and business worlds, individual merit and performance have always been the crucial qualifications in the civil service.

The British bureaucracy also offers lifetime employment; an able person can rise to the highest civil service position of Permanent Secretary and serve there for ten to fifteen years before retiring at sixty. There are only a few such high-level positions, however, and since turn-over is slow, the sluggishness of promotion often drives more ambitious civil servants out of the bureaucracy. By contrast, Japanese bureaucrats unfailingly retire at 54

---

*R.K. Kelsal, *Higher Civil Servant in Britain*, 1955.

or 55, and even appointment as vice-minister, the highest civil service post in Japan, is only for a period of two years.

Like Japanese bureaucrats, retiring British civil servants often take executive positions with public corporations, but few ever enter politics, preferring bank-related or business work. Cases are numerous in Japan in which a retiring bureaucrat takes a position of trustee in a public corporation or becomes a director or president of a large corporation. But they will almost invariably take one or two years off after leaving the civil service. While this apparent retirement allows them to enjoy the good life they have worked so hard to earn, it also serves to diffuse the legal and public censure to which the custom of "*amakudari*" (lit., "descent from heaven"; the practice of inviting retiring high-level bureaucrats to step into important private-sector positions) is so susceptible. Former officials of economy-related agencies, in particular, are much sought after by corporations which hope to benefit from the personal bonds these people have built up with the "family" of colleagues in their former ministry. A vice-minister or bureau chief is virtually guaranteed such a post-retirement job and even high officials outside the economy-related ministries can count on leadership positions in semi-governmental organizations.

As mentioned earlier, another alternative for a retired bureaucrat is to enter the world of politics. To become a politician, however, he must undergo initiation into the political world through the general elections. He does have an advantage that government agencies have branches all over the country, so that an ex-bureaucrat can count on wholehearted "family" support. If he chooses to run from the district where he was born, he is still one step ahead since, having risen high in the bureaucracy, he is already one of the most prominent figures from the area. Whatever his constituency, if he can master the techniques of cordiality and modesty in interpersonal relations—so crucial in winning an election and so different from the interpersonal relations in the bureaucracy – he is almost assured of success.

During one brief period after the War, some bureaucrats-turned-politicians ran on the Socialist Party of Japan ticket, which enhanced that party's prestige and expanded its base of support. However, today almost all former bureaucrats run as conservatives, especially as Liberal Democrats. In fact, ex-bureaucrats now account for twenty to thirty percent of Diet seats held by Liberal Democratic Party members. While this is not a particularly high ratio, these people hold the power to formulate policy, which gives them an importance out of proportion to their numbers and assures them bright political prospects.

The Trouble Ahead

Despite the bureaucracy's solid record of achievement, public esteem, and outstanding ability, its position is not altogether unassailable. The decline in the status of bureaucrats and the loss of professional pride is becoming the subject of debate among the public in general and among middle-echelon bureaucrats in particular. Two factors are directly responsible for this: increasing trivialization of bureaucrats' work and encroachments on their discretion by politics.

Bureaucrats feel their work has been trivialized because so much of their time and talent must be given over to formulating plans to help cabinet ministers and other officials respond tactfully to Diet interpellations. After the War and up until the last Kishi Cabinet of 1960, little time was necessary for such activities. The government welcomed confrontation in the Diet, vigorously refuted opposition arguments and swung the voting by virtue of its vast majority. Accordingly, almost all the very rationally worked-out bills drawn up by the bureaucracy passed the Diet just as submitted, and the bureaucracy spent far less time outguessing the Opposition and formulating defenses for their proposals.

The Cabinet of Prime Minister Ikeda Hayato is best known for the successful National Income Doubling Plan, but also as the government that abandoned the politics of confrontation and adopted what might be called "low-profile politics." The Ikeda cabinets tended to sidestep action on issues likely to arouse the Opposition and to treat Diet interpellations with the utmost deference. Government policy defenses were couched in respectful terms, and a deliberate effort was made to be unprovocative. This policy was successful and has been adopted by subsequent cabinets ever since to fend off opposition in the Diet.

At the same time, instead of incisive debate on significant policy issues, the questioning itself has become increasingly preoccupied with trivial inconsistencies. Since sessions are now broadcast live on television, Opposition Diet members have started to make the most of the opportunity to appeal to the electorate through their speeches in the course of interpellation. Government replies must be drafted with utmost care, for the questioner is apt to take issue not so much with the thrust of the proposed policy as with the way it is phrased. In addition, the Diet now sits almost without a break throughout the year, including regular and extraordinary sessions. As a result, instead of devoting themselves to the formulation of national policy, bureaucrats find themselves spending all of their time and energy drafting artful strategies and rebuttals for Diet defense. In addition, many ministers find themselves required to spend valuable time at Diet committee meetings, and ultimately most of the draft replies never see the light of day – providing fuel not for public debate but for the ministry's incinerator. Faced with such anomalies, the morale of middle-echelon bureaucrats cannot help but flag.

Unlike politicians, bureaucrats are not supposed to appear in the mass media and seldom express opinions on political affairs. Indeed, middle-rank bureaucrats have never been known to criticize the Diet, which is nominally the highest organ of state power. Diet interpellations in particular, no matter how absurd they may appear, have been considered a sacrosanct ritual of democracy immune from criticism. But bureaucratic discontent burst into the open in July 1976 when Kakizawa Kōji, then a middle-ranking official of the Ministry of Finance, published in its PR bulletin an essay entitled, "The Bespectacled Rat Pack of Kasumigaseki, or the Frustrated Elite of the Ministry of Finance." The fact that he would even dare to use so disparaging a phrase attests to the degree of bureaucratic disillusionment.

The second main factor in the decline of bureaucratic status and professional pride is the growing frequency with which their carefully-wrought policy proposals are later transformed by political pressures. Over long years of experience at the helm of government, conservative politicians have learned much from the bureaucracy. They had free access to the bureaucracy's fund of information, learned techniques of policy formation refined by the bureaucracy, and even gained a measure of control over the bureaucracy through skillful personnel administration. This in itself is not wrong, in the sense that it simply implies an expansion of legislative power. But this enhanced legislative authority has frequently been exercised solely to protect vested political interests. The preservation of government-controlled rice marketing and the protection offered non-competitive meat distribution mechanisms are blatant examples of political efforts to cater to these vested interests and the voting power which they represent. Such pressures often come from both government and Opposition politicians. Combined with the government's disinclination for confrontation with Diet opposition, bureaucratic authority has been seriously hampered, and the incentive for individual bureaucrats to formulate meaningful policy measures has been undermined.

Government and Opposition forces have gradually equalized in the Diet, and political deals and compromises to get bills passed have increased. For example, faced with concerted Opposition demands for a tax cut, the government compromised the Ministry of Finance budget draft in order to get it passed. A final compromise of half the demanded ¥1 trillion tax cut produced, to the thinking of the bureaucracy, an "unreasonable" result.

Behind these phenomena, however, is the absence of a new and overriding national objective. Following the Meiji Restoration of 1868, the imperative was to catch up with the West, and the existence of this clear objective enabled the people to appreciate and applaud the teamwork of the government and bureaucracy with the support of business. Or perhaps it would be more correct to say that success in steadily expanding the national economic pie insured that the common appetite for an ever-larger piece of pie was met.

However, now that Japan has caught up with the West in per capita income, and is beginning to overtake it in other aspects such as some industrial production techniques, average life-span, and the like, it has become harder to formulate a direction for the future. Moreover, as Japan was drawn into the mainstream of international politics by the oil crisis, currency instability and other economic problems, its own policy-making has become extremely complicated and uncertain. The decline in status and confidence experienced by the bureaucracy has undoubtedly been worsened by its admission of error in forecasting the international economic situation. The pluralization of values and increased uncertainty about the future are worldwide phenomena, and the challenge for the bureaucracy today is to determine how it can "move" Japanese society in the context of these entirely new conditions.

Editors' Note

This essay is based largely on information provided in the following three works:

Sakakibara Eisuke, *Nihon o Enshutsu suru Shin Kanryō Zō* (Modern Bureaucrats Who Move Japan), Tokyo: Yamate Shobō, 1977.

Watanuki Jōji, *Nihon no Seiji Shakai* (Politics and Society in Japan), Tokyo: University of Tokyo Press, 1967.

Sakaguchi Akira "Zaikai, Seitō, Kanryō" (Zaikai, Political Parties, and the Bureaucracy) in *Keieishi Kōza* (A Course on the History of Management), vol. 4, ed. by Morikawa Hidemasa, Tokyo: The Nihon Keizai, 1976.

Case Study:

Foreign Policy à la LDP
— The 1956 Soviet-Japanese Peace Agreement

DONALD C. HELLMANN

The key to understanding the foreign policy of Japan since the end of the American Occupation lies in the dynamics of Japanese domestic politics. At the same time, an examination of the decision-making process regarding major foreign policy issues provides some of the best windows for viewing the workings of the Japanese political system. This study focuses on the negotiation of the Soviet-Japanese Peace Agreement of 1956, but lays the foundation for understanding the foreign policy-making process in Japan throughout the entire postwar period.[1] Partly, this is because the essential features of the foreign policy-making process (especially the unbroken rule of the pro-American Liberal Democratic Party and the continuing confrontation of the essentially anti-American Opposition parties) have remained largely unchanged since the mid-1950s, despite the sweeping socio-economic changes that Japan has experienced in recent decades. Partly, it is because the main categories for analysis: public opinion, the party system, and the formal governmental institutions, provide a useful framework for examining the foreign policy formulation process regarding all major decisions in recent decades.

It should be clear from the outset that this approach to Japanese foreign policy has not been widely used and a main conclusion, that Japan plays an essentially passive role in international politics because of the

---

[1] This article draws heavily on my book *Japanese Domestic Politics and Foreign Policy: The Peace Agreement with the Soviet Union* (Berkeley: University of California Press, 1969), which is also published in translation as *Nihon no Seiji to Gaikō* (Tokyo: Chūō Kōronsha, 1970), especially Chapters I and IV.

nature of the decision-making process, is at odds with conventional wisdom. The remarkable success of Japan in gaining international status and wealth is usually assumed to be the result of shrewdly calculated responses of government decision-makers in Tokyo to the realities of world politics, or, more recently, the product of a vaguely defined coalition of business and government popularly labeled "Japan, Inc."[2] To be sure, by focusing essentially on the impact of Japanese domestic politics, somewhat exaggerated emphasis is given to the restraints imposed on Japan in international affairs, but this is a needed corrective to the image of Tokyo as a grand master in the chess game of international affairs. Even a cursory inspection of the way in which one major foreign policy decision was made underscores the inhibitions on bold leadership that are imposed by the policy-making process.

The peace agreement with the Soviet Union provides a unique opportunity for examining the postwar foreign policy-making process. Because virtually all political forces directly participated in this first major policy decision after independence and because at this time Japanese politics were undergoing rapid and fundamental change,[3] aspects of the process which commonly take place in muted fashion behind the scenes occurred openly and in exaggerated forms. Rather than elaborating the details of the negotiations chronologically, the main components of the policy-making process will be delineated and the peculiar role of each component (e.g. public opinion) in this decision explained.

The most important component of the Japanese foreign policy formulation process is the political party system. Under the Constitution of 1947, the majority party in the Diet and its president, the Prime Minister, are allocated central roles in decision-making. The unwavering party discipline in Diet votes together with the responsibilities of the Prime Minister, both in selecting the Cabinet and in assuming day-to-day policy leadership, have made the politics and policies of the ruling party the main domestic influences on Japanese foreign policy. Nevertheless, to deal fully with foreign policy formulation it is also necessary to give attention to

[2] See, for example, Herman Kahn, *The Emerging Japanese Superstate: Challenge and Response* (Englewood Cliffs: Prentice-Hall, 1970); the countermanifesto, Zbigniew Brzezinski, *The Fragile Blossom: Crisis and Change in Japan* (New York: Harper and Row, 1972); and Robert E. Osgood, *The Weary and the Wary: U.S. and Japanese Security Policies in Transition* (Baltimore: Johns Hopkins University Press, 1971).

[3] For elaboration see Masumi Junnosuke, "1955 Nen no Seiji Taisei" (The Political Structure in 1955), *Shisō*, June 1965 (Tokyo: Iwanami Shoten), pp. 55-72.

the role of pressure groups and to the patterns of interaction with the Opposition parties.

The Role of the Conservatives

The most striking feature of the Soviet-Japanese peace negotiations is the extreme degree to which control of policy was concentrated within the ruling conservative party. All other components of the political system — the Opposition, public opinion, pressure groups, and the bureaucracy — were able to affect policy to the extent that they could affect intraparty decision-making. Before elaborating on the specific circumstances among the conservatives during the Soviet peace negotiations, it is first necessary to set forth some general features of the *modus operandi* of the Liberal Democratic Party — particularly regarding the fragmented composition of the party and its impact on the formulation of policy on critical international issues.

Structurally, the Liberal Democratic Party and its various postwar conservative precursors have been essentially alliances of factions (*ha* or *habatsu*) operating together primarily for political expediency. Factions are in a basic sense autonomous parties, having their own independent sources of finance, running their own candidates under the Liberal Democratic Party label, and regularly caucusing for discussion of political strategy and, more recently, of policy matters. The causes of factions are many and varied. In part, they reflect traditional social mores, for similar factional groupings appear in all Japanese organizations. The leader-follower relationship in the party *habatsu* — the leader providing funds, political positions, and services extending beyond economic assistance in exchange for personal loyalty — is a particular manifestation of general behavioral norms common in Japanese society. *Habatsu* have also developed in response to the peculiar conditions of the postwar political system. Perhaps their primary practical *raison d'être* is to provide the funds necessary for securing and holding office that usually neither the individual nor the party can fully supply. No person can long remain a successful faction leader without business connections or substantial personal wealth. Factions are most directly concerned with the distribution of power and positions in the party and in the executive offices of the government, with the election of the party president (hence the Prime Minister) the event of major concern. Finally, the multimember electoral system, which makes open competition between conservative party candidates within the individual constituencies inevitable, works to perpetuate factional rivalries. The Liberal Democrats remain essentially a parliamentary party without a broad popular base or a strong national organization, and party leadership is recruited from those members of the Diet who can best operate in the complex and constricting world of the *habatsu*.

All major postwar foreign policy decisions — particularly the Soviet peace negotiations — as issues over which there is no broad consensus, have been deeply affected by factional politics. The commingling of factional politics with foreign policy-making imposes serious restraints on the Prime Minister's capacity for leadership; for as the head of a coalition, he must seek at least the tacit agreement of other faction leaders concerning not only the merits of policy but also the current balance of power within the party. Limits are placed on the *kinds* of policies that are undertaken. Except in extreme and unusual circumstances (the Soviet negotiations are the prime example), initiative tends to be confined to issues with minimum risk and controversy and having relatively calculable costs. Moreover, by confounding domestic and international considerations, the policy debate gives undue emphasis to the specific and short-term effects of each decision. This style of policy formulation has led to success only because Japan has dealt with issues free from the imperatives of long-term strategic planning and decisive action required of a nation fully engaged in international politics.

The Soviet-Japanese peace negotiations provide an example *par excellence* of the extensive degree to which intraparty politics fundamentally shapes foreign policy-making in Japan. It should first be emphasized that this was a time (1954-56) of great fluidity in conservative politics. With the return of prewar party leaders at the end of the Occupation in 1952, the ruling Liberal Party became divided into factions centered around older "depurged" political figures; and at the same time, a rival conservative group, the Progressive Party, also was able to challenge more effectively the heretofore dominant Liberals. In November 1954, a loose group of factions split from the Liberal Party and formed the Democratic Party. Hatoyama Ichirō, an elderly prewar politician with strong popular appeal, was chosen as president. The Democratic Party absorbed the Progressive Party and, securing the parliamentary support of the Socialists by promising a general election in two months, shakily took hold of the reins of government. The Democrats had two overriding concerns when they came into power, the maintenance of party solidarity and the strengthening of the party's Diet representation in the forthcoming general election. To establish an identity separate from the Liberals and to introduce a fresh issue for the election, Hatoyama announced that normalization of relations with the Soviet Union would be top priority for his government.

This slogan, which embittered the Liberal Party and was not fully accepted even within the Democrats, projected foreign policy toward the Soviet Union deeply into the intra-conservative power struggle, where it remained for the next two years. The election results were a triumph for the Democrats and for Hatoyama personally and, at the same time the Prime Minister and his faction became fully identified with the policy of early normalization of relations with Moscow — a posture that virtually insured subsequent conflict. The policy initiative toward normalization clearly was not a carefully calculated diplomatic action, but rather was introduced in the form of a slogan for domestic political effect. Moreover, the government's moves in the ensuing months were guided almost exclusively by considerations of internal politics. As a result, the Soviets held the diplomatic initiative from the outset and, from an international viewpoint, it was in response to their maneuvers that the changes in Japanese policy took place. Japan's role was to prove an extremely passive one.

The extent of this passivity is clear from an examination of the major policy shifts taken by Tokyo during 1955 and 1956. The formal talks which began with the Soviets in mid-1955 in London, were abruptly ended in August after the Russians claimed, seemingly with justification, that the territorial demands of Japan regarding the Kurile Islands had suddenly changed. This change in policy by Tokyo resulted from a bitter struggle among the conservatives related to an effort to merge the Liberal and Democratic parties. As one of the conditions for joining the merger, a move forced on the conservatives by the merger of the two socialist parties, the Liberals successfully demanded an expanded territorial claim be pressed in London. When this was implemented, it surprised the chief Japanese negotiator and infuriated the Russians — and led Moscow abruptly to suspend the talks.[4]

Immediately following an abortive second set of formal talks in early 1956, the Soviets skillfully exploited the divisions within the newly merged conservatives by imposing restrictions on Japanese fishing in the waters off the Soviet maritime provinces. This provoked a fishery conference in Moscow, in which the Japanese representative was the Minister of Agriculture and Forestry, Kōno Ichirō, the most powerful ally of Hatoyama in the cabinet and one who had close ties with the fishing industry. The result was a fishing agreement tied to the reopening of normalization talks, conditions which strengthened the hand of the Soviet Union and the Hatoyama faction by opening the door to a compromise settlement which avoided the territorial issue.

---

[4]For elaboration see Hellmann, *op. cit.*, pp. 58-60.

However, the press of politics in Tokyo again intruded into the policy-making process. Because the conservatives remained deeply divided over this issue and because in the ensuing weeks the Prime Minister was preoccupied with a House of Councillors election, the responsibility for devising an appropriate policy fell to Shigemitsu Mamoru, the Foreign Minister and plenipotentiary to the normalization talks to be held in Moscow in August 1956. Shigemitsu, as president of the Progressive Party, had joined the Hatoyama Cabinet with a strong expectation that he would eventually become Prime Minister, but he proved to be ineffective in the intraparty factional struggle. Although he had openly voiced reservations about early normalization with the Soviet Union in Moscow, Shigemitsu unexpectedly accepted a peace treaty arrangement, which concept he and the majority of the conservatives had previously rejected. Again the basic reasons behind this policy *volte face* seem to have been lodged in Japanese domestic politics, that is a desperate attempt by one man (Shigemitsu) to gain the political capital to become Prime Minister.[5] This tentative agreement with the Soviets was rejected by the party leadership and the issue then became fully and openly caught up in the struggle for party control. Ultimately, an agreement was signed with the Soviet Union only after Prime Minister Hatoyama promised the other faction leaders in the party that he would resign upon the conclusion of a normalization pact, and he then set off on a successful trip to Moscow in the face of continuing political turmoil among the conservatives and no real consensus on the proper policy.

What is noteworthy about this process is the way in which this foreign policy issue came to be defined almost completely in terms of intraparty considerations. In the end Hatoyama was able to successfully force a decision only through personal capitulation (i.e. resignation) and not through channels of responsible party leadership. Not only was the process of foreign policy-making essentially a narrow trade-off of factional interests, but the nature and momentum of intraparty decision-making made the decision "self-contained," that is, only peripherally affected by political forces outside the party.

The Role of Business

The role of business in the Soviet peace negotiations had two dimensions. The first involved the activities of the national business organiza-

---

[5] Kōno Ichirō, *Ima dakara Hanasō* (Now I Can Speak, Tokyo: Shunyōdō Shoten, 1958), pp. 55-56.

tions, while the second encompassed the actions of the fishing industry. The business world, as the main supporter of the conservatives, sought influence primarily through the party.

In fact, the impact of business on the negotiations was extremely small. Two unusual circumstances partially explain this: the limited connections between "party politician" Hatoyama and the main elements in the business world and the then-limited economic interests by Japan in the Soviet Union. However, the failure of business to gain effective access to the policy-making process underscores that there is no automatic or easy agreement between the government and the business world on foreign policy matters in which political considerations are important. After being drawn into the public debate over Soviet policy in mid-1956, the businessmen were virtually obliged to intervene publicly when the Shigemitsu mission failed ignominiously and precipitated such chaos among the conservatives that questions were raised about the capacity of the Liberal Democrats to retain control of the government. In a series of public statements, the leaders of the Japanese national business organizations opposed Hatoyama's trip to Moscow until the political situation within the conservative party was settled. These opinions were totally repudiated by the conservatives as unwarranted intervention into politics. Thus, neither the fragmented financial ties between business and the *habatsu*, nor the diffuse personal contacts among the business and political elites, nor the basic shared conservative ideals were able to reach the intraparty decision-making process, which by August and September of 1956 had gained a momentum of its own.

One economic issue, Japan's fishing rights in the northern seas, did figure significantly in the Soviet negotiations and the fishing industry actively worked for its own benefit as an interest group. Three conditions provided them with special advantages: (1) personal and financial connections with Kōno Ichirō and the Prime Minister's faction; (2) their clear and tangible electoral threat to the Liberal Democrats (unlike the business groups); and (3) the use of fishery restrictions by the Soviets to force early normalization of relations. Indeed, the unusual role of the fishery industry in Japanese politics was fully appreciated by the Russians, who added a new dimension to the negotiations by using a domestic pressure group to achieve a diplomatic aim that had proven beyond their reach through normal governmental channels.

The Role of the Socialists

The Socialist Party of Japan, the leading Opposition party at the time of the Soviet negotiations, was in a difficult political and ideological position. Indeed, when Hatoyama first raised the issue of normalization of relations, the Socialists were formally split into two groups over differences of foreign policy relating primarily to the Japanese-American alliance. Although these differences were overtly resolved through the merger of July 1955, personal and ideological animosities from the split were not far below the surface. Such differences aggravated the factional rivalries, which also divided the Socialists. In aggregate, the Socialists found common ground in opposition to the undeviatingly pro-American posture of the Liberal Democrats, but they were faced with a more difficult tactical situation as a result of a government policy which they had long favored, *viz.* normalization of relations with the Soviet Union.

Through the Shigemitsu mission, the Socialists acted as constructive policy critics and a loyal Opposition party. However, when confronted with internal conservative strife focused on Soviet policy, they chose to use this issue to harass the Liberal Democrats and to strengthen their own position. At no time did they issue an unambiguous statement on behalf of normalization or Hatoyama, but instead they concentrated on the political and policy shortcomings of the conservatives. Whatever this implies for the opportunistic disposition of a supposedly ideologically rigid party, it served to insure that Soviet policy would indeed be essentially a function of Japanese domestic politics and not careful calculation. Moreover, by failing to take a forthright position on a policy they had favored, they vitiated whatever constructive influence they could have exerted in the decision-making process. Like the other elements in the party system, except for the special case of the fishing industry, the Socialist Party of Japan left the Liberal Democrats' control of policy largely unaffected.[6]

The Role of Public Opinion

Before turning to the role of the public in the Soviet-Japanese peace negotiations, it is first necessary to consider the general role of public opinion in foreign policy in democratic polities. Public opinion is a prominent term in most discussions of foreign policy, in part because it is closely connected with democratic ideals and slogans. Because public opinion provides a direct link between the people and specific political decisions, it seems to exemplify a basic kind of democratic procedure and at the same time dignify the individual by projecting him immediately into the governmental process. Scholars and journalists try to educate it;

[6] For elaboration see Hellmann, *op. cit.*, pp. 118-119.

politicians claim to speak in its name or attempt to unify it; polls try to measure it. Nevertheless, most studies of public opinion in Western nations see its impact on policy as complex and, in aggregate, quite limited. It can be assumed that the Japanese public does not differ in politically significant ways from those in other democratic societies.

To evaluate how Japanese foreign policy is affected by public opinion, it is necessary to distinguish between effective public opinion and opinions held by the public. Public opinion polls deal with the latter. That is, they simply set forth a description of the opinions held by the people on specific issues. Whether these opinions have influence on the government depends on other factors. There are two kinds of effective public opinion; that is, there are two forms in which the people can influence the decision-makers and have an impact on policy. One is the mass mood or climate of opinion, while the second is made up of the articulate expressions on policy of specific individuals and organized groups including the media of communication.

The mass mood exerts influence only on the most general goals of foreign policy and is of importance only in those few decisions (e.g. an immediate threat of war) which are of both dramatic and far-reaching significance. The policy-makers may be affected by the climate of opinion in two ways. All tend to respond instinctively to broad attitudes which are an integral part of the political and social milieu of which they are members (e.g. the traditional French feelings regarding Germans or the popular antipathy toward massive rearmament in postwar Japan). In addition, as politicians, they are influenced by the overt expression of these opinions in public opinion polls and in election trends. The overwhelming majority of the public in Western democracies is uninformed about and uninterested in foreign policy, and the views expressed in the vast numbers of polls regarding foreign affairs are shallowly held and expressed largely in response to the prodding of the questioners. As the Soviet-Japanese peace negotiations illustrate, Japan falls into this pattern as well.

Articulate opinion has an activist dimension, and in Japan it has been employed primarily by the opposition, especially through demonstrations, policy pronouncements in the mass media, and interpellations in the Diet. These tactics have, of course, also been used on occasion by opposition factions within the conservative party and various interest and opinion groups. Both the style, and to a large extent the impact, of articulate opinion are basically shaped by the mass media, who report and distill the opinions expressed, provide much of the factual background immediately relevant to the issue at hand, and are able to present forcefully their own views to the policy-makers and general public alike. These exchanges constitute the essence of the public foreign policy debate in Japan, but whether or not they affect the decision-making process is the function of a party system continuously dominated by the conservatives, an electoral system in which personalities and domestic issues continuously take precedence, and an elite political culture (involving bureaucrats and conservative party leaders) that lacks a tradition of open, democratic decision-making. In the Soviet peace negotiations, and throughout the recent history of postwar Japan, the government has made the critical foreign policy decisions with only peripheral reference to expressions of articulate opinion.[7]

Given these general characteristics of public opinion, it is not surprising that a mass mood strong enough to influence the policy-makers did not and could not emerge during the Soviet-Japan peace talks. Highly negative, historically rooted feelings toward the Soviet Union (earlier Imperial Russia) and antipathy toward Communist policies, were held not only by the elite but by the general populace. (e.g. Public opinion polls consistently showed Russia as the foreign nation most disliked.) However, these attitudes were balanced by equally strong opinions favoring peace, the settlement of issues still outstanding from World War II, and a desire for Japan to play a more independent role in world politics. Public attitudes toward specific problems were not intensely held and were shaped by the specific turns of events during the negotiations rather than shaping them. Perhaps the most dramatic evidence of the shallowness of popular opinion regarding the negotiations is an *Asahi Shinbun* poll of November 1955 (almost a year after the issue became the central concern of Japanese foreign policy), in which 62% of the sample could not name a single item that had become a matter of contention in the talks.[8] This absence of strongly supported opinions allowed policy initiative to rest almost entirely in the hands of the government — a tendency that was abetted by the closed nature of the conservative party's decision-making process previously discussed.

Articulate opinion consisted primarily of three groups broadly concerned with the normalization of relations between Japan and the Soviet Union. Perhaps the most distinctly Japanese aspect was provided by a group of former top-ranking Foreign Ministry officials, including ex-Prime Minister Yoshida Shigeru, who were critical both of the policy of early

---

[7] This section draws heavily on Chapter 3 in Donald C. Hellmann, *Japan and East Asia: The New International Order* (New York: Praeger, 1972), especially pp. 58-60.

[8] *Asahi Shinbun*, December 5, 1955.

normalization and the way in which the Foreign Minister was effectively kept out of the policy formulation process. Influence was sought through public statements and newspaper articles, which sought to exploit the prominent place that these individuals held in the establishment. Although there is no evidence that the timing or substance of policy was affected by their actions, they did serve to widen the split within the conservative party on the issue. The national business associations, before turning to challenge frontally the political power of Prime Minister Hatoyama, attempted to build a public consensus on policy toward the Soviet Union, thereby adding another dimension to articulate opinion. The statements issued in the name of these organizations, following a series of "conferences" of business leaders, did constitute a clear, albeit bland, policy recommendation from another element of the establishment. Nevertheless, because of the momentum of the intraparty decision-making process, this had little impact on government policy. The main influence of the various organizations formally committed to promoting ties between Japan and the Soviet Union (e.g. the Japan-Soviet Friendship Society and the National Council for the Restoration of Diplomatic Relations with China and the Soviet Union) came not from the various publications and public meetings they sponsored, but rather from the behind-the-scenes liaison which they provided between the Hatoyama-Kōno conservative faction and the unofficial Soviet mission in Tokyo. It is ironic, but instructive, that the main impact of articulate public opinion was to promote "private diplomacy."

In the Soviet negotiations, the press reported in full detail the vicissitudes of the formal talks and the related domestic political maneuvers. Although the issue was more or less continuously reported, the intensity of the coverage fluctuated widely, following closely the dramatic changes in the formal talks. The confused account which resulted paralleled the uninformed and uncommitted state of public opinion — a correlation implying the strong imprint of the press on public opinion and suggesting yet another reason for the gap between the public and the policy formulation process. Moreover, the tangled tale of intraparty rivalry mingled with and ultimately dominated discussion of substantive issues, and the newspaper editorials left undisturbed the resulting muddled picture. In aggregate, press coverage inhibited the effect of not only articulate but general opinion on the foreign policy-making process.

The Role of the Bureaucracy

The formal governmental institutions directly concerned with international affairs form the final major component of the foreign policy formulation process. Their roles in the Soviet negotiations further illustrate the fluidity which characterized Japanese politics during this period. The wide gap between the effective processes of decision-making, elaborated in the preceding chapters, and the formal structures and procedures set up for this purpose fully demonstrated the absence of established channels for communication and policy control. Indeed, rather than facilitating policy leadership, the Foreign Ministry (Gaimushō), and to a much lesser extent the Diet, inhibited the operations of the government. In the formulation of policy toward Russia, the Foreign Ministry actually came to be a rival to the government, often differing with and occasionally openly challenging the "official" policy. Underlying the competition were a variety of factors: personal political rivalries, concrete policy disagreements, and the strong dislike of prewar diplomats in the Gaimushō of both Prime Minister Hatoyama's pragmatic negotiating tactics and his constitutionally sanctioned attempts to take policy leadership into his own hands. Instead of serving as a stabilizing force, the Gaimushō further compounded the complexities of formulating Soviet policy.

In a sense, the peace agreement of 1956 marked the passing of an era. Unlike in the prewar period, the Japanese Foreign Ministry proved incapable of directly competing with the ruling party in the making of policy. As intended in the 1947 Constitution, the Prime Minister and his party were in control — the old gave way to the new, the politician replaced the bureaucrat.

In contrast, the plenary Diet sessions and committee meetings dealing with Soviet policy played relatively modest parts in the negotiations. They did provide additional stages for debate over the issue, but did not go much beyond that role and its limited influence. Decision-making was extended to include the legislature only in a formal sense and at the periphery of the effective process through which Soviet policy was formulated.

Conclusions

Are serious problems for the Japanese political system posed if the foreign policy-making process remains highly insulated from outside influences? The wide gap between the elitist practice and the democratic ideals embodied in the Constitution and now integral to the political socialization process could be a highly destabilizing influence. Unless the channels of communication and access are broadened, each major foreign policy decision will be a potential crisis in which not only policy but the viability of the system itself is called into question. Although experience in Western democracies also suggests that effective widespread political participation in foreign policy formulation is a difficult if not impossible goal, it is doubtful that an open society with democratic ideals can for long sustain a decision-making process which functions autonomously from virtually all articulate and organized elements of its political system. Although the Soviet negotiations constitute a special case, displaying to an extreme degree the potential autonomy of conservative decision-making, nevertheless, the underlying structural and attitudinal forces operative in 1955 and 1956 have persisted. The problem which dramatically emerged in the Hatoyama era is still pertinent to foreign policy-making.

Despite the danger to the political system inherent in a decision-making process largely restricted to a party elite, this may well be the characteristic pattern for Japan. A party-centered pattern similar to that seen in the Soviet negotiations characterized the decision to normalize relations with South Korea and dominated the protracted moves regarding ties with Communist China. The mass involvement in the 1960 the U.S.-Japan Security Treaty incident represents, in one sense, a deviation from this pattern; but effective policy control in that instance remained in the hands of the Prime Minister, and it is doubtful that such widespread violent actions could recur in future Japanese foreign policy decisions without producing basic changes in the political order. Short of such revolutionary upheaval, in Japan as in the open societies of the West, the style of foreign policy-making is best understood by concentrating on the apex of the political order and on the political culture of the elite, not on the more visible mass base.

To evaluate the efficiency of the Japanese political institutions and processes in the peace negotiations, the most useful criteria are those of policy leadership and control. In this regard the crucial question is to what extent the Hatoyama government's accommodation of domestic attitudes and pressures weakened Japan's position in bargaining with Moscow. Although Japan was internationally in a weak position vis-à-vis the Soviet Union, this was a period of thaw in the cold war, leaving some latitude for diplomatic maneuver. To understand the almost wholly passive and reactive role of Japan in the negotiations, it is necessary to ascertain whether the limits imposed on policy leadership by the domestic political process left open even the possibility of another kind of agreement.

With the locus of power in Japan so centered in the ruling Liberal Democrats, the foreign policy formulation process was virtually identical with party decision-making. The task of balancing the semi-autonomous factions within the party in order to maintain conservative unity continuously served as a check on strong policy leadership by Hatoyama. As the question of Soviet policy became a focal point for factional contention, the issue became deeply involved in the struggle for party control. Government policy eventually was determined as much by *habatsu* maneuvers as by international considerations. Indeed, the timing and the content of the changes in the Japanese position came about almost totally independent of the bargaining at the negotiating table — almost, it would seem, independent of the substantive issues involved. This focus on intraparty problems induced a kind of international myopia and, at the same time, produced *immobilisme* in decision-making. Hatoyama eventually succeeded in forcing a decision, but only at the cost of his political life and after the issues in the party power struggle had been concomitantly resolved. Under these circumstances, Japan could not but play a passive role, for the Prime Minister was effectively denied the opportunity for maneuver toward any form of agreement other than that desired by the Soviets. International constraints left Japan in a weak negotiating position, but passivity was assured by the nature of her foreign policy formulation process.

Several of the factors underlying this policy *immobilisme* were unique to the Soviet negotiations. First, the peace talks occurred during a period of extreme fluidity, at a time when the new political institutions were undergoing their first major test after the Occupation. In established constitutional states having relatively permanent institutions, the duties of officials in policy formulation are carefully defined, placing inexorable restraints on their actions. No such limitations were operative during the Soviet negotiations. Conservative leaders consistently circumvented the Foreign Ministry and the formal diplomatic channels; the official party institutions and policies were ignored or bypassed. Institutional procedures were largely circumvented, and foreign policy-making came to depend on the actions of, and rivalries between, politically powerful individuals and groups. The resulting unregulated pattern of decision-making is characteristic of a system in which the roles of the political participants are not clearly established, of a transitional society in which there is a sizable gap between the constitutional and actual patterns of politics. Japanese politics continues to undergo change, but the structure and processes of the political system have become more settled with the passage of time. Barring a major political or economic upheaval, a recurrence of the turbulence of 1955 and 1956 seems quite remote.

Secondly, the prewar party leaders and bureaucrats who dominated conservative politics at that time have since passed from the political scene. To most of these individuals (e.g. Hatoyama, Shigemitsu, and

Yoshida) the old ways were most natural, and functioning in the new political milieu was a profoundly difficult and unsettling experience. Inevitably, their confusion aggravated the confusion of the entire political process and, as previously suggested, at least partially explains the inordinate concern for power and position displayed by conservative party leaders. Future foreign policy decisions will rest in the hands of men more adapted to and skilled in the politics of the post-independence period.

Because normalization of Soviet relations did not basically challenge the alliance with the West, Japan was left relatively free from international pressures and internal political forces were undoubtedly allowed exceptional latitude for policy influence. Even if the Japanese had explicitly intended to use a Soviet settlement as the basis for a more independent foreign policy, in the context of the mid-1950s such a move could have been only symbolic. With the development of a pluralist international order and Japan's sharply rising importance in Asia and the world, a major foreign policy decision in Tokyo now necessarily involves greater and more varied outside influences. This may not diminish the effect of domestic politics on foreign policy, but it means that an important dimension virtually absent in 1955 and 1956 now has to be taken into account.

In these ways, the Soviet peace negotiations are a special case; in other ways, they are not. That the issue became the shuttlecock of conservative politics is only partially attributable to the special circumstances of the immediate post-independence period. The conditions within the political world in general and the conservatives in particular were unsettled, but this is properly viewed as an extreme not a unique situation. The inextricable commingling of domestic politics with foreign policy formulation is simply the result of the form in which the postwar Japanese political system has developed. The absence of established institutions for resolving conflict in an ordered fashion, the nature of the *habatsu* struggle, and the peculiar relationships between the government and the Opposition, the parties and the interest groups, the public and the government, all had the combined effect of drawing this issue into the center of domestic politics. Moreover, these have become permanent features of the Japanese political landscape (albeit in slightly altered or attenuated forms) and integral to all major foreign policy decisions.

It is important to emphasize that this pattern of decision-making did not emerge *de novo* in the post-independence political world, but, owing to the persistence of traditional Japanese attitudes and behavior, had direct links with the past. A reciprocal relationship existed between these vestiges of tradition and the "modern" political institutions (e.g. the party and the Diet) in which they operated, producing distinct hybrid political practices. Because these new patterns of behavior were the product of the political and organizational forces of the national government and the central party organs, they are correctly viewed as parts of the political sub-culture of the upper echelon of Japanese politics. Particularly significant examples of modernized-traditional political phenomena were the *habatsu* and the concept of consensual authority. The former underlay the fragmented structure of the Liberal Democratic Party, while the latter exacerbated the problem of policy leadership in the conservative coalition by demanding the participation of all the leading political actors and at least their tacit acquiescence on major decisions. There are surprising parallels between the procedural values and practices of the conservatives and the general pattern of decision-making in the immediate prewar period as described by F. C. Jones:

> Policy was formulated by discussion and compromise between various groups in the ruling caste. It was a system which militated against swift decisions and clear-cut policies as well as against sudden changes of front.[9]

In the Soviet negotiations, the party factions replaced the then-ruling oligarchy of the military, the Court officials, the Foreign Ministry, and the party leaders; but the process of policy formulation was strikingly analogous in form as well as result.

This diffuse style of Japanese decision-making, which proscribes strong policy leadership, continues to obstruct efforts to play a more positive part in world politics. Policies involving greater independence from the United States, whether neutralist or as an armed intermediate power in East Asia, will require the kind of effective leadership which a conservative government or a conservative-dominated coalition will find extremely difficult to provide. Unless the pattern of policy formulation and leadership displayed in the Soviet negotiations is radically reversed, Japan seems destined to remain a passive actor on the international stage, reacting to, not leading, events despite increasing potential for autonomous action.

---

[9] Francis C. Jones, *Japan's New Order in East Asia: Its Rise and Fall, 1937-45* (London: Oxford University Press, 1954), p. 110.

PART II
ECONOMICS

"Japan, Inc.": Reality or Facade?

NAMIKI NOBUYOSHI

Foreword

In an attempt to explain the astonishing success of Japan's rapid postwar economic growth, many journalists and scholars have advanced the notion of a "Japan, Inc." By focusing on Japan's unique government-business relationship, the idea has proved a useful one for explaining all sorts of separately unaccountable phenomena. Success stories about Japan so often refer to this "unique collaboration" between government and business, that it has come to be almost universally accepted. The works of James Abegglen (e.g., *Management and Worker: The Japanese Solution*) have been particularly influential in popularizing the notion of a "Japan, Inc.," and numerous others such as Håkan Hedberg (*The Japanese Challenge*) and Herman Kahn (*The Emerging Japanese Superstate: Challenge and Response*) have expanded on it.

The 1973 oil crisis, however, has rendered this usage out-of-date, for ever since that time Japan, Inc., in its strict sense, has been on the decline. Although to all outward appearances Japan, Inc. would still seem to be a viable institution, recent events have seriously shaken government-business relations, thus robbing the notion of its very foundations. While labor-management relations can be said to have remained distinctly Japanese, government-business relations have begun to look more and more like their counterparts in the West.

In this article I would like to attempt to describe the rise and fall of Japan, Inc. since World War II and to extrapolate from this historical process some of the issues that a Japan which is no longer "incorporated" must face in the future.

The Genesis of Japan, Inc.

"Japan, Inc." is usually used to refer to the close relationship which government and business developed after the Second World War in the drive for national reconstruction and economic growth. Admittedly, the phrase has its derogatory overtones. But it should not be forgotten that it was precisely this combined effort by the public and private sectors which enabled Japan to catch up with, and in some areas even surpass, the advanced industrial nations of the West.

Ever since Commodore Perry opened up Japan to the outside world, the Japanese have always been extremely conscious of the economic gap between their country and the countries of the West. Defeat in war provided a fresh opportunity to begin the task of "catching up." When Japan started on its road to recovery, it already lagged far behind the West not only in technology but also in providing the basic necessities of daily life. But the Japanese were quick to learn from the West — especially from the Americans, whose armed forces were occupying their country — and the traditional way of life began to change drastically. Without giving up its essentially "Japanese" core, Japan gave itself over increasingly to adopting Western ways. People moved in ever-growing numbers from the peaceful countryside to the bustling city, and the large, extended households began to split up into small nuclear families. Rice gave way to bread, tatami to carpets, and geta to shoes. Industry too was largely modernized, with the result that Japan was soon producing not only capital and industrial goods but also durable and non-durable consumer goods every bit as good as those produced in the West.

During this period of reconstruction, Japanese industry saw as its primary task the importation of Western technology and the implementation of Western methods of production. They were playing the game of catchup with a vengeance and their aims were clear — a fact more easily understood when one remembers that they had no choice but to live cheek by jowl with the Occupation forces. This in turn provided concrete incentive for cooperation between government and business. Defeat in war spelled the end of protective competition — in business, between the established and the emerging *zaibatsu*; in government, between military activists and bureaucratic conservatives; and in society, between the old nobility and the newly privileged classes. In its place, a new leadership structure emerged, dubbed Japan, Inc., in which business leaders, bureaucrats and politicians remained pivotal in determining the nation's future.

In accordance with the new Anti-Monopoly Law (more accurately, the Act Concerning Prohibition of Private Monopoly and Maintenance of Fair Trade, as enacted in 1947), the leading *zaibatsu* were disbanded and top corporation leaders were removed to be replaced by younger men. Individual corporations plunged into a race for survival. The banks and financial institutions which had served the former *zaibatsu* did what they could to preserve their role as the link between corporations in this new competitive climate, but their control has been considerably weakened. In contrast, it was the fast-growing companies in the manufacturing and service industries which held supreme power within corporate groupings. With this realignment, Japanese business recovered from wartime devastation and grew into a formidable competitor in the international marketplace.

Power within the government was shifted from the military and the Home Office to economic agencies, including the Ministry of Finance, Ministry of International Trade and Industry (MITI) and the Bank of Japan. Officials of these agencies, who had exercised extensive power over the private sector during the War, continued to dominate Japan, Inc. Only when the economic controls of the Occupation were lifted in 1951 did the influence of these bureaucratic financiers begin to decline. More progress was made in the liberalization of capital and trade after 1960, and by the time of the oil crisis in 1973 most economic controls had been done away with. The Ministry of Finance and the Bank of Japan continue to maintain their power of direct financial intervention, but MITI's once notorious "administrative guidance" has virtually disappeared with progress in trade liberalization.

In building Japan, Inc. and rejuvenating the nation, the bureaucracy teamed up with young business executives. As time went on, however, private business grew stronger and the influence of these mature business executives increased, while the influence of their counterparts in the bureaucracy gradually waned, thus upsetting the balance between government and private enterprise.

In a sense, the politicians have been the primary beneficiaries of this transformation, inasmuch as the authority of the "democratic" politicians who came to power after the fall of the prewar privileged class increased steadily during the heyday of Japan, Inc. By placing the bureaucrats under political control and stripping them of their once unchallenged status, the politicians at the same time enhanced their own authority. In part, this was made possible because as priorities shifted from industrialization to improved public welfare, politicians were quick to extend their base of support from the business sector to the grassroots electorate and to take a greater interest in local as well as national politics. Constituencies reciprocated this new concern with their welfare with broad support, and as mass politics picked up momentum, the position of politicians grew stronger and their status higher, while that of the bureaucrats declined.

In the process of the "massification" of political issues, however, the absolute status of politics is actually lowered. As the general standard of living rises, the marginal utility of politics in improving people's living conditions is inevitably decreased. True, the more government policies for welfare become institutionalized, the further the mass appeal of politics progresses. Yet this does not mean that the absolute status of politics in the eyes of the people will necessarily rise. Once vested interests become institutionalized, they are taken for granted; and since all political parties, in order to compete in the struggle for power, must offer something more than what is taken for granted, their importance in the eyes of the people naturally decreases.

How are we to characterize, then, the relationship between business and politics? For most of the years in which Japan, Inc. prospered, business maintained close ties with the conservative political parties, and in the early stages supplied virtually all of their political and campaign funding. In the period prior to 1960 the Japanese Socialist and Communist Parties were still politically quite vigorous, and the close alliance of business and conservative politics may be seen as a response to the perceived need to work together in averting the possibility that Japanese society might veer to the left. Since 1960, however, the internationalization and rapid growth of Japan's economy have radically altered the nature of Japanese society, and the free market principle of economic development based on private enterprise has been firmly established as the optimum mode of management for the Japanese economy. This principle is so deeply rooted now that no one political party can overthrow it.

When the question of revising the Anti-Monopoly Law came up for deliberation in the Diet, for example, the Socialist Party of Japan and Japanese Communist Party made far stricter proposals than did the Liberal Democratic Party. In fact, adoption of their programs would even have made Japanese capitalism still more solidly based, to the point of delaying the advent of socialist government. From the point of view of these parties, it would seem more consistent with their doctrine to allow monopolistic capitalism to show its worst side, thereby generating anti-capitalist sentiment, winning them victories in the elections and eventually making it possible to nationalize the monopolies. In actual fact, though, the efforts of the Socialist and Communist Parties are probably doing more to humanize capitalism and to put the free market on a sound basis than is the Liberal Democratic Party. Amidst the prosperity of Japan, Inc., the leftist parties seem to have lost sight of their traditional policy objectives and to be searching for ways to cope with affluency. Although the precepts of classical egalitarian socialism are still marginally upheld, it has grown increasingly difficult to incorporate them into coherent programs in the struggle for power.

By the 1970s, Japanese business no longer feared the possible overthrow of the established political system. With the emergence of mass politics, the conservative parties realized the necessity of avoiding the impression of collusion with business. It was this that led the government of Prime Minister Miki Takeo to strengthen regulations concerning political contributions.

Should this weakening of ties between business and politics be taken to mean that the big business organizations have strengthened their positions vis-à-vis the politicians? Quite the contrary — the business organizations themselves are experiencing an erosion of their raison d'être as the common imperative has been attained. Today, ties within the giant bank-led industrial groups are weak, and it is impossible for them even to take concerted action all the time as a community of common interests. When such supposedly unified groups are characterized more by competition than by cooperation, how can organizations like Keidanren (Federation of Economic Organizations) be expected to coordinate their various member businesses? It seems that all Keidanren can do is to make studies and to advance recommendations. And even here, while it may be effective in dealing with issues of common interest to all of its member companies (such as petitioning the Japanese government to stimulate the economy or maintaining liaison with foreign governments and business organizations), yet it is surprisingly ineffective in dealing with the most urgent domestic issues. In most cases, these issues are resolved through market competition among private enterprises.

The decline of bureaucratic and political influence over the economy notwithstanding, no compensating force of unification in the business sector has emerged to provide direction. Although Japan became economically very strong during the Japan, Inc. period, this growth was in fact achieved solely through competition among the various private corporations involved. In turn, the strengthening of these diverse corporate entities has made it increasingly difficult for them to cooperate and has further diminished the influence of those business organizations which are supposed to represent their common interests. Indeed, collective business organizations continue to exist and to retain a modicum of prestige simply because they offer honorary posts for successful businessmen (it is still considered a mark of peer recognition to hold an appropriate office in Keidanren or one of the other business organizations), and perhaps also because of a residual inertia to change. However, the amount of respect or honor accorded material success (i.e. promotion) in the giant business corporations or management organizations will almost certainly continue to decline as Japan becomes increasingly affluent. As time goes on, the position of business vis-à-vis politics will neither improve nor worsen. Both business and politics will lose in the eyes of the general public, although neither as much as the bureaucracy.

As explained above, during the Japan, Inc. period the country had come to achieve an economic status equal to that of the industrialized Western countries, making democratization and modernization both a political and a social possibility. This meant a strengthening of the social, political, and economic position of the people, and in particular of the individual. Since Japan is still in a transitional period, there are still those among the elderly power elite who themselves do not share this individualistic consciousness, but we can safely expect that concern for the individual will have an increasing impact on politics, business, and the bureaucracy.

There is no particular "group-consciousness" inherent in the Japanese character, and even the phenomenon of Japan, Inc. only *appears* to be a form of collectivism. On closer examination, it turns out to have been primarily an expedient for catching up with the West. That the legacy of Japan, Inc. should be an increased individual awareness will remain one of the great anomalies of history. To replace outmoded Japan, Inc., a multifaceted knowledge-centered society will emerge, such as is already developing in the United States and Western Europe. But before discussing the future, let us first examine the phenomenon that was Japan, Inc.

The Truth about Japan, Inc.

In describing the birth and operations of Japan, Inc., it is convenient to divide Japan's postwar history into four periods. The first is the immediate period of transition between the end of World War II and 1952. It was a period of reconstruction during which, under the control of SCAP the *zaibatsu* were disbanded, the system of land ownership was reformed, and other steps were taken to democratize the country and provide it with tools for survival. At the same time, the harsh economic circumstances which prevailed while these free-market mechanisms were being established necessitated, paradoxically, stringent economic controls in order to ensure the efficient and equitable use of resources. This period ended, politically, with the restoration of Japanese independence; and economically, with the termination of price and distribution controls when the Temporary Demand and Supply Adjustment Law was allowed to expire.

The second period extends to the end of the 1950s. If the first period is viewed as one of reorientation, this second period may be described as one of rehabilitation and internal renovation. During the first period, priority was given to reconstituting such basic industries as coal, electricity, steel and shipping. This completed, the second period emphasized rationalizing and modernizing key industries as well as introducing and promoting new ones. Japan, Inc. got its start in this second period and lasted through the third period that followed.

A brief listing of some of the specific initiatives enacted in this second period includes the following: In the steel industry, determined efforts were made under the First (1951-55) and Second (1956-60) Rationalization Programs. As development progressed in these programs, an open sales system was introduced in 1958 and efforts were begun in 1959 to coordinate steel manufacturers' plant investments. This in itself indicates that Japan had attained considerable production capacity. In the machinery industry, the Temporary Law for the Promotion of the Machinery Industry (Kikai-kōgyō Shinkō Rinji Sochihō) was enacted in June 1956, followed by the Temporary Law for the Promotion of the Electronics Industry (Denshi-kōgyō Shinkō Rinji Sochihō) in June 1957 and the Temporary Law for the Promotion of the Aircraft Industry in May 1958. In the automobile industry, a policy giving priority to domestic assembly was adopted in October of 1952, the "people's car" concept was announced in 1955, and automobile mass-production plant was constructed in 1959. Finally, in the petrochemical industry, a Five-Year Plan for Fostering the Synthetic Textile Industry (Gōsei-seni Ikusei Gokanen Keikaku) was adopted in March of 1953. Measures were taken in July of 1955 to stimulate the petrochemical industry, and the Special Law for the Synthetic Rubber Industry (Sekiyu-kagaku Gōsei-gomu Seizō Tokubetsu Sochihō) was instituted in June of 1957.

The main thrust of these efforts in the period from 1952 to 1960 was to promote basic industries as well as some industries new to Japan (e.g., electrical appliances and automobiles). It was thus during this period that the foundations were laid for the automobile, electronics and precision-machinery industries — the three industrial sectors which have since seen steady expansion and are in large part responsible for Japan's trade surplus after the 1973 oil crisis. Moreover, because both core and peripheral industrial sectors had yet to be developed, Japan offered investment opportunities double those available in the United States or Western Europe. These opportunities were further increased by the rapid economic growth which followed.

Industrial development was carried out through a series of laws designed expressly for that purpose. Under these laws, medium and long-term estimates of capital outlay for plant and equipment investment were made, and goals were set for industry-wide rationalization. Plans worked out by private business in accordance with these laws were awarded tax and financial incentives to promote their implementation.

The third period, whose start was marked by the adoption of the General Plan for the Liberalization of Trade and Foreign Exchange (Bōeki Kawase Jiyū-ka Keikaku Taikō) for the period of 1960 to 1973, was one of active internationalization as industry consolidated and built upon the gains made in the second period. Industry took advantage of the successful policies of the second period and embarked upon a program of trade and capital liberalization. Industrial policy-makers had long been trying to deflect pressures to liberalize from the United States and Western Europe by insisting on the prior need to strengthen the capacity of Japanese industry for international competition. When Japan, Inc. was finally compelled to yield to foreign pressures and promote liberalization in both the trade and capital fields, it was, as might be expected of MITI, a very conservative program beginning with the least sensitive areas and proceeding gradually.

Parallel with this reluctant liberalization went efforts to coordinate production levels so as to avoid "excessive" competition. We may again look to the steel industry for an example. In the early years of the 1960s, a system of government-recommended production curtailments was introduced (with actual cutbacks made from July 1962 to October 1963 and again from July 1965 to August 1968). Along with coordinating capital investment plans, these were symbolic of Japan, Inc. during this period. Although later decried by some as possible violations of the Anti-Monopoly Law (Dokusen Kinshihō), these measures went unquestioned when they were first introduced. Active competition among Japanese steel manufacturers was generally accepted as the best way to introduce the most up-to-date production facilities so that Japan might catch up with the West, but it was also feared that too much competition might result in the creation of surplus production capacity and the danger of overproduction. In such cases, the Japanese government was expected to coordinate capital investments and to recommend production curtailments commensurate with the extent of surplus capacity. Since it was necessary to go as fast as possible to catch up, these measures were merely considered as emergency brakes which would allow the machines to run safely at full speed.

Below the surface, however, a disharmony was evident during this third period which had not existed in the second when Japan, Inc. was functioning most efficiently. The Tokushinhō incident of 1962-64 and the Sumitomo Metal Industries incident of 1965-66 are illustrative of the trend.

The Tokushinhō incident occurred when MITI tried to have legislation enacted which would provide tax and other financial incentives to encourage certain designated industries to merge or otherwise to rationalize their operations in preparation for liberalization. MITI's plan was defeated in a barrage of hostility from financial and other institutions concerned. The Ministry of Finance refused to cooperate for fear that its powers would be infringed upon, and private financial institutions did not like the prospect of government interference in their lending policies.

In the Sumitomo Metal Industries incident, Sumitomo Metal alone bucked a generally compliant industry and refused to go along with MITI's recommended steel production curtailments, holding out even when the Ministry tried to command obedience by reducing Sumitomo's coking coal import quota. Both sides finally compromised and Sumitomo went along with a modified production cutback, but this resistance and the fact that the recommendations could not be enforced raised serious doubts about the very legality of government coordination of production levels. As a result, the Ministry became very cautious about recommending production curtailments, and the feeling spread in business circles that such recommendations were illegal and did not need to be followed if inconvenient.

These two incidents serve to illustrate how private business grew less and less willing to follow the government's lead during this third period. Of course, this should not be taken to suggest that private businessmen suddenly decided to act in total disregard of the government's wishes. For the overwhelming majority of businessmen, the safest policy was to follow government recommendations, if only to avoid being held responsible for the consequences. Strong-willed leaders among Japanese executives are few; most would prefer simply to go along with the general consensus. Moreover, it should also be pointed out that the type of businessman best suited to leadership in the period when Japan had the clear and obvious goal of catching up with the West was perhaps the organizational coordinator. Nevertheless, the seeds of disunity were already taking root in this third period.

In the fourth period, the years since the oil crisis of 1973, Japan, Inc.

seems to have lost its very basis, at least domestically. As the Japanese economy "caught up," government and private business no longer shared a single overriding objective. Accordingly, insofar as the government tries to act in the public interest, conflict of interest between government and private industry is inevitable. For example, the government must impose increasingly stringent standards on industry if it hopes to control pollution. As public criticism of the abuses of big business mounts, the government will have to call upon industry to look to its social responsibilities and conflict will undoubtedly ensue.

In some areas, including research and development and international economic policy, government and business interests more readily agree. Government efforts in basic research are obviously to industry's benefit, and it is difficult to conceive of any fundamental conflict of interest in this area. In international economic policy, however, some Japanese enterprises still entertain the vain hope that Japan, Inc. will remain a viable entity. There has been an endless stream of complaints that the governments of United States and Western Europe are effectively assisting their nation's companies to bid successfully in international tenders for industrial plant facilities in the Middle East and other developing nations, while the Japanese government does little to help Japanese firms. Typical examples cited to support this contention include efforts being made by the U.S. government in Saudi Arabia, especially the drafting of a Saudi Economic Development Program by the Stanford Research Institute, and American corporate participation in its implementation, as well as the visit to Saudi Arabia by Queen Juliana of the Netherlands when Phillips was bidding for a telecommunications contract there, and similar efforts on behalf of French interests by President Valéry Giscard D'Estaing. Japanese businessmen feel that there is a conspicuous lack of such government support in their own case. Hence, they contend, although the notion of a Japan, Inc. may no longer work at home, such government-business cooperation is essential overseas. Still, without denying that Queen Juliana and President Giscard D'Estaing did make these extraordinary efforts, it is difficult to believe that these trips arose out of any formalized rules. The professional diplomats of other nations are probably as little involved in this field as Japanese diplomats are, and it is hard to conceive that Japan, Inc. will become more active overseas.

Another issue in international economic policy which complements that of export promotion is import restrictions, both foreign restrictions on imports of Japanese goods and Japanese restrictions on imports of foreign goods. In the case of foreign restrictions, it has by now become customary to respond to foreign attempts to limit imports from Japan with voluntary export controls, and the Japanese government has asked Japanese companies to rein in their exports when over-concentration threatens to become a problem. So far, these requests for moderation have usually been accepted. Yet should the reverse situation arise, in which Japanese manufacturers seek import restrictions on textiles and other goods, to what extent could the government fulfill their demands in view of the broader interests of Japanese consumers? The Japanese government is bound to find it difficult to choose between consumer interests and industrial protection, and in this respect too, Japan, Inc. will have to change.

Comparison with European Industrial Policy

If Japan, Inc. is defined as a type of government-business collaboration entered into for the expressed purpose of catching up with more industrialized nations, it is only reasonable to assume that there should be similar structures in other settings. For instance, the German Empire built by Bismarck in emulation of the rising British Empire could have been called "Germany, Inc." Even in the United States, which became the prototype of a capitalist state, an era of state mercantilism prevailed until the 1830s. State governments chartered new industries within their borders and offered protection from competition. Only after these businesses had been firmly established did the states introduce legislation which provided for joint-stock corporations and the development of private-enterprise capitalism.

More recently, a similar process has been creating a "Korea, Inc." Financial interests in the Republic of Korea have accumulated the necessary capital and are now modernizing the nation's industries in close cooperation with the government. The Korean government does its part through foreign capital controls and foreign trade controls to develop local industry. Equity regulations governing joint ventures between Korean and foreign enterprises are designed very much in the interest of Korea, and the government does not hesitate to apply import restrictions in order to protect local products. Korean policies in this respect are even more all-encompassing than those of Japan, Inc. in its heyday. Since it is not hampered by the rules of the General Agreement on Tariffs and Trade (GATT), the Korean business-government coalition which forms Korea, Inc. will be able to flourish for at least the next ten years without having its success threaten relations with the advanced industrialized nations or being compelled to observe GATT rules.

Although Japan, Inc. has several historical precedents, it is perhaps more important to compare the industrial policy of Western European countries during this same post-World War II time frame with that of Japan, Inc. For, in fact, the term "Japan, Inc." originated abroad and was picked up somewhat uncritically in Japan. Had Japanese been better informed of the industrial policies then being pursued in Western Europe, they might well have reacted differently to this slightly derogatory nickname. In my opinion, Japan, Inc. is nothing more than an exaggerated myth hatched from the misconceptions of foreigners and rendered credible to the Japanese as a result of their ignorance of development practices abroad.

Examining the activities of Japan, Inc. during the second and third postwar periods (1952-73), one finds that it was primarily the efforts of industrial firms which enabled the economy to catch up with the advanced industrial nations. The Japanese government itself engaged in no industrial activity whatsoever. It drew up programs during the second period for industrial rationalization, modernization, and promotion in cooperation with the different trade and business associations; and in the third period it performed a kind of negative role by failing to liberalize Japanese trade and capital controls. Not in themselves important, these actions were faulted because Japan's overall brilliant economic success blinded critics to the insignificance of the specific measures themselves.

In considering the government's role in economic planning, a comparison with Britain may be helpful. In the early postwar years, Sir Robert Shone, Economic Director of the British Iron and Steel Federation and later Chairman of the Iron and Steel Board, drew up a plan for the British steel industry covering the years 1954-62. Although Shone was supposedly in a position to do effective economic planning, and was later made the first Chairman of the National Economic Development Office, his program had no impact whatever on the British steel industry. Nationalization of industries in 1951 and de-nationalization in 1953 had completely altered patterns of social concern in industrial management. In its narrow sense, "social concern" means the feelings of management toward their business responsibilities, of labor toward management, of shareholders toward management, and of financial institutions toward client firms. In its broader sense, it extends to the feelings of politicians, journalists, and the general public. Hence it is that a radical change in the nature of this social concern in turn could weaken the sense of responsibility among the management of profit-oriented businesses and caused a general sense of irresponsibility to spread. It was impossible for Shone's program to bear fruit in this climate.

For its part, the Japanese government did contribute to economic planning, but only marginally. During this same period plans drawn up were actually implemented, though, because conditions in Japan were favorable to smooth economic development. A combination of factors including external environment, internal conditions, inter-business relations, and intra-company harmony were conducive to their implementation.

It is not that England did not try. It attempted, by manufacturing the Calder Hall nuclear reactor and the Comet aircraft to capture world industrial leadership, but neither was a commercial success. Although the government could not be blamed, both the traditional and the advanced industrial sectors of the British economy were destined to decline. Their every effort was thwarted by shaky industrial structures, nationalization-oriented social democratic ideologies, class divisions, troubled labor relations, the reluctance of talented people to go into business, international pressures on the pound, and other factors. As a result, Britain lags behind countries like Japan which have completed a cycle of rapid growth. Britain, in fact, suffers the misfortune of a reverse cycle, and this was all the more reason for the British government to mount an even larger policy effort than did the Japanese government. Let us look at the details of this British effort.

Around 1960 the future began to look dim and Britain began to lose its postwar optimism and to doubt the feasibility of "muddling through." Disheartened, the Conservative government attempted to introduce French-style planning with the establishment of the National Economic Development Office and National Economic Development Committee in 1962, both headed by Sir Robert Shone. In 1964 the Labor government inherited these organizations and objectives, and supplemented them by establishing a Ministry of Economic Affairs on a par with the Treasury. It also instituted a National Plan. In the following year, the Labor government added the Ministry of Technology and the Industrial Reorganization Corporation. The efforts of the Ministry of Technology and of the IRC for the Concorde, shipbuilding, aluminum, and automobile industries were more ambitious than any similar efforts made by the Japanese government. Unfortunately, however, they failed.

In the period corresponding to Japan's third postwar period (1960-73), Western European countries also needed to update their industrial structures to respond to direct capital investment by the United States. Efforts made in Western Europe in this regard were far more extensive than those undertaken by Japan, Inc. Developments in Japan included the takeover of Prince Motors by Nissan Motors, the Yawata-Fuji merger to form Nippon Steel, and the merger of the Dai-Ichi and Kangyo banks, but these seem small in comparison with the drive of Western European governments to build firms of a multinational class. Both Britain and France completely overhauled their industrial structures in order to create firms large enough to compete with the multinationals. The British structure was so thoroughly reorganized that by 1970 there were only two aircraft manufacturers (Hawker-Siddley and British Aircraft Corp.), one computer company (I.C.L.), and one British automobile firm (B.L.M.C.). Similar efforts were also made in France in the 1960s to organize the entrepreneurial rabble into heavyweight coalitions capable of repelling the American capital invasion. As a result, French firms were ultimately consolidated into two steel firms, two alliances of three automobile firms, two aircraft manufacturers, and one computer company.

Likewise, Japan attempted to consolidate its industrial structure during this period, but without much success. While Japanese internationalization progressed rapidly, it did not see a consolidation into massive dominant entities. Modernization of the industrial sector may have meant a diminution of competition in other countries, but in Japan internationalization was accomplished without seriously impairing its competitive structure. That the competitive principle should survive in spite of the fact that it went against government's industrial policy was actually a victory for Japanese society, and this victory was possible only because private business and its supporting financial groups were strong enough and independent enough to reject unnecessary mergers.

British policy left no stone unturned in its efforts for consolidation and modernization. Tax incentives included a free depreciation system and investment credits; and finance measures, the Industrial Reorganization Corporation. The full array of legislation was marshalled — the Industrial Development Act of 1966, the Investment and Building Grant Act of 1971, the Local Employment Acts of 1960, 1963, 1970 and 1972, the Industrial Expansion Act of 1968, and the Industry Acts of 1972 and 1975 — all that was lacking vitality in the private business sector. (As an example of how the effectiveness of industrial policy depends on the functioning of society as a whole, witness Italy's I.R.I. [Istituto per la Ricostruzione Industriale] and E.N.I. [Ente Nazionale Idrocarburi] and the charges leveled against them of fostering careless and irresponsible managerial attitudes.)

Legislation, administrative guidance and the like plays only a minor role in determining the success of industrial policy. Institutional changes, such as nationalization, as well as social attitudes have the greater impact. In this respect, by moving steadily toward the strengthening of a market economy based on private enterprise, Japan has crippled government leadership and invited the collapse of Japan, Inc. This does not necessarily imply, however, that performance will decline. More important today than resurrecting Japan, Inc. is gaining a correct understanding of the problems which will face the post-Japan, Inc. era, and formulating and implementing policies to cope with them.

Towards a Society of Information

The mission of Japan, Inc.—to enable the country to catch up with the West and to become one of the most industrialized nations in the world — has been accomplished. Although its efforts were aimed primarily at enhancing the international competitiveness of Japanese industry and gave scant attention to social welfare, Japan was able to improve her standard of living by economizing on military expenditures. Currently, social welfare is being refurbished in the form of various types of pensions plans.

Japan's preoccupation with international competition and its neglect of balanced social development, however, have also created other problems, such as the scarcity of housing and urban congestion, which, because of their very complexity, must be solved in a systematic manner. No society which puts top priority on achieving rapid economic growth and industrial development through the release of private business energies has time to spare for problems of balanced social development. Its considerable achievements notwithstanding, Japan will certainly regret having given so little attention to these vital concerns. One can only hope that welfare and infrastructure will be dealt with zealously in the post-Japan, Inc. era.

Japan, Inc., in the narrow sense, also faces the problem of establishing a proper relationship between government and business, since lack of coordination still prevails in some non-manufacturing fields. Intervention in manufacturing sectors by MITI has been almost completely phased out. But progress in foreign trade and capital liberalization has left little room for administrative intervention in fields outside of that Ministry's jurisdiction.

Finance is the prime example. Most Americans who complain about administrative guidance in Japan are affiliated with financial institutions. Such institutions in Japan are under the jurisdiction of the Ministry of Finance, and they have yet to be adequately internationalized. The government is anxious to maintain this non-liberalized condition, issuing directive after directive in an effort to close the loopholes which private interests might take advantage of. The result is a complex and cumbersome web of interventions in the operations of Japanese, American, and other foreign financial institutions in Japan. Over the next decade or so this state of affairs should change considerably in response to the need for reorganizing the financial system and lowering interest rates to accommodate the backlog of national bond issues.

Another sore spot is agriculture. Protectionism in this area by the Ministry of Agriculture, Forestry, and Fisheries is unrelated to Japan, Inc. But insofar as foreign observers tend to associate the two, Japan's reputation overseas suffers accordingly. Numerous other areas where administrative intervention must be improved remain, but rather than detail these, let us examine the fundamental nature of government-business relations in the post-Japan, Inc. era.

Although government and business will continue to work closely on the problems of decentralization, pollution control, energy, industrial transformation, research and development, and international economic policy, the government will not play the leading role in solving such problems as the adjustment of supply and demand and the modernization of industrial structure. Facility and production controls will increasingly be subject to review by the Fair Trade Commission under the Anti-Monopoly Law, while administrative guidance from MITI will decrease.

In the future, Japanese economic management will center on a semi-planned market-economy system, in which government, private enterprise, labor, scholars and intellectual leaders, consumers, and others will all participate. Active discussion within groups, related by issue or by sector, will provide the opportunity to achieve consensus. On the other hand, failure to reach agreement will not invalidate their work; consensus will not be binding upon participants. The efforts of sector or issue-oriented councils will be mainly educational, in order to encourage both participants and observers to take constructive initiatives in the interests of both Japan and the international community.

As explained earlier in this essay, the very core of Japanese society has weakened and authority has dispersed. Politics will become progressively less important to the general public, and while lacking a strong central core the role of the economy as a whole will increase. The role of government will increase, but will also lose public credibility. In business, politics, and government bureaucracy, people will rely increasingly on informational guidance. In this sense, Japan, Inc. will be replaced by a pluralistic, knowledge-centered society.

Behind the "Made in Japan" Label

YAMAMURA KŌZŌ

I

For most Americans, as well as for many others in Asia, Latin America, and Europe, it is hardly necessary to look at the monthly government trade statistics in order to realize that Japanese exports have been increasing steadily during the past two decades. They themselves and some of their friends most likely own a Japanese automobile, a color television, or one or more of the many other products "made in Japan." Rarely an hour goes by on television in the United States without an advertisement for Toyota, Datsun, Sony, Toshiba, Kawasaki, Seiko, or some other Japanese firm's products. And newspapers invariably carry a few articles per week on Japanese steel exports, on the weakening of the U.S. dollar in Tokyo, or on one of the trade negotiating teams or missions going to or coming from Tokyo.

This situation provokes such questions as: How was Japan able to accumulate a trade surplus of nearly $20 billion? Why did the United States' bilateral deficit with Japan reach $7 billion in 1977? And why do Japanese exports continue to increase? These questions can be answered in many ways, depending on one's perspective, interest, and knowledge as well as on the purpose for which the answer is to be used.

For American consumers, as well as for consumers in other nations, the answer can be quite simple. Given their prices, Japanese products are more desirable because of their superior quality, appearance, performance, or the like. If product quality is roughly equivalent to that of domestic products, Japanese goods are preferred because prices are lower, delivery times are shorter, the "after-care" on the product is better, etc.

For economists, the answers may include a discussion of the rapid increase in Japanese productivity which resulted from the adoption of new technology and vigorous investment policies, or of such factors as the effectiveness of "improvement engineering," the high saving rate of the Japanese, the seniority wage system (which allowed growing firms to hire a large number of young workers whose real wages were lower than their productivity), etc. There is, in other words, no shortage of economic analyses of Japan's success story. Indeed, when I compiled bibliography of works in English on the Japanese economy for my students last year, it contained no fewer than 40 books and 300 articles written by economists during the past two decades.

Finally, for those journalists, businessmen, and analysts of American industry who are intent on arguing that the success of Japanese exports is based on the "unfair" practices or on special "advantages" which Japanese producers possess, the answer invariably includes a discussion of "Japan, Inc." As is now well known, "Japan, Inc." refers to a variety of government policies — subsidies, low-interest loans, cartels, and the like — that assisted Japanese industries in gaining a competitive advantage over their American rivals. When these writers focus their attention on the bilateral negative trade balance which the United States has with Japan, their discussion of Japanese "unfairness" includes both visible and "invisible" trade barriers — such as quotas on agricultural products, the "impossibly" complex Japanese distribution system, or the varieties of Japanese red tape.

Meanwhile, as the United States' trade deficit with Japan continues to worsen, American consumers are still willing to wait as much as nine months for a Honda automobile or are prepared to buy a Sony color TV at a higher price than that charged for an American set. Such purchases are seen as a contributing factor in the continued decline of the dollar. Not surprisingly, in the second half of 1978, American mass media seemed to be showing an increased interest in some aspects of "Japan, Inc.," Japanese trade barriers, and jobs lost to Japan. Influenced by such press and TV coverage, many Americans are today increasingly uneasy about the trade deficit with Japan and may even feel a twinge of guilt when they acquire another Japanese product.

All in all, however, the current situation hardly resembles that of the 1930s. Despite some strongly worded arguments by interest groups which condemn Japanese "unfairness," the basic stance of the United States government and the general public vis-à-vis Japanese exports can be called reasoned and moderate. To be sure, some Americans are loudly protesting

Japanese imports, and their tone can sometimes be harsh. A few critics, often representing American firms directly affected by Japanese imports, attempt to build their case on less than objectively selected data and on half-truths. But the public of today is generally better informed, and in general has little difficulty in seeing when an ax is being ground. With an increasing knowledge of the workings of their economy and of international trade, a large segment of the public is familiar with problems of inflation, lagging productivity, oil imports, and other ills of its own nation, and can no longer be readily enlisted in a protectionist cause that will benefit only a few Americans at the cost of raising the prices of consumer and producer goods for a large majority. (We shall not concern ourselves here with the small fraction of unintelligent, nationalistic — and at times racist — critics of Japanese export policies.)

No less important to present American attitudes toward Japanese imports is the increased knowledge which Americans have acquired of Japan and the Japanese since the end of the Second World War. While cultural and linguistic barriers between Americans and Japanese remain, especially in comparison with those between Americans and Europeans, few Americans today regard Japan and the Japanese as they did during the 1920s and 1930s. I need not detail here all the manifestations of this increased understanding. The point is simply that increased American familiarity with Japan and things Japanese has made remarkable progress during the last few decades, which accounts for the basic good will existing between the two nations and for the failure of a small segment of the society to convince the majority of an immediate need to restrict Japanese imports.

The above observation, however, can be made with much less confidence, I fear, for Japanese-European or Japanese-Southeast Asian (ASEAN) relationships. Since this essay does not intend to undertake a comparative examination of the causes and effects of differences in the degrees of understanding reached between Japan and various nations, I can only note the importance of the future efforts of Japan and other nations toward mutual understanding.

II

The above is by no means intended to imply that even the current increased American understanding of Japan and the Japanese is adequate. Economic conflict will likely be unavoidable as the economic interdependence of the United States and Japan continues to increase, and it thus will become even more important to achieve as full an understanding of each other as possible. That is, in order to resolve intelligently the seemingly intensifying economic discord of recent years, our understanding of each other must be further elevated lest we succumb to the loud voices which demand hasty actions ultimately detrimental to our mutual interests.

Thus the central goal of this brief essay is to increase our understanding of Japan by stressing Japanese culture (especially the socio-psychological characteristics of the Japanese) as an important factor in Japanese economic activities and as a crucial factor in explaining its success in international markets. In particular, I will discuss here several aspects of Japan's cultural tradition which directly or indirectly have contributed and continue to contribute to the production of the many goods successfully exported to nations around the world.

However, before we identify and discuss specific cultural traditions which have contributed to Japan's economic success, I must state explicitly why I discuss culture as an "input" in production. My interest is not to offer this discussion either as *the* explanation of Japanese economic success, or as a rebuttal to the many criticisms leveled by Americans (among others) against practices and policies which may have given Japan certain "unfair" advantages. Rather, my wish is to suggest that all of us — economists, journalists, interest groups, and consumers in the United States and elsewhere — need to understand these aspects of Japanese society better in order to discuss Japanese economic (export) success intelligently and objectively.

In their efforts to understand the cost advantages of Japanese products, economists who analyze technological change and capital investment often suffer from a certain narrowness of vision in failing to explain why the Japanese were able to adopt new technologies more rapidly than others, and why these technologies could be used in successful competition against the nations which first exported them. Profitability or the technical capability to adopt new technology can hardly explain the Japanese performance. And many non-economists, in discussing or criticizing Japanese "unfairness" or "Japan, Inc." often mistake what I believe are in effect cultural characteristics and attributes for somehow insidious and calculated acts on the part of the Japanese and their government. Accusing the Japanese of "unfairness," of course, has the virtue of conveniently absolving others of responsibility for their own problems of lagging productivity, inflation, lack of an energy policy, etc. It can, however, hardly serve as a constructive basis for an intelligent dialogue between the two nations.

On the other hand, I should add that an understanding of Japanese culture is not synonymous with absolving Japanese practices and policies of all sin. One would be a less than objective analyst if one failed to recognize that some of the charges of unfairness are justified. Without elaborating on the charges often made, I believe there exists a broad consensus, even among the Japanese, that some Japanese policies and practices provide valid grounds for criticism. For example, many would include in this category Japanese foot-dragging during the 1960s and the early 1970s in liberalizing her international trade and capital barriers; some of the assistance given to several major industries by the Japanese government in the form of low-cost loans, permission to cartelize, etc., even after such assistance was no longer justified in the name of achieving international competitiveness; and the unwillingness to devalue the yen until the early 1970s.

My point is simply this: if we better understand Japan's culture as a significant factor in its success, we will be better able to accurately identify which practices and policies contributing to Japan's export success are indeed "unfair" and which are simply the products of Japanese culture — to be recognized as such and seen as inherent assets of Japanese society in its efforts to compete in the international market.

III

It is ignorant and chauvinistic to claim that one's own culture is superior to another's. What one can say is that some cultures are better suited to certain activities than others. We often say, for example, that the American cultural milieu encourages an individualistic and competitive spirit which is highly adapted to achieving individual excellence in many endeavors, including economic growth through competition. That is, one may acquire a fairly well-defined cultural image of each nation which will convey with some accuracy the specific strengths (or weaknesses) of each culture with regard to industrial economic activities.

In this sense, I believe that we can say that Japanese culture, or its social capability, is well suited to activities which demand (1) close coordination of all available information, (2) finely coordinated planning and execution involving many parts of a firm or a number of firms, (3) meticulous attention to details, and (4) organizational ability to distribute collective gains to reward the participants in coordinated activities in such a way as not to stifle the inherent competitive spirit of each individual participant.

On the other hand, this would indicate that Japanese society is not an ideal setting for innovative or inventive activities that depend upon a flash of insight by a strong-willed individual who pursues his goal even against the doubts expressed by his colleagues, or for a rugged individualist who, perhaps by trial and error, accomplishes his chosen course for his own satisfaction. In other words, individuals who are not inclined to observe the numerous strict rules and procedures required for the close coordination and smooth functioning of the intricately balanced organization characteristic of Japanese society will find the rigidly circumscribed rules for close interpersonal relationships oppressive.

On the other hand, Japanese society is ideally suited for the production of goods for which the fundamental technology has already been invented elsewhere, and for which the efforts needed to maximize gains (GNP and individual income) are best pursued collectively. To amplify on this observation, a description and general discussion of the behavioral patterns of Japanese employers and employees within firms and *keiretsu* (i.e. groups of firms) is presented below, following a brief summary of the socio-psychological factors and institutions which I believe are significant in influencing and even determining the basic organizational structure and behavioral characteristics of Japanese society and firms.

1. Japan is a "vertical" society in which the upper-lower hierarchical (i.e. vertical) order among men of unequal social standing dominates horizontal relationships among equals. A Japanese spends most of his daily life in situations where he must be clearly aware of his relative ranking. Or, in the words of Professor Nakane Chie, a well-known Japanese social anthropologist:

> In everyday affairs a man who has no awareness of relative rank is not able to speak or even sit and eat. When speaking, he is expected always to be ready with differentiated, delicate degrees of honorific expressions appropriate to the rank order between himself and the person he addresses. The expressions and the manner appropriate to a superior are never to be used to an inferior. Even among colleagues, it is only possible to dispense with honorifics when both parties are very intimate friends.[1]

Because of the overwhelmingly vertical nature of the society which dominates their lives from childhood, the Japanese function best in situations in which relative rank order is clearly established. This means that if a Japanese finds himself in a circumstance in which rank order is not clearly established, he will take infinite pains to establish it for his psychological comfort. The need for an established rank order is such that "even a set of individuals sharing identical qualifications tends to create a *difference* among these individuals."[2] Anyone who has ever visited Japan

---

[1] Nakane Chie, *Japanese Society* (Middlesex, England: Penguin Books, 1973), p. 31.   [2] *Ibid.*, p. 26.

is familiar with numerous examples of the processes by which Japanese quickly establish at the first meeting their relative rank order, methods ranging from exchanging name cards (which invariably carry the person's title) to discreet questioning as to the other's age, occupation, and the school from which he was graduated.

This rigid, vertical social structure is a product of the past that has come to be well-entrenched in modern Japanese society, and must always be kept in mind in discussing the managerial structure and behavioral patterns observed in Japanese firms.

2. Another, better known "fact of life" in Japan is that social characteristic which has been variously termed paternalism, groupism, and familyism. This aspect of Japanese society originated in the strong tradition of *ie* or the "house." Simply put, this is the Japanese sociopsychological tendency which emphasizes (in the sense of protecting, cherishing, finding needs for, or functioning best in) "us" against "them." In the context of this essay, a firm may show this characteristic by being "paternalistic" toward its employees. Paternalism can take the form of providing various welfare programs, fostering group cohesion by providing housing for employees to live in as neighbors, holding daily pre-work sessions to recite company mottos, conducting seminars at a Zen temple, etc. Employees, for their part, place the success of the *ie* (their company, department, or section) above everything. Even an employee's family takes second place (in terms of time, mental energy, and emotional output) to his group at work. What is important is that, in Japan, this can be said even of factory workers. The ultimate form of this is the well-known lifetime employment system which is still accepted as the norm in Japan. The *ie* guarantees lifetime security, and demands total dedication in return.

This, along with its vertical organizational quality, results in a facet of Japanese society which is important in the context of this essay. That is, the person's hierarchical rank order is fixed for life, and not only is any sign of disregarding it repugnant to the harmony within an *ie*, but it is also extremely costly to ignore. In understanding the Japanese process of decision-making, this is of crucial importance. Though this brief observation of this important facet of Japanese life must suffice here, it should be made explicit that no purely economic explanation of this Japanese characteristic — such as the long-run maximization of profit or income, or labor conditions — can ever hope to suffice. The importance of *ie* is psychological as well as economic.

3. After a discussion of the vertical nature of society and the importance of the *ie*, it is easy to understand the institutions of lifetime em-

ployment and the seniority system — in the Japanese senses of these terms. Lifetime employment is only a socially expected form of membership in an *ie*, and seniority is the handiest and socially least costly (least disruptive of harmony) indicator which can be used in establishing rank order. Economic explanations of these institutions can be only partial. Though we need not describe these two well-known institutions further, we should add that they form the basis of the view which might best be summarized as "men over organization," that is, employees matter above all else in firms. As long as the functioning of a firm is circumscribed by the lifetime employment and seniority systems, the most important thing is to hire "good" men because they will in time rise to become the decision-making officers of the firm.

4. The *ringi* system of decision-making, widely used in bureaucracy, firms, and many other organizations, is a natural one for the society we have just described. For firms, this is a system by which any change in the routines, tactics, and even overall strategy is originated by those persons who are directly concerned with the change. The final decision is made at the top level only *after* an elaborate examination of the proposal and its acceptance or rejection by consensus at every echelon of the managerial structure. This process of consensus-building involves at first one's immediate colleagues. If a consensus is obtained, then the proposal goes to the head of that group, who will then circulate it among the heads of departments (or sections) that will be directly and indirectly affected by the proposed change. If a go-ahead is obtained at this level (or after a few more layers of consensus-building, if necessary to reach the top level) it will finally go to the top for sanction.

The system is ideally suited to Japanese firms because it assures harmony within an *ie* and enables senior (but not necessarily more capable) men to occupy higher-ranking positions. At the same time, the cohesion of the group is strengthened because no one person is to blame should the change end in failure. In any event, informal consensus-building is much more efficient in getting the best perspective than a committee which would be dominated by a senior presiding chairman whom others would be reluctant to oppose. In public as well as in private, a subordinate will exercise the greatest caution in efforts to change his senior's mind. The process is extremely delicate and often time-consuming, but to most Japanese, the advantages of the *ringi* system are more important than the slowness of the process, its unsuitability for long-range planning (strategy), and (from the Western point of view) its other shortcomings. The system is changing and is being complemented by other methods of decision-making, but it is still used widely by the largest firms even today.

5. As is evidenced in various forms of Japanese art — such as bonsai and architectural designs — the Japanese exhibit an intense interest, even fascination, with detail and subtle distinctions of color and shape. I believe it is also accurate to say that this concern for detail and nuance is seen also in their interpersonal relationships and communication. Since much has been written by artists, sociologists, and others on the origins and the various manifestations of this aspect of Japanese society, my interest here as a non-specialist is only to recall this well-known facet of Japanese society.

6. Finally, I should again remind readers that Japan is an extremely homogeneous and cohesive society in terms of basic values, ethnic origin, language, and many other dimensions. This fact is well known and often discussed, and plays, as will be argued below, an important role in the workings of Japanese firms and the interrelationships among firms.

IV

If the preceding characterization of the socio-psychological characteristics of the Japanese is accurate, one can readily see why such a society might excel in industrial production through the close coordination of information, coordinated execution of plans, attention to details, and the evocation of maximum efforts by individuals in collective teamwork.

Of all the socio-cultural attributes which contribute to the effectiveness of Japanese industrial firms, the sense of the group — the *ie* — which is shared by both employers and employees is perhaps the most important. Though labor mobility has risen during the past decade, an overwhelming majority of Japanese hope and expect that their employment with a firm will be permanent. To say the least, even today there is a strong presumption on the part of employees at larger industrial firms that they will work for the same firm and with the same colleagues until retirement. An employee is fully justified in believing that his employer will terminate his employment only as a last resort, even in a recession. When asked "To whom is your obligation greatest in order to assure the success and the growth of your firm?" virtually all Japanese employers will say it is to their employees rather than to their stockholders. The better one knows Japanese society, the less likely one is to dismiss this as merely a stock answer for public relations purposes.

To be sure, this implicit "cultural contract" is by no means always harmoniously adhered to. Japan has labor unions, strikes (though many less than in other industrial economies), dismissals, and bankruptcies. But the "cultural contract" serves as a strong force in determining the conduct and behavior of both employees and employers, and the presumption of both is of a life-long association.

From the assumptions that all members of a firm belong to an *ie* (the firm) and that the membership is permanent may be derived several crucial attributes which are extremely important to efficient production. As long as one's employment is guaranteed, there is little reason to object to the adoption of new technology. If a job becomes obsolete as a result, the company will shift the employee to another task within the firm. Of course, given the permanent employment system, the firm is also willing to undertake the retraining of the employee at its own expense so that employees whose skills become obsolete may still be used productively within the firm.

With the prospect of a life-long association, there is a premium on harmonious relationships with one's colleagues, superiors, and subordinates. There is little temptation to seek exclusive recognition or to monopolize credit for a success when this would mean incurring the jealousy or ill-will of others. Harmony is thus cherished, and consensus is sought wherever possible.

In Japan, the task of obtaining consensus and maintaining harmony is easier than in other nations because of the homogeneity of values, ethnic origins, language, and many other factors. To repeat, perhaps the most prominent characteristic of the corporate culture of the Japanese firm is that the Japanese are prepared to go a long way to preserve harmony, consensus, and identity of goals.

A necessary part of success at preserving these social goals is the maintenance of constant communication, i.e., intense "dialogue." Inadequate explanations or incomplete information can be a cause of disharmony, misunderstanding, and the inability to obtain consensus. Thus Japanese take great pains, during and even after work hours, to communicate with each other. Firms supplement the *ringi* system with discussion groups, study sessions, seminars, company-sponsored outings, frequent nights out for "the boys from the same section," etc. The members of an *ie* are expected to remain in very close contact with each other. However, despite the harmony and closeness of the members of a firm, observance of the vertical authority structure is deeply ingrained, so that formal lines of communication, channels of authority, and protocol for the exchange of views are not compromised. A vertical society also yields the added benefit of minimizing disciplinary problems, as the rationale of the structure and the source of authority is readily understood by all and most can expect, in time, to climb the ladder of authority themselves.

Above all, a Japanese firm with these characteristics can expect the maximum effort from its employees. The success of their *ie*, through increased efficiency and performance, is important not only in perpetuating their employment but also in increasing their income and prestige. The more successful one's firm, the larger one's wages, bonuses, and pride in working for a large and prosperous firm. To cite only two examples: employees at Toyota have decided to work on weekends to meet the demand for their cars; and the Ministry of Labor as late as the summer of 1978 issued a pamphlet urging employees to take all paid vacations to which they are entitled, whereas at present only 50% do so.

In this light, it is clear that these cultural attributes contribute greatly to making Japanese firms highly adept at producing such industrial commodities as automobiles, color television sets, complex machinery, and numerous chemical and metal products whose efficient production and marketing require close coordination in the planning and execution of minute details in all divisions and sections of a firm. Production of these goods also necessitates adherence to performance standards in each part, which reflects each employee's willingness to pay close attention to detail and his desire to assure the quality of the product.

If a given *ie* prospers, the "family" will be duly rewarded with higher wages, bonuses in June and December, and promotions recognizing the contribution to the collective task. (Though space limitations do not permit elaboration, promotion in Japan is a carefully considered reward for ability within the framework of the seniority system.) However, individual incentive is not blunted by the cultural emphasis on teamwork because not to perform to one's best is to add to the burden borne by the other members of the team, whose approval and respect are absolutely essential if one is to work with them throughout adult life.

For many of the products successfully exported by Japanese firms, Japanese advantages in technology are either non-existent or too limited to explain Japanese success in international markets. This can only mean that the cultural input described above must have contributed to a substantial degree to the rapid increase in Japanese exports. If a Japanese automobile or color television is preferred over a car or TV produced elsewhere and sold at a similar price, we must give due recognition to the cultural input that made the Japanese automobile or color television preferable to the competing product exported by other nations.

V

Moreover, I believe that the socio-psychological characteristics manifested in the *keiretsu* also contributed significantly to Japan's rapid postwar growth and the steady increase in exports. *Keiretsu* refers to the organization of Japanese firms into readily identifiable groups. Each one of about a dozen such groups usually has a large bank and a general trading company as its core, and includes major industrial firms from among a score of heavy, chemical, energy, machinery, and other "key" industries. Japanese often refer to this phenomenon as "one-setism," i.e., each of the *keiretsu* has at least one firm in each of all the "key" industries. As of now, among the best known of the *keiretsu* are Mitsui, Mitsubishi, Sumitomo, Fuji, and Dai-Ichi Kangyo. Even so-called "independent" firms, such as Sony, Honda, Matsushita, and others have developed, if not a complete set, at least an increasing number of satellite companies and close connections with a few of the largest banks.

A number of Western scholars have observed that the *keiretsu* and *keiretsu*-like interfirm relationships seen in Japan are little different from the conglomerates and subcontracting relationships seen in many industrial nations. Yet to view them this way is, I believe, totally to miss the significance of these Japanese interfirm relations in the rapid postwar growth of the Japanese economy. Though it comes as no surprise to readers familiar with the socio-psychological fabric of Japanese society, these interfirm relationships, as exemplified by the formations of the *keiretsu*, are different in many respects from similar arrangements found among groups of firms elsewhere.

To put it simply, the most significant difference to be emphasized between *keiretsu* relationships on the one hand, and conglomerates and subcontracting relationships as seen in the West on the other, is the degree of coordination which firms in *keiretsu* and *keiretsu*-like relationships maintain with other firms in the group. By international standards, the coordination achieved among the *keiretsu* firms on matters relating to financing, technological development, personnel, purchasing, marketing and distribution, and new project planning and development is unmatched elsewhere.

Mutual shareholding and borrower-lender relationships among member firms and banks are limited. Indeed, it is rare for more than several percent of the total shares of a firm in a *keiretsu* to be owned by any other member of the *keiretsu*, and most firms in any *keiretsu* borrow from banks outside of the *keiretsu* as well as from the "main" *keiretsu* bank. Nonetheless, each member of a *keiretsu* consults the others as closely as if they were all, to put it perhaps a little too strongly, wholly owned divisions of a giant conglomerate in the United States. In short, each *keiretsu* group is seen as an *ie* which is to work together in all possible activities for the benefit of the group. Led by a "breakfast session" or by monthly meetings of the presidents of the member firms of each *keiretsu*, each group plans, executes, and often finances joint ventures in areas and projects of mutual interest. These would likely include: investments in nuclear energy development, large foreign operations, a new major chemical plant, etc.; joint planning of new investments in raw material development or in production facilities for intermediate input (i.e., in coordination of investments in the capacities of firms making use of the raw material or intermediate inputs); exchanges of information concerning new technology (sources, problem solving, coordinated adoption, etc.); the "loan" of experts (both managerial and technical and even skilled and semi-skilled blue collar workers) to *keiretsu* member firms (the most revealing examples of which were the recent "loans" of surplus skilled employees from the recession-struck iron, steel, and shipbuilding firms to booming automobile and electronics firms within the same *keiretsu* group); the joint purchase of raw materials and intermediate input; the coordination of campaigns to develop markets in Japan and abroad; the establishment of priorities in acquiring required input and services for member firms in the same *keiretsu*; and joint training for employees. Given the extremely close communication and coordination maintained among member firms, the above listing of joint or coordinated activities is not exhaustive.

The basic incentives for such coordination can be explained in economic terms. This cooperation among members enables each to use its resources (capital, expertise, skilled manpower, information, etc.) more efficiently, and enables all to realize economies of scale and advantages accruing from experience, among other things. Of course, the economies realized and new ventures undertaken because of this coordination give Japan added competitive abilities in the international market. In contrast to the world of the economics textbook, in which perfect competition and costless information is assumed, the real world is one where dynamic competition continues and access to resources and information is less than perfectly competitive. Here, such coordination and joint activities enable the member firms of the group to adopt more new technology more quickly and to use resources more efficiently than in an economy where no such coordination is undertaken. The gains realized by this cooperation — more rapid growth of the economy and the consequent rise in income — accrue to the population as a whole. And, one can also argue with considerable justification, the ability of these Japanese firms to adopt new technology to economize resources and to make effective use of information, also benefits the purchasers of goods exported from Japan.

The central point of the preceding is, however, that the competitiveness of Japanese products, realized in part through the Japanese ability for coordination and cooperation among firms, is a product of Japanese culture. Had it not been for the socio-cultural traditions of Japan as described earlier, economic incentives alone could not have produced the *keiretsu*. Put differently, economic incentives alone (in the absence of the Japanese socio-psychological characteristics) would have provided only an awareness of the desirability of interfirm coordination and cooperation, but not the necessary socio-psychological foundation on which the success of such group activities must depend. For this reason, even an American conglomerate, motivated as it is by ownership interest, does not seem to reap all the economic gains realized by the *keiretsu*. It would be a serious error to explain the *keiretsu* and their advantages solely in economic terms, because the seemingly successful functioning of the *keiretsu* depends crucially on the Japanese socio-psychological attributes which encourage cooperation and coordination through close communication, as well as the pride employees take in working for a member firm in a large and successful *keiretsu* group.

VI

I am fully aware that some scholars may take exception to some specific observations made and arguments advanced in this essay because of the general nature of my discussion. Also, one could readily prepare a long list of exceptions and qualifications to the views and analyses which I have presented. For example, we all know that the Japanese are capable of planning and building an oddity like the Narita airport, that giant firms do go bankrupt due to mismanagement, and that there are individualistic and even lazy Japanese. But I believe the central points of my essay are essentially valid since it is primarily concerned with the majority of employers and employees who produce, mostly in larger firms, the goods being exported abroad.

In brief, I have argued that in discussing the postwar success of Japanese exports, we must be better informed about the socio-psychological characteristics of the Japanese and the uniquely Japanese institutions which determine the behavior patterns of employees, employers, and firms. This is so, because I believe that as we learn more about Japanese society and how it functions, we will be better able to discriminate which policies and behavior characteristics of the Japanese economy are products of a conscious design to compete in international markets and which are reflections, not consciously adopted, of Japanese cultural attributes that happen to be useful and even effective in producing goods requiring the closely coordinated and cooperatively planned adoption of new technology and investments among firms, and careful, detailed coordination and minutely specified performance, design and other characteristics among many parts of a firm.

If I am correct, all this would mean that Japanese success in the world's export markets depends much less on the "unfair" policies of "Japan, Inc." than has been thought or argued. It is more than likely that, as the Japanese government discontinues those criticized policies, we will discover that much of what we have loosely called "Japan, Inc." is actually "Japanese culture." (Though I was unable to discuss it here, even the form of government-business relationships is often the product of Japan's cultural environment and historical legacies.) We must realize that Japan's cultural attributes have made valuable contributions to augmenting Japanese international competitive abilities. The extent of these contributions cannot be measured, but to deny their existence is to commit the error of failing to recognize the unique assets of Japanese culture which happen to make it highly suitable for the industrial production of a wide range of export goods.

Perhaps I should end this essay with the following note to those who are concerned by the current "excess" of Japanese exports. I believe it is possible that the days when Japan can continue to enjoy its advantage — the conduciveness of Japanese culture to efficient industrial production — may be numbered. After having so long depended on its former cultural patterns (along with its unique institutions), Japan is now entering a difficult new age. The growth of the world's industrial economies has slowed, the pool of readily borrowable technology abroad has all but been exhausted, and Japanese culture itself seems to be changing perceptibly.

Visibly slowed economic growth is already severely testing the institution of permanent employment and the seniority system of promotion. In the increasingly competitive post-OPEC era, the luxury of the time-consuming *ringi* system can less and less be indulged as more and quicker decisions are called for; more firms are becoming aware that the virtues of cooperative and harmonious teamwork can be preserved only at the cost of detracting from the innovative efforts which now need to be encouraged more than ever; the new generation of employees seems to take less pride in their firm or in *keiretsu* than their fathers did; the ability of Japanese firms going abroad to "transplant" their corporate culture is in serious doubt at best; etc. The implications of these recent developments for the near future of the Japanese economy may prove to be profound.

Culture can be likened to athletic skill. Often a superb baseball player can hope to be only a mediocre football player. Skills suitable for one game are transferable to another only with great difficulty. Japanese culture could very well be in the position of the baseball player as the rules of the game of international competition — if not the game itself — are changing rapidly. Will Japanese culture successfully adapt to the new game? Or will it fail to adapt and thus limit its success in the international markets? These are questions which I believe are worth pondering instead of merely bewailing the current trade deficit with Japan and condemning "Japan, Inc." for its large trade surplus.

Japan's Labor Unions:
The Meeting of White and Blue Collar

KŌSHIRO KAZUTOSHI

The typical Japanese labor union is an "enterprise union" organized along company lines rather than according to divisions of industry, craft or trade. Despite this structural peculiarity, or perhaps because of it, the Japanese union has shown a high degree of flexibility in responding efficiently to economic change and technological innovation.

The "enterprise union" in Japan is distinguished first of all by its membership, which is limited to employees on the regular company payroll. Temporary workers are not admitted to this union; they either remain unorganized or else belong to a separate union. In the second place, union membership tends to be automatic, not optional. All new full-time employees in an enterprise are thus, by definition, drawn into the union. Third, an enterprise union includes both the white-collar and blue-collar workers employed by the enterprise. Finally, although frequently the unions of large enterprises not only embrace smaller unions within the company (e.g., factory or business office unions) but are also commonly affiliated with an industry-wide union federation, union members attach more importance to their enterprise union than to the industry-based federation.

The Japanese labor union has been both the object of high praise and the target of severe criticism. Many economists in Japan and elsewhere praise the Japanese pattern of labor-management relations, which is characterized by enterprise unionism, seniority and permanent employment, as being one of the major factors responsible for the nation's rapid economic growth in the 1960s and for the nation's relatively quick recovery from the 1973 oil crisis. Other economists, however, criticize Japanese labor unions for being too eager to do the bidding of management and not caring enough for the needs of their own members. Some even blame Japan's huge surplus in the balance of payments and the yen's soaring exchange rate, as well as such domestic ills as insufficient housing and inadequate public works, on labor's failure to influence policy decisions concerning the national economy.

In this chapter we would like to re-evaluate this praise and criticism, but to do this we must first ask how these enterprise unions came into being and what their inherent advantages and disadvantages are.

Historical Overview

1. Prewar Heritage

The first moves to create some kind of labor union in Japan came toward the end of the 1880s, and resulted in the establishment of the Rōdō Kumiai Kiseikai (Association for the Formation of Labor Unions) in 1897 by Takano Fusatarō and Katayama Sen, both repatriates from the United States. Modeled after the American Federation of Labor (AFL), their organization brought together three craft unions: the Printers' Union, the Railway Engineers' Union, and the Ironworkers' Union. Despite its initial successes, however, the Kiseikai went into sudden decline soon after the enactment of the Public Peace Police Law in 1900, which provided for severe restrictions on labor union activities (Article 17).

As Japan's industrialization progressed, the number of factory workers increased drastically. This growth of an urban working class paved the way for the formation of the Yūaikai (Fraternity Society) in 1912, which was a direct precursor of the modern labor movement. Founded by Suzuki Bunji, a graduate of Tokyo Imperial University's law school and a fervent member of the Unitarian Church, the Yūaikai initially stood for moderate reformism. As its name suggests, it was based on the Christian beliefs of its founder. After World War I, however, as the impact of the Russian revolution reached Japan's shores, Marxist influences grew rapidly stronger and intense ideological confrontations between right and left broke out, undermining the unity of the Yūaikai. In 1919 it was renamed Dai-Nippon Rōdō Sōdōmei Yūaikai (Greater Japan General Federation of Labor Fraternity Society), and again in 1921, Nippon Rōdō Sōdōmei (Japan General Federation of Labor). By that time, the labor organization had come to be divided into two factions. One was led by Nishio Suehiro, Matsuoka Komakichi, and others from working class backgrounds who favored trade unionism based on the British pattern. The other centered around college-educated leaders and was more inclined to revolutionary radicalism. In 1925, the left-wing faction finally broke away to form the Nihon Rōdō Kumiai Hyōgikai (Council of Japanese Labor Unions), often abbreviated to simply Hyōgikai. This split set the basic pattern of ideological conflicts for the subsequent history of the labor movement in Japan.

Five labor union bills were presented before the Imperial Diet between 1921 and 1931, but they all failed to pass. That meant that labor's right to unionize was never legally sanctioned. Thus in 1936, when the strength of organized labor was at its prewar peak, only 420,000 workers were unionized, accounting for less than eight percent of the nation's industrial labor force. A relatively insignificant force though it was in Japanese society, the labor movement was dissolved by the government in 1940 as part of its total war effort and placed under the charge of the Sangyō Hōkokukai (Industrial Patriotic Association).

2. Postwar Growth

After World War II, the Allied Occupation forces encouraged the development of labor unions as part of Japan's democratization. Labor unions (organized by factory or office rather than by trade) mushroomed throughout the country. In December, 1945, the Diet enacted the Labor Union Law, which took effect in March of the following year. This legislation provided the impetus for the organization in August, 1946 of the Zen-Nihon Sangyōbetsu Kumiai Kaigi (abbr. Sanbetsu Kaigi; All-Japan Federation of Industrial Organizations) with a membership of 850,000. Sanbetsu Kaigi grew rapidly with the support of the influential Japanese Communist Party (JCP), but it suffered serious setbacks as the Occupation's labor policy underwent drastic changes. The first sign of change was SCAP's ban on the general strike of February 1, 1947. The shift in attitude became still clearer with MacArthur's letter to Prime Minister Ashida Hitoshi in July of the following year, disapproving political activities of civil servants and government workers. Encouraged by the changing Occupation policy, anti-mainstream forces opposed to JCP control of Sanbetsu Kaigi organized the Minshuka Dōmei (Democratization League). In July, 1950, these groups, together with the left-wing faction of Sōdōmei, formed Nihon Rōdō Kumiai Sōhyōgikai (abbr. Sōhyō; General Council of Trade Unions of Japan).

At its inception, therefore, Sōhyō was a national center for anti-Communist unions, but it soon evolved from a moderate to a militant group in the course of the Korean War and the controversy over the 1951 San Francisco Peace Treaty, to which the Soviet Union and other communist nations as well as some neutralist countries were not signatory. Four Sōhyō-affiliated groups of unions, including the Japan Federation of Textile Workers' Unions and the All-Japan Seamen's Union, opposed

146 ECONOMICS

Figure 8-1. Genealogy of Major Labor Organizations

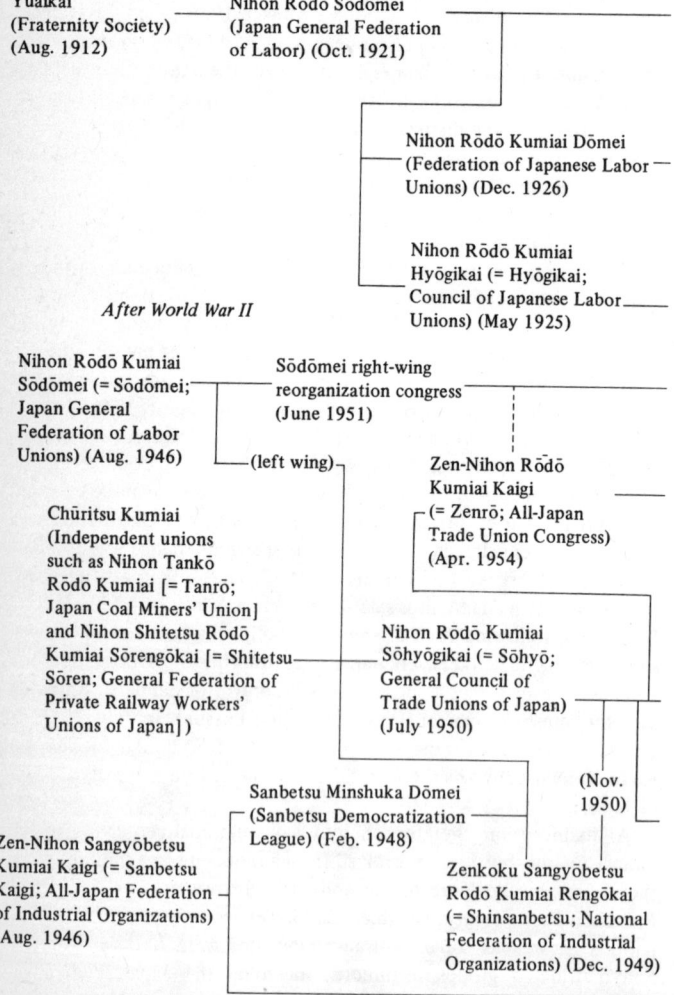

Source: Adapted from *Encyclopedia EPOCA*; Ōbunsha, Tokyo, 1975, p.336.

```
┌─ Rōdō Kumiai Dōmei
└─ (Federation of Labor Unions)
   (Sept. 1929) ──┐
                  ├── Zen-Nihon Rōdō Sōdōmei
┌─ Zenkoku Rōdō Kumiai    (= Sōdōmei; All-Japan General ─┐
└─ Dōmei (National Labor ─┘  Federation of Labor)
   Union Federation)         (Jan. 1936)                  dissolved
   (June 1930)                                            (June 1940)
```

```
                      Nihon Rōdō Kumiai
   meeting prohibited  Zenkoku Kyōgikai (= Zenkyō;      in disarray
   (Apr. 1928) ──────  National Conference of Japanese ─ (1934)
                       Labor Unions) (Dec. 1928)
```

Membership as of
June 1977

```
┌─ Zen-Nihon Rōdō Sōdōmei
└─ Kumiai Kaigi (= Dōmei Kaigi;
   All-Japan General Federation
   of Labor Unions Congress)
   (Apr. 1962) ─────────┐
                        ├── Zen-Nihon Rōdō
┌─ Zenkoku Kankōshokuin │   Sōdōmei (= Dōmei;
└─ Rōdō Kumiai Kyōgikai ┘   Japan Confederation ── 2,210,000
   (National Council of     of Labor) (Nov. 1964)
   Government and
   Public Workers' Unions)
   (Sept. 1959)
                                                ── 4,556,000

   Zenkoku Chūritsu
   Rōdō Kumiai
   Renraku Kaigi
   (= Chūritsu Rōren; ─────────────────────────── 1,330,000
   National Federation
   of Independent
   Unions) (Sept. 1956)

┌─ Shinsanbetsu ──────────────────────────────── 65,000
└─ (National Federation of
   Industrial Organizations)    (In addition, there
   (July 1952)                  are also 4,660,000
                    dissolved   members in
                    (Feb. 1958) unaffiliated unions)
```

Table 8-1. Growth of Labor Unions (1921-1977)

Year	Total union membership	Estimated % of unionization	Year	Total union membership	Estimated % of unionization
1921	103,412	?	1950	5,773,908	46.2
1924	228,278	5.3	1955	6,285,878	35.6
1926	284,739	6.1	1960	7,661,568	32.2
1931	368,975	7.9	1965	10,146,872	34.8
1936	420,589	6.9	1970	11,604,770	35.4
1940	9,455	0.1	1975	12,590,400	34.4
1945	378,481	4.1	1976	12,508,731	33.7
1946	3,936,815	46.8	1977	12,437,012	33.2
1948	6,677,427	53.0			

Sources: Labor Policy Bureau, Ministry of Labor, *Rōdō Tōkei* (Labor Statistics), Tokyo, 1946; Institute of Statistical Mathematics, ed., *Nihon Keizai Tōkeishū* (Japanese Economic Statistical Almanac), Nihon Hyōron Shinsha, Tokyo, 1958, p.298; and Labor Policy Bureau, Ministry of Labor, *Rōdō Kumiai Kihon Chōsa* (Basic Survey of Labor Unions), Tokyo, 1958-77.

Note: Figures for 1946 and after are from June of each year.

Sōhyō's change of policy and broke away in 1954 to form the Zen-Nihon Rōdō Kumiai Kaigi (abbr. Zenrō; All-Japan Trade Union Congress) along with the right wing of Sōdōmei. Today's Zen-Nihon Rōdō Sōdōmei (abbr. Dōmei; Japan Confederation of Labor) grew out of Zenrō.

3. The National Centers

Of the national centers, Sōhyō is the largest, with 4.56 million members (36.6% of organized labor) as of 1977. In the same year, Dōmei had 2.21 million members (17.8%). However, three million of Sōhyō's members are employed in the public sector by the national government, local governments, the three public corporations (Japanese National Railways, Nippon Telegraph and Telephone, and Japan Tobacco & Salt Public Corporation), and the five government enterprises (Postal Service, State Forestry Service, Government Mint Bureau, Printing Bureau, and Japan Monopoly Corporation's Alcohol Division). Only 1.56 million of Sōhyō's members are in the private sector, as compared with more than 90% (2.04 million) of Dōmei's membership. Thus, in terms of the private sector alone, Dōmei has been larger than Sōhyō since 1967. Especially noteworthy is the fact that many unions from the advanced sector of industry, such as automobiles, ship-

Table 8-2. Union Membership by Applicable Law
(1 = 1000)

Law		1949 Membership	1949 % of total	1953 Membership	1953 % of total	1963 Membership	1963 % of total	1973 Membership	1973 % of total	1975 Membership	1975 % of total	1977 Membership	1977 % of total
Labor Union Law		5,230	78.6	3,822	64.5	6,519	69.7	8,841	73.1	9,183	72.9	8,991	72.3
Public sector	Public Corporation and National Enterprise Labor Relations Law	609	9.1	861	14.5	973	10.4	1,014	8.4	1,020	8.1	1,020	8.2
	Local Public Enterprise Labor Relations Law	...	...	73	1.2	166	1.8	220	1.8	229	1.8	230	1.8
	National Public Servants Law	817	12.3	221	3.7	285	3.0	284	2.3	287	2.3	288	2.3
	Local Public Servants Law	*932	14.0	951	16.1	1,415	15.1	1,738	14.4	1,871	14.9	1,909	15.3
	Public sector sub-total	*2,447	36.8	2,105	35.5	2,838	30.3	3,257	26.9	3,407	27.1	3,446	27.7
Total		6,655	100	5,927	100	9,357	100	12,098	100	12,590	100	12,437	100

Source: Ministry of Labor, *Rōdō Kumiai Kihon Chōsa* (Basic Survey of Labor Unions), Tokyo, annually.
Notes: *In 1949, the Labor Union Law was applicable to local government employees and to 89,000 people employed by the Occupation authorities. However, because these people were essentially employed by the national government, they have been double-entered in the public sector sub-total.

building, and electrical power, belong to Dōmei. The two national centers also differ considerably in their political inclinations. Sōhyō supports the Socialist Party of Japan (SPJ), and its left-wing faction favors the JCP. By contrast, Dōmei is aligned with the more moderate Japan Democratic Socialist Party (DSP).

In addition to Sōhyō and Dōmei, there are two more national centers: Zenkoku Sangyōbetsu Rōdō Kumiai Rengōkai (abbr. Shinsanbetsu; National Federation of Industrial Organizations), and Zenkoku Chūritsu Rōdō Kumiai Renraku Kaigi (abbr. Chūritsu Rōren; National Federation of Independent Unions). Shinsanbetsu is the smallest of the four national centers with a membership of slightly over 40,000, while Chūritsu Rōren claims to represent 1.33 million workers. They differ in their political stance both from Sōhyō and Dōmei as well as from each other. A most striking feature of the Japanese labor movement is that the largest group of union workers, (4.66 million or 37%), are not affiliated with any of these national organizations, including Chūritsu Rōren. They belong to enterprise unions which are independent or members of *tansan*, the industry-wide labor federations that are independent from the national centers.

Since the mid-1960s, there have been several councils organized outside the framework of the existing national centers. Two of the better known among them are the Kokusai Kinzoku Rōren Nihon Kyōgikai (abbr. IMF-JC: International Metalworkers' Federation-Japan Council) organized in 1964 and the Nihon Kagaku Enerugī Rōdō Kumiai Kyōgikai (Japan Council of Chemical and Energy Industry Labor Unions) launched in 1977. These new councils were formed to facilitate realignment in the labor front and ultimately its reunification, but at the present time they are no more than loose associations that in no way replace the national centers.

Problems of Enterprise Unions

1. Legal Aspects

There is no question that the enterprise union is the form of organization chosen, in most cases, by the majority of eligible company employees. The Japanese Constitution expressly guarantees the freedom of assembly and association (Article 21) and the right of workers to organize and to bargain and act collectively (Article 28); and the Labor Union Law spells out these guarantees in further detail. Anyone who feels that any of these rights has been infringed upon is entitled to request the local Labor Relations Commission or the court to conduct an investigation of alleged

Table 8-3. Numbers of Unions and Union Members by Type of Organization

	Number of unions	% of total	Membership	% of total
Enterprise unions	31,295	93.6	10,382,000	82.5
Industry-wide unions	451	1.3	141,000	1.1
Trade unions	1,107	3.3	1,664,000	13.2
Others	571	1.7	404,000	3.2
Total	33,424	100	12,590,000	100

Source: Ministry of Labor, *Rōdō Kumiai Kihon Chōsa* (Basic Survey of Labor Unions), Tokyo, 1975.

unfair labor practices. In fact, this procedure has been used to good effect on a number of occasions. Given the overall legal framework and the way the provisions are actually applied, some observers would go so far as to claim that Japanese unions are overprotected. Overprotected or not, they are certainly blessed with one of the most favorable legal systems in the world. It would thus be wide of the mark to try to attribute the emergence of enterprise unions in Japan to some flaws or inadequacies in the legal system.

At least in form, the enterprise union resembles the employee representation plans common in the mass-production industries of the United States during the 1930s. But the passage of the National Labor Relations Act (Wagner Act) in 1935 and the organizing efforts of labor leaders combined to transform the American "enterprise unions" into locals of national industrial unions. In postwar Japan, both national centers (e.g., Sanbetsu Kaigi, Sōdōmei) and *tansan* strongly pushed for labor-management negotiations on an industry-wide basis — as opposed to an enterprise basis — in hopes of transforming enterprise unions into locals of national industrial unions. But few have succeeded aside from the Japan Coal Miners' Union, the All-Japan Seamen's Union, and a handful of others where workers join the national industrial union directly through their memberships in a local. Even these unions are not free from the fetters of enterprise unionism, however, because their major locals, organized at the plant level within large corporations, are usually more loyal to the intraenterprise labor federations than to the national organization. In this respect, they are little different from the other, more typical *tansan*, which are by nature loose federations of enterprise unions in a given industry.

Japan has some craft, industrial and general unions, but the overwhelming majority are enterprise unions. Table 6-3 gives a breakdown of Japanese labor unions by organizational features. There has been absolutely no change in the overwhelming predominance of enterprise unions during the more than three decades since World War II. Although a few craft unions do exist in certain fields, most workers in carpentry, catering, handicrafts, hairdressing, and similar occupations join in trade syndicates along with master craftsmen and employers.

2. Mixed Membership

Membership qualifications are the key feature of the enterprise union. Membership is, in principle, limited to full-time, non-managerial employees of the enterprise (be it a private company, a government office, a public corporation, a government enterprise, a nonprofit organization, or whatever, *regardless* of job description.) Since only full-time employees of the enterprise qualify as members of its union, neither temporary workers nor those from subsidiaries who have been assigned to do the same work side by side with employees of the parent company are eligible for membership in the union. As employees of subsidiaries, the latter may belong to their own enterprise unions.

That all the non-managerial employees of a given enterprise or plant are in the same union means of course a mixture of blue-collar and white-collar workers in its membership. Yet if this is one of the enterprise union's strengths, it can also be one of its weaknesses.

In the inflation-ridden years immediately after World War II, blue-collar and white-collar workers had to unite in the struggle for subsistence wages and reconstruction of their war-devastated factories. This system of mixed membership was also very much in keeping with postwar democratization in which abolishing such kinds of status discrimination between employees was of paramount importance. In fact, the better educated white-collar workers often assumed positions of leadership in the unions in the early postwar years, and it was not uncommon for a man in a middle-management position to become president of the company's union. In 1949, however, the Labor Trade Union Law was revised so as to restrict tightly the use of company funds and facilities for union activities, and most companies took the opportunity to exclude employees in management posts from union membership.

One of the most serious problems with membership in enterprise unions is that it is premised on one's employment status. As noted above, temporary workers and workers from subsidiaries are not eligible for union membership even though they may do the same work at the same place. Likewise, a worker who retires or resigns, automatically forfeits eligibility for membership in the union upon leaving the company. Indeed, this particular brand of unionism prevents the unemployed worker from belonging to any union and receiving any benefits from it. The inability to protect the interests of the unemployed is perhaps the most vulnerable point in an enterprise union, and it is here that the Japanese unions differ from their American and European counterparts which have been formed to insure the freedom of their workers to change jobs, and to help them in that process.

3. Rights of Workers in the Public Sector

The far-reaching dispute concerning employment status and eligibility for union membership is one that touches upon freedom of association for workers in the public sector. In the case of the postal service and the Japanese National Railways, the unions themselves, in their immediate postwar regulations, restricted membership to employees. The Public Corporations Labor Relations Law instituted in 1948 also stipulated that "union members must be employees" (Article 4, Paragraph 3). No one objected to this provision at that time, and in fact it was widely used to drive JCP members and sympathizers out of the labor movement during the Red Purge of 1949-50.

Later, from 1953 to 1958, there was a spate of incidents in which union officials who had led illegal actions in wage disputes were fired, rendering them ineligible for future union posts. It became evident from such events that this provision of the Public Corporations Labor Relations Law posed a serious threat to the workers' right of free association. Accordingly, the unions concerned and Sōhyō took the matter to the International Labor Organization (ILO) and urged the government to ratify ILO Convention No. 87 guaranteeing workers' freedom of association and the right to organize. The heated dispute between the government and Kōkyō Kigyōtai-tō Rōdō Kumiai Kyōgikai (abbr. Kōrōkyō; Council of Public Corporation and Government Enterprise Workers' Unions) continued until 1965 when the government ratified the ILO Convention and repealed the offending provision. However, in the early 1960s, during the process of this protracted and bitter struggle, Sōhyō and Kōrōkyō also began to demand that the government recognize the right of public-sector employees to strike, a matter which is still unresolved.

The connection between employee status and eligibility for union membership is a major limitation affecting union officials. People dismissed for illegal actions can now continue to serve as union officials in public-sector unions; but in the private sector, such people are almost always automatically barred from union offices. At the same time, workers in the private sector who take up union posts are usually retained on their company's employee rolls and given a "leave of absence" for the period they are paid by the union. Even *tansan* officials are retained on their company rolls, and it is customary for a chairman of a *tansan* to retire from the union upon reaching his own company's mandatory retirement age.

Officials of an enterprise union are most often chosen from among those workers who have been promoted to some lower-echelon supervisory position. They do not have as much authority as a foreman in an American factory, but at the first rung of the management organization, they generally feel a strong sense of loyalty to the company.

Functions of Labor Unions

Although Japanese labor unions appear weak, they have played an important part, both politically and socially, in Japan's postwar history. In particular, they have actively sought to maintain and improve wage levels and working conditions, which are, after all, the basic purposes of a labor union.

1. Employment Security

One of the most significant changes brought about by the development of the labor movement is that the employers' freedom to dismiss employees has been severely restricted. Many fierce disputes over personnel cuts occurred in the 1950s, from which management has learned to avoid dismissal of their employees at all cost. In the present recession, for example, companies are relying upon natural attrition processes and the reassigning of existing staff in an effort to avoid the ready recourse to layoffs commonly used in the United States.

Employees in Japanese companies are often moved around within the organization, frequently into widely different fields. This is possible because there are no conflicting interests of different craft unions when all the company's employees are members of the same union. It also means that employees can be given full on-the-job training to handle the widest range of work.

Mandatory retirement at age 55 or 60 has also contributed to smooth labor turnover. Since 1970, however, the trend has been toward later compulsory retirement, and this trend is likely to continue as Japan's elderly population increases.

2. The Spring Labor Offensive

In 1955, at the initiative of Sōhyō, unions combined their efforts for the first time in the "*shuntō*" or spring offensive. Designed to bring unions together in concerted action in order to compensate for the weak collective bargaining power of individual enterprise unions, this unique formula achieved considerable results. Although only 730,000 workers joined the offensive in its first year, participation increased to 4.39 million in 1961 and 9.68 million in 1975. While Sōhyō and Chūritsu Rōren joined to form the Shuntō Kyōtō Kaigi (Spring Struggle Committee), Dōmei and the unaffiliated unions have also begun to time their wage negotiations since 1960 to coincide with these spring offensives.

The success of the spring labor offensive is not limited to wage increases. These annual skirmishes have also made wage settlements more uniform, thus narrowing wage differences among different industries and between large and small companies. Similarly, they have encouraged the establishment of standards for intra-company wage differentials. Born of post-World War II democratization, Japanese labor unions base their wage negotiating positions on the egalitarian philosophy that each worker should be provided for according to such considerations as age, length of service, and number of dependents. They have consistently opposed position, responsibilities and efficiency as wage determinants.

3. Political and Social Roles

Along with securing better wages and working conditions for their members, labor unions also have had a strong impact on national economic and social policies. In 1974, Sōhyō and Chūritsu Rōren, concerned about the high rate of inflation, attempted with considerable success to expand the spring offensive into a "people's campaign," calling for pension indexing and various other welfare improvements. Meantime, Dōmei and IMF-JC are pushing for a "social contract" policy under which wages would be determined in accordance with the state of the economy and negotiations would concentrate on real rather than nominal wage increases. As employment and pollution problems have grown more serious, an increasing number of people have begun to advocate greater policy-making participation by unions.

As of the end of 1975, 63 members of the House of Representatives and 46 members of the House of Councilors had union backgrounds. Among them, 59 in the Lower House (including two from Chūritsu Rōren) and 38 in the Upper House were affiliated with the Sōhyō-SPJ bloc. By union, the Japan Teachers' Union (Nikkyōso) is politically the strongest with 12 representatives in the Lower House and 14 in the Upper House, while there are only four in the Lower House and seven in the Upper House with Dōmei backgrounds. By sector, public-sector unions are far stronger than private-sector unions in the Diet; in particular, the Japan Teachers' Union, National Railway Workers' Union (Kokurō), Japan Postal Workers' Union (Zentei), and the All-Japan Prefectural and Municipal Government Workers' Union (Jichirō) are heavily represented. However, the average union member's interest in politics is gradually waning, and in several individual unions there has been more support for the Liberal Democratic Party (LDP) than for the SPJ, which is backed by Sōhyō. From the other side, JCP supporters are urging Sōhyō to abandon its exclusive support of the SPJ and to allow the locals greater freedom in deciding which parties to support.

Although reformist governors elected with labor support head the governments of such heavily populated areas as Tokyo, Yokohama, and Osaka, there has been a significant swing in public opinion back in favor of the conservatives, as evidenced most clearly in the 1978 Kyoto gubernatorial and Yokohama mayoral elections. This trend can be taken as a reflection of a new realism among Japan's private-sector unions.

The Unsung Mainstays (1)

Small Businesses

KIYONARI TADAO

Introduction

Big business today is such a prominent and structurally well-established part of all major industrialized economies that the small business[1] sector is often the victim of neglect, misunderstanding and even disdain. In Japan too, the economic role of small business has not been fully appreciated, even though it has made a substantial contribution to economic growth.

Japan's high population density has been conducive to role specialization, and small enterprises proliferated from very early on. Today, small business accounts for a larger percentage of the total number of enterprises in Japan than in any other industrialized nation. The level of education had been high even before industrialization began in the latter half of the nineteenth century, and the know-how and creative ingenuity of small businesses became a powerful force in the building of a modern industrial nation. In the 1860s when late-blooming Japan began its industrialization, no large indigenous industries existed. It was the small businesses which took the initiative in adopting and adapting the advanced technology of the West and making use of native skills in order to speed the process of

[1] The Basic Law for Small Businesses in Japan defines small businesses as those transportation, mining, or manufacturing companies having ¥100 million or less in capital *or* less than 300 employees; those wholesale companies having ¥30 million or less in capital *or* less than 100 employees; and those retail or service industry companies having ¥10 million or less in capital *or* less than 50 employees.

modernization. This pattern has persisted to the present day. Japanese small business in general is highly capable of absorbing new technology and has become the mainstay of economic growth precisely because it is very adaptable to changing market conditions.

During the rapid growth of the 1950s, small business became closely associated with big business, forming a truly unique industrial organization. Yet in this partnership, big business did not necessarily dominate; it may even be said with some justification that big business could not have developed as it did without the dynamic development of the small business sector. I hope that the following outline of historical development of small business and description of the sector particularly since 1960 will provide a better appreciation of its role in Japan's economy.

Historical Development

1. A Profile of Small Business

Let us look first at the development of the small business sector since the turn of the century as reflected in government statistics. Inclusive and reliable statistics which can be used to show small business trends over long periods are difficult to come by, and this is especially true of the period before the national census was instituted in 1920. Nevertheless, the *Census of Works* and the *Census of Manufacturers* provide a clear understanding of trends in the manufacturing sector and indicate the change in the number of establishments by size (see Table 9-1 and Figure 9-1).

As the charts show, the total number of establishments increased steadily every half-decade except during and immediately after the Pacific War. Small businesses have consistently accounted for approximately 95% of all establishments, and while they remain a constant proportion of a steadily expanding whole, the number of small businesses has also been steadily expanding. The increase in the number of small businesses was most marked during the 1950s and 1960s; in fact, although this period of rapid growth was characterized by the expansion of heavy and tertiary industries, the number of small businesses increased at a faster rate than the GNP in the overall postwar period. Parallel to this increase was the rapid increase in the number of people employed, both in absolute and relative terms, in small businesses (see Figure 9-2 and Table 9-2), although since 1960 the rate of small business employment growth has been slower than the increase in the number of business establishments.

As the economy grew, so did the value of industrial shipments, and the proportion of small-business shipments to total shipments has virtually held steady over the years (see Table 9-3). In manufacturing, small busi-

Table 9-1. Percentages of establishments by business scale

Year	Total number of business establishments	4-9 persons*	10-29 persons	30-99 persons	Sub-total	100-199 persons	200-499 persons	500 or more persons	Total
1909	32,032	52.4	33.6	10.8	96.8		2.8	0.4	100.0
1919	43,723	45.8	35.6	13.5	94.9		4.3	0.8	100.0
1920	45,576	83.0		12.4	95.4		3.8	0.8	100.0
1925	48,850	48.0	33.9	12.3	94.2		4.0	1.1	100.0
1930	61,768	57.6	27.6	10.6	95.8	2.2	1.3	0.7	100.0
1935	84,625	54.9	30.1	11.1	96.1	2.1	1.1	0.7	100.0
1940	137,142	55.6	31.5	9.5	96.6	1.7	1.0	0.7	100.0
1945	57,980	—	—	—	—	—	—	—	—
1950	156,223	55.2	32.4	9.5	97.1	1.5	0.9	0.5	100.0
1955	187,112	48.5	39.7	11.3	96.8	1.7	1.0	0.5	100.0
1960	238,320	40.7	40.9	14.1	95.7	2.4	1.3	0.6	100.0
1965	345,120	55.7	29.2	11.4	96.3	2.1	1.1	0.5	100.0
1970	405,515	57.2	28.4	10.5	96.1	2.1	1.2	0.6	100.0

Sources: Compiled from *Census of Works* and *Census of Manufactures*, Ministry of International Trade and Industry.
Note: Figures prior to 1945 are for businesses of 5-9 persons.

160 ECONOMICS

Figure 9-1. Numbers of establishments

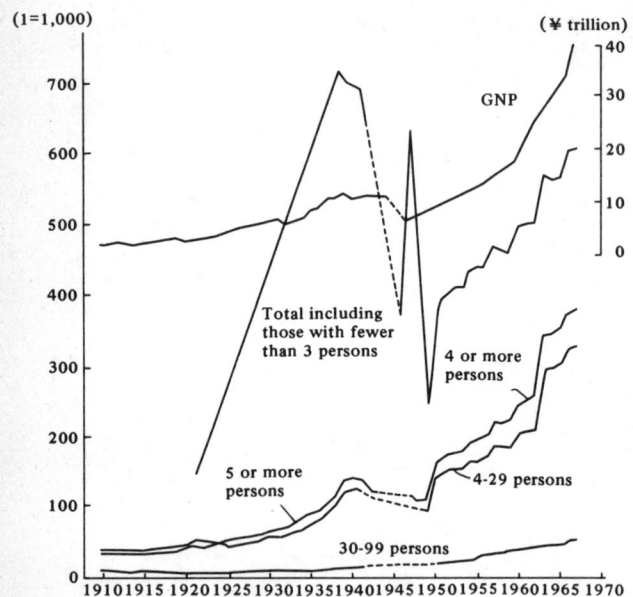

Sources and Note: Same as Table 9-1.

ness achieved considerable expansion in relative terms and held its own in absolute terms. Japanese economic growth was characterized by the deliberate use made of small businesses which became a mainstay of economic growth.

Table 9-4 shows the changing composition of the industrial structure by type of manufacturing industry. Except during World War II, the rapid expansion in Japan's heavy industrial sector is obvious. Whereas light industry accounted for 80.4% of manufacturing output by value in 1909, this was down to 41.8% in 1967. Around 1960, heavy industry replaced light industry as the dominant sector of the economy, but it is significant that the heavy-industry sector was led by the machinery industry, in which small business is heavily represented and which was expanding into other areas as well.

Table 9-2. Percentages of employees by business scale

Year	Total number of employees (1=1,000)	4-99 persons				100-199 persons	200-499 persons	500 or more persons	Total
		4-9 persons*	10-29 persons	30-99 persons	Sub-total				
1909	821	14.1	21.8	22.0	57.9	21.4		20.7	100.0
1919	1,808	8.7	16.6	19.9	45.2	23.3		31.5	100.0
1920	1,758	26.9		19.2	46.1	21.5		32.4	100.0
1925	1,996	8.9	14.8	16.9	40.6	21.9		37.5	100.0
1930	1,875	12.4	16.3	19.9	48.6	11.3	14.5	25.6	100.0
1935	2,620	10.9	17.2	19.7	47.8	10.1	12.1	30.0	100.0
1940	4,486	11.6	17.0	16.3	44.9	8.1	10.8	36.2	100.0
1945	2,200	—	—	—	—	—	—	—	—
1950	3,861	13.3	21.0	18.8	55.1	8.6	11.4	26.9	100.0
1955	4,964	11.1	23.9	20.7	55.7	9.1	11.4	23.8	100.0
1960	7,602	8.3	20.8	22.0	51.1	10.5	12.3	26.1	100.0
1965	9,481	12.2	17.8	21.0	51.0	10.7	12.5	25.8	100.0
1970	11,163	12.5	17.1	19.7	49.3	10.7	12.8	27.2	100.0

Sources and Note: Same as Table 9-1.

162 ECONOMICS

Figure 9-2. Numbers of persons engaged by business scale

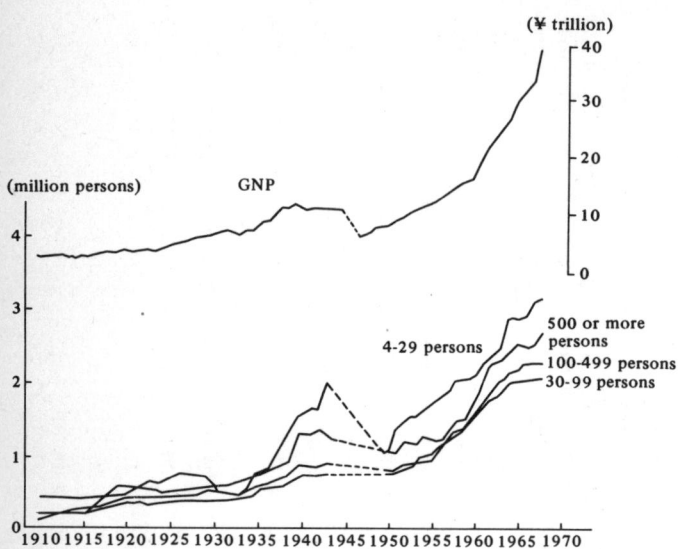

Sources and Note: Same as Table 9-1.

Although no adequate statistics are available to illustrate trends in non-manufacturing sectors, it is possible to get an idea of what was happening to non-agricultural self-employed businesses (*jiei-gyō*, independent enterprises managed by self-employed businessmen), as shown in Table 9-5. Despite some fluctuation, their numbers have increased considerably over the years, and the ratio of people in non-agricultural self-employed businesses to total employment, although generally stable, has recently been on the increase. By industrial category, small businesses have shown absolute expansion in commerce and service, while their representation in manufacturing has fluctuated.

A detailed tabulation of employment in self-employed businesses in both the agricultural and non-agricultural sectors since 1940 is given in Table 9-6. The sharp decline in the number of owners and family workers in agriculture since 1960 is conspicuous, and this trend is especially

Table 9-3. Percentages of shipping value by business size

Year	4-99 persons				100-199 persons	200-499 persons	500 or more persons	Total
	4-9 persons	10-29 persons	30-99 persons	Sub-total				
1929	8.0	12.5	18.9	39.4	11.5	17.8	31.3	100.0
1930	9.0	13.4	19.9	42.4	11.8	16.4	29.5	100.0
1935	6.2	12.1	17.1	35.4	10.6	14.4	39.6	100.0
1940	8.0	13.4	16.6	38.0	8.6	12.5	40.9	100.0
1950	6.6	13.6	16.7	36.9	9.7	15.7	37.7	100.0
1955	5.0	14.7	17.5	37.2	10.3	16.7	35.8	100.0
1960	3.3	11.4	16.4	31.1	10.3	14.9	43.7	100.0
1965	4.8	10.7	16.6	32.1	10.8	15.4	41.7	100.0
1970	4.8	10.5	15.5	30.8	10.2	14.9	43.3	100.0

Sources: Same as Table 9-1.
Note: Figures prior to 1950 are percentages of production value.

prominent with respect to family workers. On the other side of the table, there was an equally sharp increase in non-agricultural self-employed owners after World War II; their numbers more than doubled between 1948 and 1974. Although there was some relative decline in the 1950s, the number of self-employed businessmen remained steady, at approximately 14% of all non-agricultural employees, throughout the 1960s. The absolute number of family workers has risen steadily. 1974 marked the first decline since World War II. The total number of owners and family workers combined has consistently been about 20% of the total non-agricultural employment, typical figures being 21.6% in 1965, 22.1% in 1970, and 19.9% in 1974. Including non-family employees, such self-employed businesses accounted for 31.4% of all non-agricultural employment in 1965, 32.3% in 1968, 31.1% in 1971, and 29.9% in 1974, according to the government's *Basic Survey of Employment*. Nearly one-third of all workers were employed in such small self-employed businesses. Despite the large increase in the number of corporations during this period, self-employed business employment expanded steadily in absolute terms, thus maintaining its representation in relative terms.

From these data may be derived two observations: (1) the absolute number of self-employed businesses in the agricultural field has declined, while that in the non-agricultural field has increased; and (2) there is a limit to how much modernization of the industrial structure can induce

Table 9-4. Percentages of production value by industrial sector

Year	Light industries				Heavy industries				Total
		Foodstuffs	Textiles	Wooden products		Chemicals	Metals	Machinery	
1909	80.4	18.4	50.6	2.7	19.6	10.2	4.2	5.4	100.0
1919	73.0	10.8	51.0	2.9	27.0	10.5	6.5	10.0	100.0
1920	72.8	13.4	44.4	3.4	27.2	11.9	5.6	9.7	100.0
1925	75.4	15.9	50.2	2.7	24.6	11.1	6.9	6.6	100.0
1930	64.6	16.1	38.0	2.8	35.4	15.3	9.6	10.6	100.0
1935	52.3	10.8	32.3	2.3	47.7	16.8	18.4	12.5	100.0
1940	30.0	9.1	18.4	3.8	70.0	17.1	21.8	31.2	100.0
1945	21.6	5.3	5.9	5.0	79.4	9.2	18.8	51.3	100.0
1950	55.8	13.5	23.2	4.6	44.2	12.9	16.0	13.9	100.0
1955	55.3	18.0	17.5	5.1	44.7	11.0	16.9	14.8	100.0
1960	43.6	12.4	12.4	4.5	56.4	9.4	18.8	25.8	100.0
1965	43.5	12.5	10.3	5.0	56.5	9.5	17.8	26.6	100.0
1970	37.8	10.4	7.8	4.7	62.2	8.0	19.3	32.3	100.0

Sources: Same as Table 9-1.
Note: Same as Table 9-3.

a decline in the number of self-employed businesses and an increase in outside employment.

Not only have self-employed businesses survived in the highly industrialized environment, they have obviously thrived. Self-employed businesses, no matter how small, are not dying out in either absolute or relative terms. On the contrary, they constitute an expanding stratum as the economic scale rises, and it is almost inconceivable that they might degenerate into insignificance as a consequence of economic development. Rather, the mechanics of economic growth are such as to generate even more small businesses.

2. The Role of Small Business in Industrialization

The important role played by small business in Japan's belated industrialization may be summarized as follows.

a. Small businesses manufacturing textiles and sundries sprang up throughout the nation and gradually developed into export industries. These exports in turn enabled the country to import the resources and machinery required for industrialization. In this way small businesses

Table 9-5. Percentages of non-agricultural independent enteprises (owners and family workers) by industry

Year	Non-agricultural industries total		Manufacturing sector		Wholesale and retail sector		Service sector		Percentage of non-agricultural independent enterprise employment to total employment
	Number (1=1,000)	Percentage	Number (1=1,000)	Percentage	Number (1=1,000)	Percentage	Number (1=1,000)	Percentage	
1920	5,175	100.0	1,657	32.2	2,001	38.8	622	12.0	20.4
1930	6,279	100.0	1,860	29.6	2,834	45.1	616	9.8	21.9
1940	5,723	100.0	1,468	25.7	2,675	46.6	608	10.6	15.7
1947	4,300	100.0	1,280	29.8	1,504	35.1	897	20.9	–
1950	5,342	100.0	1,232	23.0	2,453	46.0	1,100	20.6	16.2
1955	6,187	100.0	1,286	20.8	2,967	48.0	1,289	20.9	16.8
1960	6,983	100.0	1,337	19.1	3,237	46.5	1,339	19.2	16.0
1962	6,744	100.0	1,232	18.2	3,103	46.0	1,284	19.0	15.7
1965	7,095	100.0	1,390	19.6	3,148	44.4	1,377	19.4	15.8
1968	8,533	100.0	1,856	21.8	3,653	42.8	1,681	19.7	17.4
1971	8,982	100.0	2,050	22.8	3,641	40.5	1,797	20.0	17.7

Sources: *Koyō to Shitsugyō* [Employment and Unemployment], Shōwa Dōjinkai for 1920-1955.
National Census, Prime Minister's Office, 1960.
Basic Survey on Employment Structure, Prime Minister's Office, 1962.

Table 9-6. Structure of employment (1=1,000 persons)

Year	Agriculture							Non-agricultural industries						
	Self-employed owners		Family workers		Employees		Total number	Self-employed owners		Family workers		Employees		Total number
	No. of people	% of total	No. of people	% of total	No. of people	% of total		No. of people	% of total	No. of people	% of total	No. of people	% of total	
1940	4,690	34.3	8,466	62.0	498	3.6	13,654	3,757	20.5	1,799	9.8	12,803	69.7	18,359
1948	5,117	29.9	11,343	66.3	641	3.7	17,101	3,066	19.4	1,588	10.1	11,133	70.5	15,787
1950	5,449	33.0	10,372	62.7	711	4.3	16,532	3,835	20.2	1,875	9.9	13,245	69.9	18,955
1955	5,127	33.3	9,616	62.4	665	4.3	15,408	4,267	17.9	2,278	9.6	17,305	72.6	23,850
1960	4,999	36.9	8,047	59.3	514	3.8	13,560	4,635	15.4	2,430	8.1	23,056	76.5	30,121
1965	4,456	40.1	6,288	56.6	369	3.3	11,113	4,880	13.4	2,995	8.2	28,534	78.4	36,418
1970	4,064	42.6	5,190	54.4	284	3.0	9,538	6,080	14.3	3,341	7.8	33,233	77.9	42,654
1974	3,272	47.9	3,095	45.3	461	6.8	6,828	6,200	13.9	2,657	6.0	35,622	80.1	44,479

Sources: *National Census*, Prime Minister's Office for years prior to 1974. *Basic Survey on Employment Structure*, Prime Minister's Office, 1974.

played a pivotal role in Japan's industrial structure until the 1920s.

b. Simultaneously, small businesses achieved rapid growth as import-substitution industries.

c. An increasing number of small businesses subsequently moved into advanced, technology-intensive export industries.

d. The number of small sub-contractors in assembly fields increased.

e. A large number of technology-intensive small businesses which could meet diversified popular demand flourished.

f. Small businesses offered important opportunities for employment in the labor-intensive service sector.

Yet despite their importance within the economy, or perhaps because of it, small businesses encountered more than their share of difficulties during the process of industrialization. Because industrialization was largely equivalent to Westernization, traditional industries which had existed since the 1880s met with a declining demand for their goods and services. Decline was inevitable for those that failed to adapt. Although the system of cooperative societies was introduced to alleviate the problem, the effectiveness of these societies in turn depended primarily upon how astute their members were in dealing with change.

In the early 1900s, the industrial revolution drove an additional number of petty industries into bankruptcy, and the introduction of the German historical school of economics prompted considerable debate over the *Kleingewerbe* (small business) problem. Big businesses as we know them today were established in the 1920s and qualitative differences began to emerge between the traditional small businesses and the new big businesses, differences which were later seen as characteristic of the "dual structure."

This evolving economic structure was eventually disrupted by the financial panic of the 1930s. More and more workers were thrown out on their own, and in a desperate effort to stave off unemployment, many banded together, producing a new expansion of the small business world. It was during this same period that Japan made her bid for an empire. The economy became more centrally controlled and many small businesses in light industry were forced by the government to switch to munitions or other wartime production. In the devastation of war, however, the productive capability of the small business sector was largely destroyed. The decade after the War was thus one of gradual rehabilitation for the small business sector.

Modernization of Small Businesses

1. Rapid Economic Growth and Small Businesses

Small business management as a whole was completely transformed during the period of rapid economic growth that began in the mid-1950s. Profits improved and areas of activity diversified. Most noteworthy of these many changes was the increase in the absolute number of small businesses and the outstanding corporate growth some of them achieved. Many of the new small businesses that sprang up in this rapidly expanding economy kept pace with the total economic scale, eventually shedding their small business status and developing into medium-sized or even larger corporations.

The number of small businesses, as indicated by the number of non-agricultural individual enterprises (*kojin kigyō*), rose by nearly one-third, from 4.76 million in 1956 to 6.2 million in 1974 (see Table 9-7). The number of individual enterprises was only 3.84 million in 1950, and despite expectations that the number of small business would subsequently decline, the growth of this sector has been spectacular. During this same period, the number of corporations (*hōjin kigyō*) increased even faster than did the number of individual enterprises, tripling in the 20-year period from 1954 to 1974. Yet 98% of these corporations were small businesses of ¥50 million or less in capital. Since all individual enterprises are also small businesses, it is reasonable to assume that over 99% of all business enterprises were small businesses. At present, the number of small businesses is estimated to be in excess of 7.5 million.

Table 9-8 shows the changes in the number of business establishments with 100 or more employees in the rapidly growing manufacturing sector. As the table shows, businesses with 100-299 employees more than doubled in number between 1958 and 1973 — from 4,400 to 10,139. The greatest percentage of increase was in manufacturing firms with 300-999 employees, which nearly tripled during the period. At the same time, the number of manufacturing firms with 1,000 employees or more in 1973 was more than double its 1958 figure. Clearly the medium-sized business stratum expanded more rapidly than either the small-business or big-business strata. Moreover, since productivity rose faster than in the past, actual corporate growth was even greater than these figures indicate. Of the 1,747 businesses listed on the nation's stock exchanges as of 1975, 564, or nearly one-third, are firms established since 1945, including a number which started as small businesses.

These phenomena illustrate the rapid expansion of the small business

Table 9-7. Numbers of businesses

(1=1,000)

Year	Individual enterprises (unincorporated business)	Corporations	Total
1956	4,762	407	5,169
1959	4,823	510	5,333
1962	4,684	624	5,308
1965	4,932	753	5,685
1968	5,680	898	6,578
1971	6,108	1,058	7,166
1974	6,200	1,292	7,492

Sources: *Basic Survey on Employment Structure*, Prime Minister's Office and *Annual Statistical Report*, Tax Administration Agency.

Note: "Individual enterprises" figures are for non-manufacturing businesses only.

field. The striking changes which rapid growth induced in the industrial structure made possible specialized division of labor, thereby stimulating expansion of small business operations. Even as expanded demand prompted integration into big businesses, it also accelerated diversification into new small business fields.

As a result of the growth of heavy and chemical industries, diversification took place both in the fabrication and assembly of investment goods and durable consumer goods. At the same time, higher income levels promoted expansion of the non-durable consumer goods industries. In addition, increases in production and consumption led to further expansion of the service sector. While established industries diversified, new businesses came into being as specialization spread. This process is illustrated in Table 9-9, which indicates the fluctuations in the number of small businesses by industrial field. Slightly over three-quarters of these businesses were in the tertiary sector, and they contributed approximately 72% of the total increase. Growth was especially noteworthy in the areas of real estate and construction. Even with the minor decreases registered in mining and utilities, the number of small businesses rose more than 50% over a period of fifteen years.

Along with GNP growth, technological advances contributed greatly to expansion of the small business sector. As mass production became firmly entrenched and mass-marketing systems organized, many small businesses

Table 9-8. Numbers of medium-sized, medium-large, and big businesses (manufacturing only)

Year	100-299 employees	300-999 employees	1,000 or more employees
1958	4,400	1,133	395
1959	5,102	1,299	438
1960	5,660	1,460	498
1961	6,534	1,807	629
1962	7,543	2,060	665
1963	8,216	2,264	722
1964	8,524	2,319	726
1965	8,548	2,499	704
1966	8,941	2,406	734
1967	8,989	2,463	764
1968	9,216	2,581	803
1969	9,596	2,761	841
1970	10,106	2,825	866
1971	9,826	2,780	809
1972	10,033	2,831	850
1973	10,139	2,944	857

Source: *Census of Manufactures*, Ministry of International Trade and Industry.

were created, others were integrated into big businesses, and some evolved into big businesses.

In Table 9-10, market changes are shown in terms of changes in net production by industrial category. Growth was especially good in the labor-intensive small business sector, particularly in the construction and the service industries.

While Japan's rapid economic growth provided a favorable climate for small business, it was not uniformly taken advantage of. Small businesses prospered only to the extent that they were able to change. Particularly in the years during which Japan achieved almost full employment and when there was no longer a large pool of talented workers to draw upon, small businesses faced difficult times. As the excess labor pool dried up, wages tended to equalize throughout industry and the wage differentials between large and small businesses narrowed. As a consequence, the "dual structure," insofar as it included a separate small business sector characterized by lower wage scales, was virtually eliminated. Equivalent wages

Table 9-9. Numbers of small business establishments by industrial category

Industrial category	1960	1975	Numerical increase	Percentage increase	Percentage of total increase
Mining	9,553	7,197	−2,356	−24.7	−0.1
Construction	195,220	446,516	251,296	128.7	13.9
Manufacturing	549,778	809,309	259,531	47.2	14.3
Wholesale & retail	1,842,463	2,622,635	780,172	42.3	43.1
Financing & insurance	51,119	65,877	14,758	28.9	0.8
Real estate	38,472	176,565	138,093	358.9	7.6
Transportation & communication	66,101	104,627	38,526	58.3	2.1
Electricity, gas, & water supply	7,563	5,570	−1,993	−26.4	−0.1
Services	786,230	1,119,716	333,486	42.4	18.4
Total for non-primary industries	3,546,499	5,358,012	1,811,513	51.1	100.0

Source: *Statistical Survey on Establishments*, Prime Minister's Office.

Table 9-10. Domestic net production by industrial category

(1=¥100 million)

Year Industry	1960 Value of production	1960 Percentage of total	1975 Value of production	1975 Percentage of total	Rate of increase	Elasticity value
Primary industries	19,412	14.6	85,472	6.7	440.3	0.46
Secondary industries	48,368	36.4	458,574	35.9	948.1	0.99
Manufacturing	38,911	29.3	341,100	26.7	876.6	0.91
Construction	7,332	5.5	112,133	8.8	1,529.4	1.59
Tertiary industries	67,154	50.5	731,704	57.4	1,089.6	1.14
Wholesale and retail	21,506	16.2	242,746	19.0	1,128.7	1.18
Services	14,328	10.8	184,671	14.5	1,288.9	1.34
Total value	132,934	100.0	1,275,750	100.0	959.7	1.00

Source: *Annual Statistical Report on National Income*, Economic Planning Agency.

Note: Rate of increase = $\dfrac{\text{Value of production (1975)}}{\text{Value of production (1960)}} \times 100$

had to be paid to attract quality employees and one of the most important problems of small businesses was how to cope with rapidly rising wage levels.

2. Independent Measures by Small Businesses

Small businesses have devoted great effort to adapting to such changes in the business environment as expansion and diversification of demand, technological advances, labor shortages, higher wages, and so forth. For example, they have handled higher costs, especially in wages paid out, through a combination of tactics: (1) raising capital-plant ratios and productivity, (2) emphasizing higher-quality goods and services, and (3) raising prices to offset these higher costs. An inevitable consequence of such adaptation to market changes was that competition intensified. Small businesses had an unprecedented need for managerial ability, because those which could not institute any of the above three responses invariably fell by the wayside.

Although as a whole the small business sector adapted well to the changes in the business environment, there has been considerable corporate turnover. While many more businesses have failed to adapt and have gone bankrupt, been taken over, or otherwise ceased operation as distinct entities, they have been replaced by an ever-larger number of new businesses which can meet expanding market demand. This cycle has accelerated since 1963, and since more new businesses were being formed than were breaking up, there has been a net increase in the absolute number of small businesses. Although it is impossible to trace the details of this replacement process in the statistics, Table 9-11 gives a rough picture based upon the numbers of closures and new business openings for three 33-month periods.

The number of new businesses has decreased both in absolute and in relative terms. As the rate of economic growth slowed, so did the rate of establishment of new businesses, and yet even in the 1972-75 period, new businesses were increasing by 6% per annum. On the other hand, the number of business closings, which had declined slightly in the 1970-72 period, rose to record heights between 1972 and 1975. As a consequence of these conflicting trends, the rate of net increase fell from 3.3% per annum in 1966-69 to 1.9% per annum in 1972-75, and there was actually a decline in the absolute net increase. Nonetheless, it is quite obvious from Table 9-11 that the 1966-75 decade was a vigorous period for the nonagricultural sector.

A closer survey of these new businesses reveals that the majority were managed by young persons possessed of business acumen and specialized

Table 9-11. Private-sector non-agricultural business openings and closings

	Openings	Closings	Net increase
66-69	884,101 (7.6)	499,324 (4.3)	384,777 (3.3)
70-72	863,915 (6.7)	461,638 (3.6)	402,277 (3.1)
72-75	847,605 (6.0)	572,028 (4.1)	275,577 (1.9)

Source: Same as Table 9-9.
Note: Actual 33-month figures. Figures in parentheses are per-annum rates.

know-how, and who were able to respond creatively to the challenges of changing circumstances. These regenerative powers made it possible for small business to adapt. Overall, small businesses coped successfully with the varied demands made of them by trade liberalization, preferential tariffs, capital liberalization, fluctuations in the currency exchange rate and so on. At the same time, they benefited considerably from the rapid growth of the total economy, for expansion enhanced the foundations upon which small business operations rested.

The benefits to small enterprise are perhaps best illustrated statistically. As a starting point, Figure 9-3 charts the income of the average individual enterprise proprietor. Annual income, which was around ¥1 million in 1965, rose to more than ¥3 million in manufacturing and nearly ¥4 million in commerce a decade later. It was a satisfactory increase, but major disparities between high-income and low-income proprietors persisted. As Figure 9-4 reveals, the non-agricultural individual enterprise sector is characterized by considerable income discrepancies; while some small business owners thrive, most must struggle to get by.

Although the average annual income was ¥1,197,000 and ¥2,221,000 in 1971 and 1974, respectively, this does not imply that all non-agricultural proprietors were earning as much or as little as the average. For example, in 1971, when the average was ¥1,197,000, 56% of individual enterprise proprietors were earning less than ¥1 million (approximately 10% lower than the average) and 7.9%, ¥2.5 million (more than double the average) or more. In 1974, when the average had risen to ¥2,221,000, 21.8% were still earning less than ¥1 million (less than half the average) and 26.2% over ¥2.5 million (approximately 10% over the average). While incomes had risen overall, considerable discrepancies remained.

Corporate profits, as illustrated in the ratio of profits to capital in the manufacturing sector, indicate that small businesses with 50-299 employees consistently enjoyed a higher profit ratio than larger businesses (see Table 9-12 and Figure 9-5). Conversely, large businesses with 1,000

Figure 9-3. Incomes of individual enterprise proprietors (with three employees)

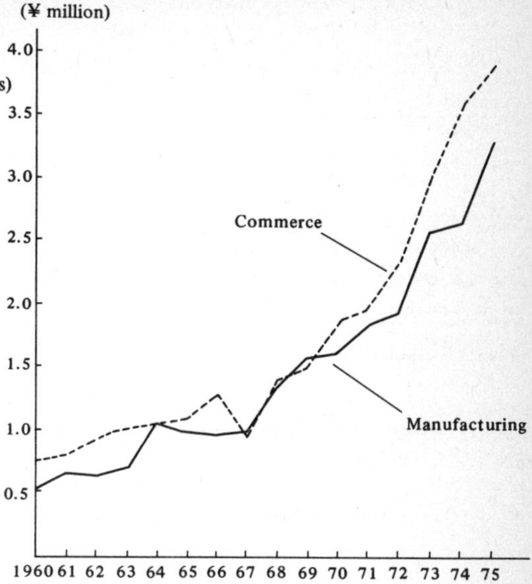

Source: *Economic Survey on Individual Enterprises*, Prime Minister's Office

Figure 9-4. Incomes of non-agricultural individual entrepreneurs

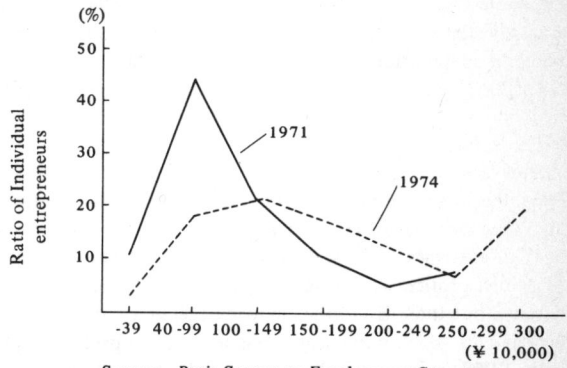

Source: *Basic Survey on Employment Structure*, Prime Minister's Office

Table 9-12. Ratio of profits to total capital in manufacturing

Year No. of employees	1972	1973	1974
50-99	6.0	10.6	7.9
100-199	5.5	9.8	6.9
200-299	5.6	9.5	5.5
300-499	4.5	7.7	4.7
500-999	4.3	7.0	3.8
1,000-4,999	4.3	6.5	3.8
5,000 or more	4.3	5.9	3.7
Average	4.5	6.9	4.3

Source: *Management Analysis of Business by Scale*, Bank of Japan.
Note: Ratio of profits to total capital

$$= \frac{\text{Net profit for current period (before taxes)}}{\text{Owned capital + liabilities at end of preceding and current periods} \div 2} \times 100$$

or more employees showed the lowest profit ratios in every year since 1968. Far from being hurt by a profit squeeze, small businesses actually outperformed larger companies, and profit ratios appeared to be in inverse proportion to corporate size. Table 9-12, where the profit ratio of companies having 5,000 or more employees is seen to be approximately one-half that of those having 50-99 employees, shows this most clearly. While it is traditionally asserted that exploitation by monopoly capital means that the smaller the business the lower the profit ratio, these figures, although admittedly averages, indicate that this conventional notion is false.

Nor is this true only of average values. Even on an individual corporate basis, there was considerable discrepancy between the profit ratios of small and large firms (see Figure 9-6). Small businesses were heavily represented at both extremes of the scale, many with running deficits and many others with high profits. By contrast, a smaller percentage of large businesses run deficits, but there is not the compensating sharp upturn on the high profit end as with small businesses. Thus the average profit ratio for businesses with 1,000 or more employees was only 3.7%. While only 22.2% of all

Figure 9-5. Ratio of profits to total capital in manufacturing

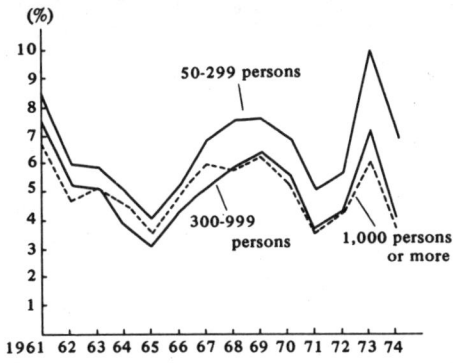

Source: Same as Table 9-12.

large businesses had profit ratios at least double that, 39.6% of small businesses had profit ratios of 8% or more. In effect, there were proportionately more small businesses than large businesses with high profit ratios. Some of these small businesses were able to accumulate considerable capital and to achieve quite rapid growth as a result of their favorable profit performance. Despite the sharp discrepancies among small businesses and the large number operating with a deficit, there are also many highly profitable ones, and it is just as erroneous to paint an entirely bleak picture of the sufferings of small business as it would be to claim that small balance sheets are always beautiful.

Part of the disparity among small business profit ratios is regional in nature. Small businesses in heavily populated areas, for example, achieved highly profitable ones, and it is just as erroneous to paint an entirely bleak costs, while those in sparsely populated areas had low productivity which could not make up for high costs. Further, more new businesses were started in heavily populated areas, perhaps as a result of the larger market and more abundant profit opportunities.

The main source of executive talent for emerging small businesses was

178 ECONOMICS

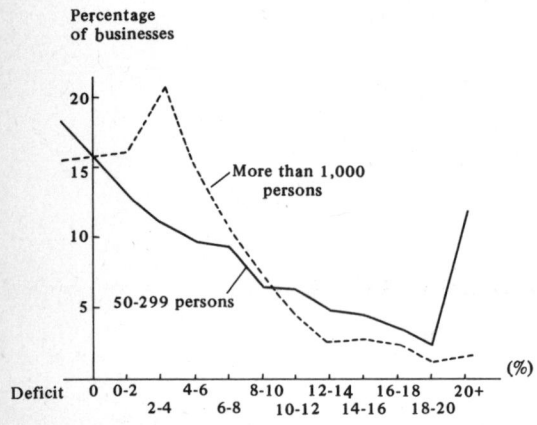

Figure 9-6. Numbers of small and large businesses by ratio of profits to total capital (1974)

Source: Same as Table 9-12.

other small businesses. As rapid economic growth generated expanded business opportunities and held out the lure of larger profits, highly profit- and independence-minded employees, especially younger ones, tended to go into business for themselves. As a result, acquisition of skills intensified, and efforts expended for independence gave these small businesses a firm grounding in management know-how. Moreover, the steadily expanding number of such emerging small businesses meant that consistently higher levels of managerial skill were required for survival and success, thus pushing standards ever higher. While it is true that a considerable number of these new businesses failed to make the grade as independent entities, this persistent striving for independence distinguished Japanese small business under conditions of rapid economic growth.

3. Small Businesses: Problems and Solutions

As rapid growth altered the economy's dual structure, it also wrought irrevocable changes in the nature of problems facing small businesses. Before discussing these changes and their ramifications, let us first focus on how the dual structure eventually broke down.

The "dual structure" is variously defined, but most interpretations agree on the distinction between big business and small business sectors. The term "dual structure" was coined by Arisawa Hiromi in 1957[2] to describe the residual existence of an unmodernized (small business) sector in Japan's postwar economy. He further defined dual structure as the relationship which evolves between these big and small businesses in a period of underemployment when big corporations take advantage of small businesses, which supply cheap labor. As such, he postulated that the survival of small businesses is prolonged by the threat of unemployment and the low wages prevailing under such circumstances, and that they are bound to the larger companies by close commercial ties.

This dual structure concept became widely used after it was cited in the *Economic White Paper*[3] of 1957, which stressed the need for resolution of the contradictions of this dual structure through economic growth. According to the *White Paper*, wage and productivity differentials became pronounced for different-sized companies, and it was desirable to take advantage of economic growth in order to raise small business wage levels. As employment became tighter, these higher wages should be paid as part of management efforts to improve productivity by raising the capital-plant ratio. Modernization for these small businesses was therefore seen as a process of improving productivity through investment in more modern plants and equipment.

Although there was some controversy around the turn of the decade as to whether rapid economic growth would actually mitigate or exacerbate the dual structure, when growth did finally generate full employment and equalize wages regardless of company size, the duality was considered to have been resolved. Of course, however, this did not mean the end of problems faced by small business.

New problems lay ahead, the most pressing of which were labor shortages and high wages. As noted above, three measures were adopted to cope with this situation: (1) a shift of emphasis from labor-intensive to capital-intensive fields, (2) a concentration on production of higher-quality goods, and (3) a raising of prices which made higher wages supportable. Companies which failed to institute an effective combination of these

---

[2] See his article, "Nihon ni okeru Koyō Mondai no Kihon-teki Kangaekata" (A Basic Approach to Employment Problem in Japan), in *Nihon no Keizai Kōzō to Koyō Mondai* (Economic Structure and Employment in Japan, Tokyo: Nihon Seisansei Honbu, 1957).

[3] *Economic White Paper*, 1957. Part I, Chapter 4, Section ii, p. 33 ff.

three basic responses soon found themselves out of business.

Another problem facing the small business sector was the need to adapt to new technological innovations which had far-reaching impact on both production and management. Complex changes also took place simultaneously in the structure and climate of both domestic and international markets, among them trade and capital liberalization, increased competition from newly industrializing nations, currency fluctuations, and spiraling oil prices. At the same time, heightened concern for the environment meant that small businesses were also subject to pollution regulations. Moreover, the mass of problems afflicting all small businesses was further complicated by the special requirements of location including high or low population densities and the needs for regional development. Even as small business management changed, new problems were constantly arising which demanded ever more resourceful management and still further change. Ultimately, the success or failure of small businesses in meeting these modern challenges will determine future patterns of corporate growth.

Coinciding with this transition in small business management was a shift in government policies vis-à-vis small business. The 1957 *Economic White Paper* had already advocated that medium-sized businesses be nurtured to bridge the gap between large and small businesses, and substantial assistance was made available from 1960 on for small businesses that wished to modernize their facilities. The Small Business Law (*Chūshō Kigyō Kihonhō*) and the Law to Promote Small Business Modernization (*Chūshō Kigyō Kindaika Sokushinhō*) enacted in 1963 detailed practical steps necessary to achieve modernization in the small business sector. According to the dual structure theory, small businesses were both too small and too numerous to be efficient, and accordingly the sector was to be modernized by investing in new plants and expanding operations. Small businesses were to be given both the facilities and the operational scale to shed their second-class status. Capital investment was intensified and a major effort made to achieve greater labor productivity through expansion. While these policies did benefit some companies, others not so favorably situated found it difficult to modernize (i.e. expand) on their own, and even cooperative efforts achieved only limited success.

By 1967, the dual structure theory gave way to an emphasis on broad structural improvements such as in the textile industry, to strengthen international competitiveness and revitalize particular regions by expanding their economic foundations. Yet no matter how efficient operations were, overall expansion could not occur without commensurate expansion in demand, and production-oriented capital modernization openly invited

Table 9-13. Numbers of non-agricultural individual enterprises and corporations

(1=10,000)

	1963		1966		1969		1972		1975	
	Number	Percentage of total	Number	Percentage of total	Number	Percentage of total	Number	Percentage of total	Number	Percentage of total
Individual enterprises	495	88.4	537	87.2	596	86.5	605	84.6	615	82.3
Filing blue returns	54	9.6	96	15.6	141	20.5	177	24.8	217	29.0
Unestablished	197	35.2	222	36.0	252	36.6	246	34.4	238	31.9
Others	244	43.6	219	35.6	203	29.5	182	25.5	160	21.4
Small corporations	65	11.6	79	12.8	93	13.5	110	15.4	132	17.7
Total	560	100.0	616	100.0	689	100.0	715	100.0	747	100.0

Sources: *Survey on Labor Force and Statistical Survey on Establishments*, Prime Minister's Office and *Annual Statistical Report*, Tax Administration Agency.

Note: Small corporations are those capitalized at less than ¥50 million.

trouble in the recession which followed.

In 1969, the Law to Promote Small Business Modernization was revised to provide structural improvements for a broader range of small businesses. Nevertheless, most of the industrial fields where small businesses predominate are by nature unreceptive to capital-intensive modernization, and when this did not succeed, serious reevaluation took place. Small business owners took an especially dim view of the all too automatic resort to plant modernization, although they recognized the need to develop new products with greater market acceptance.

When these efforts proved inadequate in coping with the currency fluctuation inherent in floating exchange rates, in 1973 the Law to Promote Small Business Modernization was again revised to emphasize knowledge-intensive development. Priority was now on "software," including development of new products and marketing techniques. Nevertheless, such "software" development does not lend itself easily to collective efforts, and the results so far have been disappointing for the small business sector.

Conclusion

Although Japan's economic growth rate has stagnated somewhat since the oil crisis of 1973-74, it has been an era of profound transformation within the industrial structure. With rapid improvement in wage levels, higher oil costs, the dramatic progress of South Korea and other industrializing nations as market competitors, the yen's startling appreciation, and other changes, Japanese industry has been forced into value-added fields since higher production costs have largely vitiated any advantage they may have had vis-à-vis the emerging industrial powers.

In this process of adaptation to fluid circumstances, disparities among different industries have grown more obvious, and ever-widening differences have developed among companies in the same industry. Although there have always been differences of both style and substance among small businesses, these differences have recently become sharper.

A new industrial order is emerging from these economic trials. While on the one hand an increasing number of small businesses are going out of business, on the other hand, there are indications that new types of businesses are opening up new fields, especially, for example, in the knowledge-intensive businesses and new service industries which have emerged in quick response to new conditions of urban demand.

It is no longer possible to generalize that a company is safe simply because it is big or, conversely, that it must be shaky because it is small.

While an increasing number of big businesses have been stagnating, quite a few small businesses are enjoying rapid growth. What is clear is that big business overall is losing its leadership position in the economy. Historically, the development of the big business structure was thus but one facet of one stage of Japan's industrial development. And in today's industrial society, the situation is characterized by strata diversification which makes it impossible to apply uniform criteria to all businesses. Now, more than ever, it is important that the role and significance of the small business sector be properly understood.

The Unsung Mainstays (2)

Agriculture

YAMAJI SUSUMU

One of the crucial questions besetting a nation on the road to modernization is how to deal with its agricultural sector, since the process of modernization necessarily involves the transformation from an agrarian to an industrial society. Japan began modernizing in the 1880s, and had made significant progress by the time of the Second World War. Her industrial base was still weak, however, and rural areas continued to suffer from poverty and over-population. After the War, Japanese agriculture was faced with two immediate tasks. The first task was food production. Japan had lost all her former territories, and millions of overseas nationals and soldiers crowded back into the homeland at once. The entire nation was in a state of near starvation. The people had to be fed. The second task was land reform. Nearly half of Japan's cultivated area was worked by tenant farmers. The aim of the land reform was to transfer ownership of the land to the poor tenants who made up the bulk of the rural population in order to defuse revolutionary pressure and to provide incentives for increased food production.

The land reform proved to be an enormous success. The relative wealth of farmers increased, and the industries could now count on a base of rural purchasing power. An expanded domestic market and a stabilized society paved the way for a period of rapid industrial growth that followed. In the 1960s, however, Japan was faced with a new problem. Industrial and commercial growth had created a gap in living standards between the urban and rural populations. The Japanese government sought to resolve this problem by encouraging increased agricultural productivity and conversion to profitable cash crops, and by providing price supports for rice. These measures have met with some success, but they have by no means provided an entirely satisfactory solution.

In this essay I would like to describe the current state of Japanese agriculture, the rural responses to government policies, and the changes wrought in the lives of farmers by Japan's rapid industrial growth, in the hope of shedding new light on this most important part of Japan's economy.

Japanese Agriculture's Setting

Traveling the length of the Japanese archipelago by air or rail, the visitor to Japan quickly discovers that the rural landscape differs markedly from that of the United States, Canada, Australia, or Western Europe. While almost all of the farmland in these countries consists of fields or pasture, Japan's is mostly wet rice paddies, the remainder being dry fields used for farming other crops.

Recent statistics (1977) show that of the 5,500,000 hectares of farmland in Japan, a total of 3,100,000 hectares are wet paddies for cultivating rice, the staple crop. Of the remaining 2,400,000 hectares, 600,000 are orchards and 530,000 are pasture. Only 1,270,000 hectares are crop fields, most of them are small and scattered, often tucked away in some secluded place.

Farmhouses are generally grouped together in clusters of 30 or 40 among the paddies. (In industrial regions, however, it would probably be more accurate to say that paddies are clustered among houses and factories.) The single exception to this rule is Hokkaido, the northernmost island, which was developed by pioneers from the southern islands a little more than a century ago. Here, dry fields and pastures outnumber the paddies, farms are larger, and farmhouses stand one to a farm rather than in groups. In short, farms in Hokkaido resemble those in the West. I must repeat, however, that Hokkaido is an exception, and agricultural statistics treat it separately from the rest of the nation in recognition of this fact. Outside of Hokkaido, relatively large expanses of farmland can be found only on the Kantō Plain near Tokyo, in the rice bowl of Niigata along the Japan Sea to the north, on the plain around Nagoya in central Japan, and in northern Kyushu to the west.

Except for these areas, Japan is extremely mountainous, with the result that most farmland is made up of small rectangular plots or is located along the banks of rivers and streams that cut through rugged terrain. Because of the lack of flat land, many paddies are terraced along the valleys and up into the foothills.

A glance at Table 10-1 clearly reveals the conditions of scarcity which agriculture in Japan faces. It is not merely that Japan has a relatively small land area and a large population; 80% of the land is mountainous and unsuitable for farming. Compared to West Germany, for example, Japan is

Table 10-1. Populations and land areas in the major nations

Nation	Population (millions)	Total area (million ha)	Arable land (million ha)	Arable land as percentage of total area	Cultivated fields (wet & dry) (million ha)	Per-capita arable land (ha)	Per-capita cultivated fields (ha)
China	800	959	288	30	112	0.36	0.14
France	52	55	33	60	19	0.63	0.37
Japan	107	37	6	16	5	0.06	0.05
U.K.	56	24	18	75	7	0.32	0.13
U.S.A.	209	936	436	47	192	2.09	0.92
West Germany	61	25	14	56	8	0.23	0.13

Source: Adapted from 1972 Food and Agricultural Organization statistics.

half again as large; but whereas forests cover a mere 29% of West Germany's total land area, they cover a full 69% of Japan's total. Thus, Japan has only half the total arable land (cultivated fields plus orchards and pasture) that West Germany has. Further, Japan's population is 107 million against West Germany's 61 million, meaning that Japan has only 0.06 hectares of arable land per capita compared to West Germany's 0.23. The disadvantages which these conditions entail should be obvious.

Although Japan is fortunate in having abundant rainfall and a temperate climate, the fact remains that its population is extremely large for the amount of available arable land. Japan's arable land, which as we have seen totals some 5.5 million hectares, is shared by 5 million farming households. Thus, the average holding per family is only 1.1 hectares. On the other hand, the holdings of households which make a living by farming alone (13% of the total farming households) average two hectares, and those of Class A part-time farmers, i.e., households whose farm income exceeds their non-farm income (27% of the total farming households) average 1.5 hectares. But neither group is very far removed from the overall one hectare per family average. It is this feature — intensive farming on a small plot of land — which more than anything else sets agriculture in Japan apart from that in the industrialized nations of the West.

Of course, these conditions are not unique to Japan, but are characteristic of much of Asia. In China and in South Korea, the average holding of cultivated fields is roughly one hectare per family. In North Korea, the Philippines, Thailand and Pakistan, the holdings are only slightly larger — perhaps two or three hectares per family — although lower production levels (less irrigation and technology is used in these countries) cancel out the advantage of size. Thus, they too are essentially one hectare per family farms. Indonesia, where 12 million families farm 12 million hectares of land (primarily wet paddy), perhaps most closely resembles Japan.

In one crucial respect, however, Japan differs radically from her Asian neighbors: the degree to which she has become industrialized. Japan is one of the world's great industrial powers, with a GNP second in the Free World only to the United States. And despite her large population, Japan's per-capita GNP also ranks among the highest in the world. This in turn raises the question of how a labor-intensive agricultural system can exist in a highly industrialized country like Japan. (In the United States, the average farm size is 158 hectares; in France, 25 hectares; in West Germany, 14 hectares; and in Italy, 8 hectares. Some farms in Australia are as large as 2,000 hectares.)

How large a yield can be wrought out of one hectare of land? If we take wheat as our example, the maximum yield is about 5 tons. This will fetch roughly $200 on today's market. Such a yield is economically viable only if the farm is large enough to offset the operational costs. How do the tiny Japanese farms manage to stay in business? The answer is twofold. On the one hand, there is an increase in non-agricultural income earned by farming households; on the other, a high level of government price support. An examination of these two factors will reveal the Japanese farmer's predicament and the basic posture of Japan's farm policy.

The one-hectare farm is by no means a recent phenomenon in Japanese agriculture, but a condition which has prevailed since the late nineteenth century. The late Dr. Yokoi Tokiyoshi of Tokyo University, a distinguished pioneer in Japanese agronomics, has written: "The three basic statistics in Japanese agriculture have remained constant from the Meiji Restoration (1868) to the present (1920), and they will no doubt remain constant in the future."[1] The statistics Dr. Yokoi refers to are the nation's 5.5 million farming households, 6 million hectares of farmland, and the 14 million farmers. Dr. Yokoi's prediction has proved correct. These three figures have indeed held constant since the Meiji Restoration to the present in spite of the tremendous changes Japan has experienced: the Pacific War, the sweeping Occupation agrarian reforms, and the dizzying industrial growth of the 1960s and early 1970s. In 1975, there were still 5 million households cultivating 5.5 million hectares of farmland. One figure has changed, however: the total permanent farming population has dropped from 14 million to 7 million. If seasonal labor during the busy periods of planting and harvesting is included, however, the actual farming population numbers about 13 million.

One must, of course, not overlook the great changes that have taken place. The traditionally high proportion of land used for sharecropping declined drastically following the postwar land reform. Moreover, the number of full-time farmers has decreased dramatically during the economic boom of the last quarter century. As late as 1950 (the year in which the Korean War broke out), 50% of all farming households farmed full-time; 28%, part-time as Class A farmers; and 22%, part-time as Class B farmers (i.e., whose non-agricultural income exceeds their farm income). By 1975, however, these figures had changed to 13%, 27%, and 66% respectively.

In spite of these changes, the one-hectare farm pattern has remained constant, and in most cases the increase in part-time farming households has meant simply that one or two members of the household are engaged

---

[1] Quoted from a lecture Yokoi Tokiyoshi delivered at Tokyo Imperial University in 1920.

in other occupations during the off-season (e.g., working at a nearby factory or construction site). Virtually all of Japan's roads are now paved, even in rural areas, and it is easy to commute large distances by car. Consequently, as tertiary industries expanded into the countryside, a new labor market was created which the part-time farmers were able to supply. This has been possible also because educational levels are as high in rural as in urban areas. The average farmer in Japan is well prepared for and highly adaptable to change.

The Postwar Agrarian Reforms

Along with labor reform and the dissolution of the mighty *zaibatsu* (business conglomerates like Mitsubishi and Mitsui), land reform was one of the most far-reaching economic reforms to come from the era of the Occupation following World War II. The tenant system was dismantled, landlords divested of most of their holdings, and independent farmers given the opportunity to farm their own land.

One might easily imagine that the postwar land reform altered decisively the one-hectare farm system. Such was not the case, however, as the land reform in fact further buttressed the system.

Preparations for agrarian reform began immediately after Japan's acceptance of the Potsdam Declaration on August 14, 1945, and the reforms were implemented between 1946 and 1949. As the Agricultural Land Law of 1952 makes clear, the basic philosophy of these reforms rested on private ownership.

Unlike most other postwar reforms, which were undertaken only after much prodding by the Occupation authorities, land reform was initiated by the Japanese government. There are several reasons for this. First of all, the wartime defeat shook the landed establishment to its very core, and it was feared that conflict between landlords and tenants might escalate into an outright revolution unless appropriate measures were quickly taken. Moreover, even before World War II, government policy makers had been studying ways to relieve sharecroppers from high rents (paid out as a percentage of the total harvest) and from the constant threat of eviction. The basic reform measures had already been worked out, and merely awaited implementation. Finally, Japan suffered from severe food shortages after the War, and government leaders saw land redistribution as a strong incentive for increased productivity. Thus, land reform was in fact a combined effort of government and Occupation authorities.

The land reform comprised four principal measures. First, landlords were required to sell all sharecropped land outside of their own villages to the state, which in turn sold it to the former tenants. Second, landlords were required to sell all sharecropped land in their own villages in excess of one hectare (the national average). Third, payment of rent in kind was outlawed and replaced by greatly reduced cash rents for the land that remained in tenancy. Fourth, land sales and purchases were put under tight controls in order that no landowner could expel a tenant from his land except in extreme circumstances and only then with the permission of the prefectural governor.

The results were considerable. Of the 2,400,000 hectares of land sharecropped before the reform (46% of the total land cultivated at that time), 80% was sold to the state and then back to the tillers. Only 10% of the nation's total farmland was now farmed by tenants. 1.25 million individual and 140,000 corporate landlords were involved in the transactions. 4.3 million farming households, 73% of the total, bought land from the state.

Because of these reforms, the number of landless tenant farmers was reduced from one-third of the total farming households to a mere 5%. Even if one includes those part-time tenants who owned some land of their own, tenancy was still below 10%. The share of total agricultural products paid out as rent was reduced from 30% to only 1%. In 1948, Laurence I. Hewes, Jr., a consultant to the Supreme Commander Allied Powers (SCAP), commented on Japan's agrarian reforms: "Seldom has such a bold scheme affecting so many people been carried out so smoothly and with such dispatch."[2]

In addition to the above four measures, there was a fifth measure which stipulated that owner-cultivated land in excess of 3 hectares (the national average, Hokkaido excepted) be purchased by the state as if it had been held in tenancy. Even those landlords who tilled most of their own land and rented only a small portion to tenants were subject to this limitation in order that total liquidation of what was regarded as a parasitic landlord class be achieved. The size of holdings actually worked by farmers, however, remained unaffected by these reforms. Another SCAP consultant who exercised strong leadership in the land reform (and whom the Japanese involved referred to as "a New Dealer"), Wolf I. Ladejnsky, observed after the reform: "The distress attendant on smallness of 6 million farms crowded on 6 million hectares of land was not for land reform to relieve."[3]

---

[2] Quoted in the editorial of *The Nihon Keizai*, December 12, 1952.

[3] Quoted in Danno Nobuo, *Nōgyō, Nōson, Nōmin*. (Tokyo: Asahi Shinbunsha), 1973, pp. 76-77.

To make matters even more difficult, rural areas were overflowing with repatriated, demobilized troops and refugees from the bombed-out cities. It was all the authorities could do to turn land over to tenant farmers. Had Japan faced a socialist revolution at this time, it might also have experienced the rise of the Soviet-style *kolkhoz* and *sovkhoz*. But even so — given the prevailing socioeconomic conditions — the total area under cultivation would have probably worked out to one hectare per family.

Rampant inflation quickly eroded the compensation that landlords received for selling their tenant farms to the government. This same inflation reduced to almost nothing the payments former tenants made on their land, which they had bought on extremely liberal 24-year terms to begin with. Both the rural landlords and the farmers' leagues (which had been active in defending tenant interests) rapidly lost their power. Agricultural cooperatives, which recruited members chiefly from among the new owner-cultivators, took their place. An extension service modelled after the American system was created to spread technical improvements. It was the dawn of a new era.

The Japanese agricultural cooperatives (collectively known as *Nōkyō*) form a comprehensive organization which assists the farmer in a variety of ways. *Nōkyō* acts as a go-between for business transactions, provides credit and loans, and acts as a clearing house for complaints and technical advice. Cooperatives first appeared at the beginning of this century, but they were not widespread until the government passed the Agricultural Cooperative Societies' Act in 1947.

At first local cooperatives were on rather shaky financial footing. But through the Food Administration Act (Shokuryō Kanrihō) of 1942 the government designated these agricultural cooperatives as its purchasing agent for price-controlled rice, and they then became depositories for government money which could be used for loans and credits. Cooperatives capitalized on this lending business to consolidate their positions, so that to this day the agricultural cooperatives remain intimately involved in the price-support system. Cooperatives played an important role in the development of agriculture in the immediate postwar years by providing a framework in support of the newly independent cultivators generated by the land reform.

"[The] magic of property turns sand to gold,"[4] writes the British agronomist Arthur Young. And so it was with the tenants whom the land reform turned into landed farmers. Now that they were able to keep for them-

[4] Quoted in J.S. Mill, *Principles of Political Economy, with Some of Their Applications to Social Philosophy.*

selves crops that previously had to be handed over as rent (in the case of rice as much as 40% of the harvest), they became much more concerned with increasing their output. In many villages groups began studying ways of improving rice harvests, raising seedlings, and using the new chemicals, fertilizers, and machinery that were appearing on the market. At the same time, the government worked to increase the rice crop by investing in programs to augment fertilizer output and to improve irrigation. Farm incomes rose, as did the farmers' purchasing power. Industry was thus able to count on rural demand to support increased manufacturing, something that would have been an impossibility before the War.

1955 marked a turning point for the Japanese economy as a whole and for agriculture in particular. In its 1956 *Economic Survey of Japan*, the government made its famous statement that the postwar reconstruction period had ended. Indeed, by 1955 Japan had emerged from the recession that followed the Korean War, had achieved a 9% real increase of the GNP with virtually zero inflation, and had accumulated a $500 million surplus in its overall balance of payments. Exports, particularly shipbuilding, were a major factor in this about-face. New ship orders jumped from 59,000 tons (worth $130 million) in 1954 to 223,000 tons ($520 million) in 1955. Also in 1955, steel replaced cotton textiles as Japan's leading export. And in 1956, private-sector investment increased by an unprecedented 58% (39% in real terms).

The agricultural sector too was on the upswing. Since the War's end, Japan's rice output had hovered around 9 million tons per year. In 1955, however, it jumped 36% over the previous year to 12.4 million tons — a record harvest. Even allowing for statistical errors, this was a significant increase. The 1955 crop was aided by good weather, to be sure, but this record harvest would not have been possible without the technical advances that had been made. Nowhere was Young's dictum about the magic of property better demonstrated. The land reform program had obviously worked. Increased domestic rice production meant a decrease in imported rice and thus improvement in the balance of payments. This in turn led to a relaxation of credit and provided new stimulus for vigorous production and investment in the industrial sector.

In a sense, then, the land reform was the launching pad for Japan's economic take-off. The contribution of agricultural expansion was particularly prominent in the second half of the 1950s. Not only rice but also fruit and livestock production increased during this period. Total agricultural imports went up by only $10 million in this period (from $870 million in 1955 to $880 million in 1960), so that the savings in the balance of payments could be applied elsewhere. Stable domestic food prices helped keep wages stable and hold down inflation. The remarkable growth in the latter half of the 1950s (8.1% in the period 1955-59) in turn created the momentum for even faster growth in the 1960s (10.8% in the first half and 12.7% in the second half).

The Farmer and Economic Growth

The 1960s were a decade of spectacular — one might even say tumultuous — growth. Let us look at some of the factors that made this growth possible. First, the latest technological innovations in petrochemicals and electronics were imported and adapted to the automobile and other industries. Second, there was an abundant supply of labor, particularly in the rural areas. Third, cheap energy (primarily petroleum) and food (wheat and corn) were available from abroad, thanks in part to improved shipping methods. Fourth, a generally healthy world economy provided a ready export market for Japan. And fifth, investment activity switched from light industry, the economy's traditional strength, to heavy and chemical industries.

Japan's growth can be said to have been powered chiefly by exports and plant investment. Expanded exports to the U.S. (which has traditionally consumed about 30% of Japan's exports) and to other countries in turn sparked new plant investment. Because old plants and machinery had been almost entirely destroyed in the War, the latest equipment could be installed in their place. This new equipment improved productivity and strengthened Japan's competitiveness in the international market, which then spurred further exports and plant investment. And so the cycle continued.

Another key factor promoting Japan's growth in the 1960s was the "National Income Doubling Plan" proposed by the Ikeda Cabinet in 1960. Inspired by the previous decade's economic expansion, the major corporations vied with one another for larger shares of the market, at a time when there was a high demand for consumer goods. The result was vigorous economic expansion. Nearly all the plan's major objectives were reached or exceeded (see Table 10-2). By the early 1970s, Japan had become a highly industrialized country.

Agriculture was profoundly affected by this rapid industrial growth. As late as the 1950s, the agricultural sector held sway over the entire economy. By the 1960s, however, the mover had become the moved, and agriculture began to be seriously affected by developments in other industries.

Symbolic of this change was the greatly improved position of the

Table 10-2. 1961 National Income Doubling Plan: goals and achievements

	FY 1970 targets		Actual FY 1970 figures	
	Absolute	Annual increase (%)	Absolute	Annual increase (%)
Population (millions)	102.22	0.9	103.72	1.0
Employment (millions)	48.69	1.2	50.94	1.5
Wage earners (millions)	32.35	4.1	33.06	4.3
GNP (¥bil. in 1958 prices)	26,000.0	8.8	40,521.2	11.6
National income (¥bil. in 1958 prices)	21,323.2	7.8	32,851.6	11.5
Per-capita national income (¥ in 1958 prices)	208,601.0	6.9	317,678.0	10.4
Personal consumption (¥ mil. in 1958 prices)	15,176.6	7.6	20,786.3	10.3
Per-capita consumption (¥ in 1958 prices)	147,883.0	6.7	204,079.0	9.4
Primary industry's share of GNP (%)	10.1	—	7.4	—
Secondary industry's share of GNP (%)	38.6	—	38.5	—
Tertiary industry's share of GNP (%)	51.3	—	54.1	—
Mining and manufacturing index (1958 = 100)	431.7	11.9	539.4	13.9
Agriculture, forestry, and fishery index (1958 = 100)	144.1	2.8	130.3	2.1
Domestic freight transport (bil. ton-kilometers)	217.3	6.9	343.8	10.2
Domestic passenger transport (bil. passenger-kilometers)	508.2	7.6	588.9	8.3
Energy consumption (mil. tons of coal equivalence)	302.76	7.8	574.10	12.0
Exports ($bil. customs clearance)	9.32	10.0	20.25	16.8
Imports ($bil. customs clearance)	9.89	9.3	19.53	15.5

younger sons in farming households who earned their living in the cities. Following the custom of primogeniture, the eldest son took over the farm (which was, of course, small enough for him to manage by himself), leaving the younger brothers to fend for themselves. The younger brothers looked for work in the cities, but employment opportunities were limited after the War. The government had its hands full finding jobs for these men. In the late 1950s all this changed. Rapid industrial growth created a great demand for labor, which these younger sons were there to fill. Meanwhile, the eldest sons, back on their farms, looked on with envy at the good fortunes of their younger brothers in the cities.

The industrial boom did, however, create certain economic imbalances. Farmers, who in 1952 earned roughly the same amount as other workers, by 1960 were earning only 70% of what other workers did. In the mid-1950s, farm organizations and rural-based legislators pressed the government to rectify the economic disparity that had emerged between urban and rural areas.

The expansion of mass media helped to heighten rural awareness of this disparity, and Japan began to look to the example of certain Western European countries, which had implemented basic agricultural legislation to solve essentially the same problem.

At the same time, Japanese farms underwent a demographic transition, as illustrated by the term "three-*chan* farm" which became popular about this time. As farmers flocked to the cities to augment their income, *jī-chan* (grandpa), *bā-chan* (grandma), and *kā-chan* (mama) were left behind to look after the farm. As time went by, housewives also began to seek work in the cities, and the "three-*chan* farms" turned into "two-*chan* farms."

The decline in the farm labor population became pronounced by the early 1960s. Farming as an occupation has become less and less attractive to young people. Census figures show that the number of people engaged in farming declined from 16.1 million in 1950 to 13 million in 1960, and to 11 million in 1965 — a decline of 30% in only 15 years. The number of new junior high school and senior high school graduates going into farming declined from 260,000 in 1955 to 130,000 in 1960 — a drop of 50% in only 5 years.

Still, the farms kept going. Increased mechanization temporarily offset the decrease in labor. Sales of tilling machines, for example, rose from 50,000 in 1955 to 520,000 in 1960. Moreover, the well-to-do urban population created a demand for other agricultural products besides rice and essential vegetables. To meet this demand, many farmers supplemented their rice crop with fruit and livestock such as Mandarin oranges, a perennial favorite with the Japanese, and poultry.

But further troubles loomed on the horizon. For one thing, demand for rice had reached its peak. For another, Japan faced increasing pressure to open its domestic agricultural market to foreign penetration just as it was doing with its domestic industrial market. Japan had joined the General Agreement on Tariffs and Trade (GATT) in 1955 and the International Monetary Fund (IMF) in 1962, and in 1960 drafted currency and trade liberalization plans, the provisions of which included liberalizing imports of 121 agricultural and fishery products.

These developments only fed anxiety in rural areas over the viability of the one-hectare farm system. The glowing memories of land reform and the 1955 bumper crop disappeared in the haze of unprecedented industrial growth. Pressure from farmers' organizations and rural-based legislators to eliminate urban-rural income disparities yielded success on two fronts. First, the government passed the Basic Agricultural Act, and second, it implemented a new means of determining price support levels by making use of manufacturing wage schedules to calculate the labor costs involved in rice production.

The Impact of the Basic Agricultural Act

In June of 1961 the Diet passed the Basic Agricultural Act after a two-year study of the state of domestic agriculture and of similar laws passed in West Germany and France. This landmark legislation established in a single law the basic framework for agricultural policy in a highly industrialized society.

In its preamble, the Act elucidates the ideas that guided farm policy in the early stages of postwar industrial growth. The government did not attempt to raise farm incomes through direct assistance as was done in West Germany. Rather, it strove to equalize rural and urban incomes primarily through increased agricultural productivity. To make this increase possible, the government implemented a twofold policy of selective expansion and structural change.

Selective expansion meant encouraging production of those products for which there was a growing demand. As consumer incomes continued to rise year by year, the demand for fruit and animal protein increased, predictably, as well. The government accordingly encouraged production in these areas.

Structural change meant a shift to large scale of operations, the consolidation of scattered plots, the introduction of livestock, mechanization, the rationalization of ownership, and the modernization of management—in a word, a frontal attack on the one-hectare farm system. The aim of the Basic Act was to provide the right combination of these measures in order to nurture "independent farm operators," i.e., operators who derive their entire income from agricultural sources. As such, they are the same as the "full-time farmers" in agricultural statistics, with one important distinction: the independent farm operator's income is equivalent to that earned by workers in other industries.

Many Ministry of Agriculture and Forestry bureaucrats active in the postwar land reforms felt that the industrial boom of the 1960s offered a once-in-a-lifetime chance to put an end to the one-hectare farm system. They likened the Basic Act to the transformation which the Industrial Revolution brought to rural life in England. In drafting the law, these bureaucrats expected that the size of farms would increase naturally. As they envisioned it, younger sons in farming households would depart for the cities in search of high paying jobs. The heads of households would follow, looking for work at nearby factories and construction sites. The resultant decline in the number of people engaged in farming would cause a decline in the total number of farm households, making it possible for other households to expand their own farms by renting or buying up abandoned fields. Meanwhile, a prosperous urban population would create a greater demand for animal protein, fruit, and vegetables, thus generating an expanding market for agricultural products. The number of independent farm operators would increase until they accounted for the bulk of agricultural output—or so the scenario went.

As things turned out, however, the Basic Act only served to bolster further the one-hectare farm system. Japan's economy continued to expand at an explosive pace even after the law was enacted, but it was this very growth which was the undoing of the bureaucrats' plan. The problem lay not in the nature of farming but in the structure of the Japanese economy. First, with the sudden increase in economic activity after the War, the demand for urban and rural real estate pushed prices up sharply. As farmers watched the price of property soar higher and higher, they clung all the more tenaciously to their land.

Second, although farmers had many opportunities for outside employment, most of them were short-lived. Japanese employment practices and wage scales are presumably characterized by life-time employment and seniority-based wages, but these standards are maintained only by large firms or corporate groups, which employ only 30% of the total work force. In addition, there are major wage differentials between large and small enterprises. Thus the jobs that were available to Japanese farmers were mostly in low-paying, unstable employment.

Third, very few people left the farm entirely. Those looking for outside employment usually found jobs within commuting distance of their homes. Such jobs typically paid poorly, and could never do more than supplement farm income. Hence the ties of household members to the farm were not severed but reinforced.

Fourth, the Agricultural Land Law of 1952 had so strengthened the rights of tenants that scarcely anyone was willing to rent out land. Although amendments to the Law in 1956 alleviated the situation somewhat, it was still impossible, for example, for a landlord to abrogate a contract leasing agricultural land within 10 years of its signing. (The Law provides that abrogation of the contract within the first 10 years requires the approval of the prefectural governor, who is enjoined to side with the tenant.)

It should be noted, however, that there are signs of change. In many instances, part-time farmers contract with full-time farmers to do seasonal work such as rice-planting, weeding, or harvesting. In other instances, work on a rice paddy is contracted out on an annual basis in disregard of the Agricultural Land Law. Since full-time farmers now use a wide range of equipment from seedling planters to combines and dryers, seasonal work can develop into annual contracts.

For instance, one rice farmer on the Kanazawa Plain in Ishikawa Prefecture who owns only 5 hectares of land has contracted to work another 8.5 hectares year-round and to do seasonal work on 2 additional hectares. Thus he actually works a total of 15.5 hectares. This larger scale of operation, made possible by mechanization, is beginning to appear in several parts of Japan. It means that a small number of people can now farm from 10 to 20 hectares of land.

While recent developments demonstrate that it is possible to break the one-hectare farm pattern, the outlook for dramatic change is hardly bright. The oil crisis of 1973 has radically altered the structure of Japan's economy, which had been founded on exports and plant investment. The economy continues to grow, although more slowly; and while personal consumption and public investment are strong, the demand for labor has slackened considerably. No longer are farmers needed in the cities during the off-season. Diminished job opportunities have pushed people back to the farm.

Meanwhile, conditions on the farms have improved remarkably since the land reform due to the tremendous transformation that the economy as a whole has undergone. Even those farmers who own less than 0.5 hectares (most of them Class B part-time farmers earning more from non-farm work than from farming) are already capable of supporting themselves with non-farm income alone. The average income for farming households (counting income from all sources, farming and non-farming) is actually higher than that of other households now. Nonetheless, farmers still cling tightly to their land. Their wariness to let go of it is born of experience. In the postwar agrarian reform, the government appropriated large amounts of land held in tenancy, and the subsequent strengthening of tenants' rights made it extremely difficult later to get back even those plots that were not taken.

In addition, the exodus of young people to urban areas has left many farm households in the care of older people. Indeed, surveys show that 80% of the total population permanently engaged in farming (4.73 million in 1977) are over 50 years old. These people have no desire to leave the farm and seek jobs elsewhere. And since they generally have no pensions, public or private, to support them in their old age, they cling all the more tenaciously to their land.

Politics also contributes to maintaining the status quo. Because the Liberal Democratic Party (LDP), which has been in power for most of the postwar years, depends on the rural population for the bulk of its support, there is little incentive to risk voter wrath by upsetting the one-hectare farm system. On the contrary, the LDP has sought to preserve the structure of the rural economy through such programs as the Third National Comprehensive Development Plan, drawn up in 1977. The object of this program is to disperse industries, until now largely concentrated in the cities, into rural districts, and thereby to maintain the present rural population level (and consequently, the strength of the LDP as well). Of course it is entirely possible that industrial dispersion will ultimately alter the traditional agrarian structure and encourage large-scale commercial farming, but this will depend on what kinds of factories relocate in rural areas and what sort of progress is made through further agrarian reforms. Prospects for any major transformation in the rural landscape are dim, however, for the one-hectare farm system remains as solidly entrenched as ever.

Rice Price Support and its Problems

As we have seen, the agricultural lobby's campaign to eradicate the urban-rural income disparity resulted not only in the passage of the Basic Agricultural Act but also in the adoption of a price support computation system which greatly favors the farmer. Although the legislation in the Basic Act was received with general favor, price supports were so sweeping as to provoke public backlash against the farmers and the government.

Until 1959, postwar price support levels were computed according to a parity formula indexing the price of rice to farming household expenditures (both production costs and consumer goods). In 1960, however, the agricultural lobby succeeded in passing a "production-cost and income-supplement formula" for price support. The formula's main innovation is that it computes the labor costs involved in rice production at current wage rates earned by urban factory workers. If urban wages rise, so do price supports. Of course if mechanization, a greater use of chemicals, an increased unit production, or other labor-saving measures are introduced, price support levels will tend to decline, but the sharp rise in manufacturing wages in recent years has more than offset such downward pressures. As a result, the 1976 support price is four times the 1960 support price. During this period, only vegetables and fruits remained better money crops in terms of net hourly compensation. Although rice production accounts for only 35% of total agricultural production, it accounts for over 50% of the total agricultural income.

At the same time, the incentive to grow rice has created problems unimaginable in earlier years. While technology has increased per-hectare production, per-capita rice consumption has been declining since 1962, resulting in a tremendous surplus. In 1970, the government had more than 7 million tons of rice in its warehouses in addition to the 12 million tons harvested that year. (The government controls nearly all rice distribution.) It was forced to impose production controls for a five-year period beginning in 1971. While these controls succeeded in reducing government stockpiles, they returned to their former level as soon as the government lifted its controls. By autumn of 1978, stockpiles had reached 6 million tons, and once again the government was forced to impose controls. This expanding surplus is now the most serious issue confronting agricultural policy makers. The Japanese eat less and less rice even as price supports encourage farmers to grow more. No solution is in sight.

Technological innovations continue to increase production. However, since wet rice paddies are constructed so as to retain water, it is difficult to convert them to dry crop fields, which require good drainage. Even if farmers do convert to other staple crops, such as corn, sorghum, or soy beans, they cannot hope to get the return that they get on rice — even with government subsidies for crop conversion. Price supports and the one-hectare farm system seem to have locked the agricultural economy firmly into rice production.

Meanwhile, per-capita consumption of rice continues to diminish despite vigorous efforts by both public and private organizations to reverse this trend. There are several factors responsible for this decline. Primary among these, oddly enough, is a U.S. aid program initiated after the War to relieve the severe food shortage. The United States donated surplus wheat which became the basis for a national school lunch program. Schoolchildren became accustomed to eating bread at least once a day, and so did the generations which followed, long after the food shortage had been alleviated. The dominant place of rice in the Japanese diet began to erode with the rise of wheat consumption and with the general switch in diet from carbohydrates to other foods such as animal protein, fruits, and vegetables.

Technology has also worked to increase the gap between supply and demand. By making work easier, automation has served to reduce laborers' caloric intake. Meanwhile mechanization has greatly increased rice production and made rice a safe, convenient crop for the small farmer.

Up to this point, we have focused on the one hectare per family farm as a structural characteristic of Japanese agriculture, and have briefly traced the history of agrarian reforms in order to show how farm-policy, markets, and farmers have tried to work free of the constraints which this structure imposes. No doubt farm size will continue to be a major issue well into the next century, and for the foreseeable future at least it seems that the one-hectare farm system will remain characteristic of Japanese agriculture.

The Future

Despite the structural peculiarities of the one-hectare farm system, the Japanese consume a steady diet of highly nutritious foods. It is no accident that the average life expectancy in Japan is now the highest in the world.

How is this so? We have seen that the one-hectare farm system generally entails high production costs. Hence, the price of rice in Japan is several times the prevailing international price. Such is also the case, for example, with the price of beef even though the government has taken steps to insure that these other foods are reasonably priced. This is so, first, because although Japan relies almost entirely upon foreign sources for wheat, barley, corn, sorghum, and soy beans, government regulations are such that corn, sorghum, and soy beans can be imported duty-free, making it possible for farmers to produce eggs, poultry, and pork at prices close to international norms.

Second, although milk costs more in Japan than it does in the West, the fact that 40% of the total milk consumption consists of low-cost imports has helped to keep the cost down. Powdered skim milk is an example. The government regulates imports of powdered milk to ensure that it does not undersell the domestic product. The way that importers manage to circumvent this obstacle is by importing the two major ingredients of powdered skim milk separately and reconstituting them in Japan, thus enabling them to sell their product at highly competitive prices.

Third, since the Japanese diet still consists of a higher carbohydrate intake much higher than that of other industrialized countries, the high cost of animal protein does not affect consumers as adversely as it would in the West. Carbohydrates make up over 50% of the Japanese diet in terms of caloric intake, or twice as much as that in the West. This is not considered an excessive amount in Japan; in fact, it accords with government nutritional standards. The government's suggested caloric intake ratio is 1 : 2 : 5 for protein, fat, and, carbohydrates respectively; and this ratio closely reflects the actual Japanese diet today. (It is interesting to note here that the United States government has recently recommended increased carbohydrate intake as a way of reducing fat consumption.) The Japanese are fortunate at least in that carbohydrates are generally the least expensive nutrients per calorie.

Fourth, the Japanese depend more on vegetable protein than on animal protein. Whereas the ratio of animal to plant protein consumption is 6 : 4 in the West, it is 4 : 6 in Japan. Japanese get most of their protein from grains (rice alone supplies 20% of the total), soy beans (in the form of bean curd [*tōfu*] and fermented beans [*nattō*]), and other vegetable sources. Since livestock raising is an expensive operation (it takes several hundred grams of grain to produce 100 grams of meat) a larger direct intake of plant protein means a lower food budget.

For animal protein, Japan relies heavily on fish, which supplies fully half of Japan's animal protein needs. While it is true that the price of fish has gone up considerably since the general implementation of the 200-mile limit, families that eat the more common fish, such as sardines and mackerel, can still count on an inexpensive source of animal protein.

In this way, despite the limitations on the economy imposed by the one-hectare farm system which have made agricultural products more expensive in Japan than in other industrialized countries, Japanese dietary habits and food supply mechanisms have held the Engel's coefficient (the ratio of food costs to total consumer expenditures) to an average of 30% in recent years, or only slightly higher than that in the West. Maintaining dietary standards comparable to those in the West, however, has involved certain sacrifices. Except for rice, in which Japan is completely self-sufficient, Japan is almost entirely dependent on imports for its grain consumption. Japan imports 96% of its wheat (5.8 million tons in 1977), 91% of its barley (1.7 million tons), and 100% of its corn (9 million tons) and sorghum (5.2 million tons). All told, Japan supplies only 37% of the grain it actually consumes, less than any other industrialized country. If one includes sugar (Japan imports 81% or 2.7 million tons of its total consumption) and soy beans (97% or 3.6 million tons) in the above figures, Japan's self-sufficiency is only 30%. Japan also imports 30% of its meat and 20% of its fruit.

This trend is not likely to change in the near future. On the contrary it is more likely that Japan's dependence on imports will be increased. Double-cropping is one possible way to bolster the nation's self-sufficiency. Double-cropping has already been implemented in some areas; but until improvements in paddy drainage and irrigation are carried out on a broad scale — and the investment is enormous — it would be unrealistic to expect too much here.

In the final analysis, the only way to assure secure food supplies for Japan is to make the one-hectare farm system as efficient as possible in order to minimize the cost disadvantages which it necessarily entails. While the responsibility here falls heaviest upon farmers and government, it cannot be carried out without the cooperation of the general public. Furthermore, it is essential that the understanding and cooperation of food-exporting nations such as the United States, Australia, and New Zealand be obtained. In particular, the response of the United States is pivotal. Should the United States insist on completely free trade in agriculture and absolute liberalization of all agricultural imports, much of Japanese non-rice agriculture would be crippled, leaving only the token production of a few vegetables, fruits, eggs, and other specialty products. Surely no one, not even the United States, could wish for such rural impoverishment and the dependency which it would engender.

Case Study:

How to Go Bankrupt and Still Stay Afloat

——The Ataka Affair

ZUSHI SABURŌ

Prologue

Since the end of World War II Japan's business world has experienced a number of crises, but there are two in particular which nearly plunged the nation into chaos. In 1965, Yamaichi Securities, at the time Japan's second largest securities company, very nearly went bankrupt when a stock market crash set off a run on that house. Panic was only narrowly avoided when the Bank of Japan made an emergency loan to the company on the grounds of protecting the national interest. And in 1975, Ataka & Co., a general trading company, also nearly went bankrupt when its wholly owned U.S. subsidiary, Ataka America, failed to recover oil-import loans made to a Canadian refinery. The Ataka affair in particular was one of the most serious corporate crises in the last fifty years, and could well have touched off a financial panic had not certain parties rushed to the company's rescue. The incident bears close attention not only because of its sheer scale — Ataka was Japan's ninth largest trading company at the time and presumably indestructible — but also because it provides a wealth of material for a study of the strengths and weaknesses of managing and bargaining Japanese style.

Why did the Ataka incident have such serious repercussions? One reason was a matter of timing. In 1975 Japan was in the throes of a major recession. The nation was still reeling from the so-called "oil-shock," sparked by the Middle Eastern embargo in 1973 and the subsequent spiraling cost of foreign oil, on which the nation depends so heavily for its energy needs. The wind had been taken out of the economy's sails, and the double-figure annual growth rate was suddenly a thing of the past. The collapse of a major corporation at this juncture was bound to cause general alarm. A second reason lies in the very nature of a Japanese trading company. A general trading company does far more than simply handle exports and imports. It also engages in a substantial amount of investing, commonly dubbed "trading-house financing." Although it owns little capital, it borrows heavily from banks and operates what is tantamount to its own brokerage business. The bankruptcy of such a company thus could have the same impact on the economy as a major bank failure. A third reason is the Japanese economy's precariously extensive involvement overseas. In 1975, borrowings by Japanese banks and trading companies from foreign banks are estimated to have been around $30 billion. The failure of a company like Ataka could have prompted foreign banks to call in these loans. Such a call-in, had it occurred, would have drained the country of precious foreign currency reserves needed to purchase oil and other resources.

In fact, the worst did not happen. Both private industry and the public sector (the Bank of Japan, the Finance Ministry, the Ministry of International Trade and Industry, etc.) joined forces to avert the ultimate crisis, and Ataka was eventually absorbed by another trading giant, C. Itoh & Co. Foreign observers may view wryly this effort by government and business to bail Ataka out of trouble as yet another manifestation of the monolithic solidarity which presumably characterizes "Japan, Inc." But this is far from the truth. In fact, the effort to save Ataka generated intense infighting among the parties involved for the simple reason that their interests came into inevitable conflict, as I shall demonstrate in the following pages. The saga of Ataka's merger with C. Itoh has all the drama of a five-act play, and I hope the reader will indulge a slightly histrionic approach to the subject. It is wise to remember, however, as the curtain rises on our drama, that what goes on behind the scenes can be just as important as the action center stage.

Act One: Enter Sumitomo

On September 26, 1975, Ataka's main bank, Sumitomo Bank, first learned that Ataka America had been unable to recover its loans to Newfoundland Refining Co. (NRC), and that it had obtained the consent of one of its other lenders (Bank of Tokyo) to roll over its trust receipts. (Ten days earlier, the President of Ataka & Co. had ordered the President of Ataka America back to Japan for a detailed report on the subsidiary's trouble with NRC, but even then the problem was too big for Ataka's management to handle on its own.) Sumitomo executives were stunned, for a company does not resort to rolling over (i.e. renewing) its trust receipts unless it is in extreme financial difficulty.

A word about trust receipts ("TRs") may be in order here. Generally, an importer cannot receive shipping documents — and thus the benefit of usance — until an import bill is settled. To get around this problem, the importer can ask its bank for a special chattel mortgage — the trust receipt — on the goods it is to import, and thereby receive the shipping documents in advance subject to certain conditions. Having obtained possession of the documents, it receives the goods, sells them, and uses the funds thus procured to settle the import bill with its bank. However, if for some reason the importer cannot sell the goods and is unable to settle with the bank, its only alternative is to ask the bank to extend the repayment period by "rolling over" the TRs. This is exactly what happened to Ataka America when NRC failed to pay up. On top of that, Ataka had kept Sumitomo Bank, its main bank, in the dark about its troubles until it was too late. An almost unthinkable breakdown in communications had taken place.

A word here too about the importance of a main bank. A company's main bank is generally the bank which has the most financing outstanding to a particular company. Every company has its main bank or banks. The institution began late in World War II, when the Finance Ministry designated certain banks to be responsible for all the financial needs of each company with defense contracts. It was discontinued in the immediate postwar period, but revived in the early 1950s. The institution is unique in that the bond between bank and corporation is ethical as well as economic, cemented by loyalty as well as by loans. A main bank is obligated to do all in its power to help its client company, in much the same way that a gangland boss covers for a henchman in trouble. But just as the boss is responsible for his henchmen, so the henchmen are duty-bound to carry out the boss's bidding and report to him their every move. Ataka had neglected its duty.

Incensed at Ataka's breach of faith, Sumitomo Bank immediately began probing Ataka's finances and asked a U.S. investment company, Morgan Stanley, to investigate Ataka America's business partner, NRC. Their findings were astonishing: 1) Ataka America had advanced most of its loans to NRC under unsecured and loosely worded contracts; 2) Ataka America was stuck with the colossal sum of $326,200,000 worth of bad paper for crude oil sales and other transactions, and had already written off $100 million of it as uncollectable; 3) Ataka America had already asked the New York branches of several Japanese banks to roll over loans it was unable to repay; 4) NRC was itself on the verge of bankruptcy, plagued by inefficiency, high costs, and depressed product prices. If things were left to go their own way, there was every reason to believe that Ataka & Co. and its American subsidiary would be declared in default, and that the news of a major Japanese trading house's bankruptcy would damage, perhaps irreparably, Japan's hard-earned international trust.

How did Ataka & Co., long known in trading circles for its conservative management, get itself into such a fix? A brief review of the company's history will provide part of the answer. Ataka & Co. was founded in 1904 by Ataka Yakichi, a talented merchant who graduated from Tokyo Higher Commercial School (now Hitotsubashi University). In 1926, Ataka became a "designated trader" along with Suzuki & Co., Mitsui & Co., Mitsubishi Corp., and Iwai & Co. for Imperial Steel Works (forerunner of Nippon Steel Corp.), a state-run enterprise, and it devoted its efforts thenceforth to the steel trade. In 1933 it became agent for Oji Paper Co. and went into the sale of pulp for rayon; and in 1936 it became general agent for America's Gleason Works, then one of the world's leading machine tool manufacturers. Having tied the company securely to three major industries, Ataka's management became known for its reliability.

After World War II, Ataka, like Mitsui & Co., Mitsubishi Corp. and the other corporate giants, lost all of its overseas branches and facilities. To make matters worse, the company was subject to a tax under the War Indemnity Special Measures Law assessed at three times its capitalization, wiping out overnight assets which the company had built up since 1904. Unlike many larger firms, however, Ataka escaped being split up into smaller companies under the Deconcentration Law. Nor did it undergo any merger such as which produced Marubeni, Nissho-Iwai, Kanematsu-Gosho, and other trading companies. Proud of its unbroken lineage, Ataka continued to be active in steel, pulp, and machine tool trading through the 1960s. So conservative was Ataka's management during this period that it might have been likened to the timid person who taps a stone bridge before crossing it — except that this company hesitated to cross even *after* tapping it.

Around 1970, however, when the Japanese economy entered into another period of rapid growth, Ataka's management suddenly turned adventurous. Why the about-face? In a word, oil speculation. Former Ataka Board Chairman Izaki Kyūtarō, who is credited with having made Ataka one of Japan's top ten trading houses, recalls the decision in this fashion: "Our goal was to top the ¥1 trillion mark in semi-annual sales — and we finally made it, in 1974. But even so, we were afraid that we would still remain forever tenth in the 'Big Ten' unless we went into oil." At a time when the major trading firms were nearly doubling their gross sales every year, Ataka tried frantically to keep pace. In an attempt to improve its sales ranking, the company diversified and in effect staked its financial life on the booming oil business.

Besides oil, Ataka ventured into textiles, machinery, golf courses, condominiums, sauna baths, CTSs (central trans-shipment stations), and even aircraft (through a tie-up with America's Grumman Corp.). As a result, Ataka's sales grew faster than any of the top ten trading companies from FY 1970 to 1974. In 1974, its total sales passed those of Nichimen to rank ninth among the Big Ten.

As Ataka's sales increased, however, so did its debts. The company's short- and long-term borrowings increased more than three-fold in the five years from FY 1970 through 1974. As of 1974, these debts totaled ¥691,100 million and entailed a net interest burden of ¥11,500 million. When one realizes that this latter figure was roughly equal to that of Mitsui & Co. (Japan's second largest trading house) even though Mitsui's sales were four times that of Ataka's, it is easy to see how deeply in debt Ataka was relative to its sales volume. In fact, many economists believe that this heavy indebtedness would have caused Ataka to go under even without the NRC episode.

Nevertheless, it was NRC which precipitated the fall. NRC was an oil refinery located in Come-by-Chance, Newfoundland. NRC imported crude oil from British Petroleum (BP), one of the world's major oil firms, refined it and sold the products.

The relationship between these three companies — Ataka, NRC, and BP — was an intricate and potentially fragile one. Under its agent contract with NRC, Ataka America received a straight commission in return for financing NRC's crude oil imports from BP. In effect, Ataka America paid BP for crude oil on NRC's behalf with money borrowed from the New York branches of Sumitomo Bank, Bank of Tokyo and other Japanese banks. This arrangement worked fine as long as all the wheels turned smoothly, but Ataka America was in a continuously precarious position. If NRC could not earn enough to reimburse Ataka America for its oil import payments, it faced imminent bankruptcy. As it turned out, this is exactly what happened.

Informed at last of the crisis, Sumitomo Bank advised the government of the situation and began secret talks with the other banks involved during October and November. Meanwhile, the Bank of Japan and the Finance Ministry's Banking Bureau instructed Sumitomo to devise a plan to bail Ataka out of trouble. Collecting $300 million in bad debts overnight, however, proved an impossible order. The situation dragged on for weeks, and rumors of Ataka's impending collapse finally reached the press. Mainichi Shinbun broke the news on December 7 with the head-line, "NRC Takes Ataka for a ¥60 Billion Ride."

Although December 7 was a Sunday, concerned government and business leaders called a special press conference to explain the situation. The Bank of Japan, the nation's central bank, voiced its concern that foreign and domestic banks might suddenly call in their loans to Ataka and its U.S. subsidiary, but pledged that domestic banks, at least, would not make such a move. The Central Bank clearly viewed the incident as a threat to the Japanese economy, and was prepared to take any step necessary to protect it. The presidents of Sumitomo Bank and Kyowa Bank, the two major lenders to Ataka, issued a joint statement declaring their and other major creditors' unqualified support of Ataka & Co. and requesting that the Bank of Japan exempt Ataka from the usual restrictions imposed through window guidance.

Act Two: Enter C. Itoh & Co.

Excepting the major banks — and they were not in the running — the only corporations believed capable of absorbing Ataka and thereby rescuing it from financial ruin were the five largest trading companies: Mitsubishi Corp., Mitsui & Co., Marubeni Corp., C. Itoh & Co., and Sumitomo Shoji. Indeed, some bankers who knew the magnitude of Ataka's troubles claimed that only the top two — Mitsubishi and Mitsui — could do the job. The problem was that neither house could be expected to play the role of knight-errant. Both Mitsubishi and Mitsui are leaders in their respective business groups, and these two groups, the most powerful in Japan, have been competing fiercely since well before World War II, not only between themselves but also against the Sumitomo group, of which Sumitomo Bank is a member. They were not about to accept a request of this kind from their rival, Sumitomo, and thereby lose ground in the overall competition.

What about Marubeni, then? Sumitomo Bank used to be Marubeni's main bank, just as it had been C. Itoh's. In view of the past relationship between Marubeni and Sumitomo, it was not inconceivable that Marubeni could be prevailed upon to come to Ataka's rescue. Times had changed, however. After absorbing Takashimaya-Iida in 1955, Marubeni switched main banks from Sumitomo to Fuji Bank and developed into a key member of the Fuji Bank-led Fuyo group. Moreover, a number of Marubeni executives had just been implicated in the Lockheed Aircraft scandal, one of the major scandals of the postwar era, which had erupted at about the same time. Marubeni had too many of its own problems, then, to be worrying about somebody else's.

And so, the field was narrowed to Sumitomo Shoji and C. Itoh. Sumitomo Bank naturally went first to Sumitomo Shoji, also a member of the Sumitomo group. But Sumitomo Shoji refused outright the Bank's request for assistance, pleading violation of company policy — which was, simply put, to avoid unnecessary risks. This excuse was for public consumption only, however; the real reason lay elsewhere. In 1966, nearly a decade before the Ataka affair, Hotta Shōzō, then President of Sumitomo Bank, had talked Sumitomo Shoji's president into merging with Ataka to form a "Greater Sumitomo Shoji." The plan had to be aborted, however, when it met with last-minute opposition from Ataka Eiichi, Ataka & Co.'s owner. Sumitomo Shoji executives were not about to forget the earlier slight when Sumitomo Bank approached them once again on Ataka's behalf.

C. Itoh, the only corporation left, responded to Sumitomo Bank's request. On January 12, 1976, the presidents of C. Itoh, Ataka, Sumitomo Bank, and Kyowa Bank held a joint press conference and announced that C. Itoh and Ataka had agreed to a total business tie-up with the intent to merge at some future date. This announcement took many by surprise. Knowledgeable people in banking and trading found it difficult to believe that the C. Itoh management, known for its cold calculations and emphasis on profit, would take over a company approximately $300 million in debt.

What was in the deal for C. Itoh? One might note first that C. Itoh was in sympathy with Sumitomo's exhortations on the necessity for maintaining international trust in the Japanese economy. One might note further that C. Itoh no doubt recalled gratefully the bank's assistance during the depression years of the late 1920s. Yet such noble considerations seem hardly adequate cause for one company to take over another on the brink of collapse. More likely, C. Itoh saw this as a golden opportunity to bolster its standing in the heavy industries, where it had traditionally been weakest. Ataka had been a major wholesaler for Nippon Steel since before the War and had an annual sales of ¥2 trillion in FY 1975. C. Itoh no doubt dreamed of expanding its operations and replacing Marubeni as the third largest trading house only behind Mitsubishi and Mitsui. This could happen, however, only if a merger with Ataka were effected on the best of terms. Indeed, C. Itoh and Sumitomo reached an agreement only after heated negotiations. While Sumitomo repeatedly assured C. Itoh that it would not regret a merger with Ataka, C. Itoh refused to be content with

vague promises. The trading house finally presented Sumitomo three conditions:
1. C. Itoh shall not take over any disadvantageous portions of Ataka's business.
2. Ataka shall yield its Nippon Steel concession to C. Itoh.
3. Dai-Ichi Kangyo Bank shall continue to serve as C. Itoh's main bank.

The first two conditions insured that the trading company would take over only those portions of Ataka's business which would improve its own position, while rejecting those portions which would be a burden..The third condition dispelled any hopes Sumitomo Bank might have that C. Itoh would return to the Sumitomo fold after its merger with Ataka. This clear expression of C. Itoh's independence was a result of extensive consultations with its main bank, Dai-Ichi Kangyo Bank, and a pledge of the bank's continued support. Sumitomo Bank, in no position to push its own views, was forced to accept all three conditions.

Nor was that all. Until the very eve of the January 12 press conference, C. Itoh vigorously opposed Sumitomo Bank's use of the term "merger" in the press release, and insisted on using only the term "business tie-up." The company contended that there would be no merger unless Ataka's business and financial standing improved as a result of the tie-up. Sumitomo was just as vehement in its rebuttal, because it feared that assistance in the form of a mere business tie-up would not be enough to restore confidence in Ataka and that Ataka would therefore lose its valuable contracts and concessions. A compromise of sorts was reached, and thus the final wording, "business tie-up with the intent to merge." Since the usual wording in such an instance is "business tie-up preparatory to merger," one can see that the wording in the January 12 press release is a rather weak expression of intent. Here, too, Sumitomo had yielded to C. Itoh.

Ataka and C. Itoh formally signed the tie-up agreement on February 14, 1976, thus ending the first round of negotiations between C. Itoh and Sumitomo Bank. C. Itoh had clearly emerged with the upper hand. Its domination of the talks was also reflected in the director that C. Itoh nominated for inclusion on the Ataka Board of Directors as specified in the tie-up agreement. C. Itoh had been expected to send someone to represent it at Ataka in the capacity of vice-president, but the company in fact named Matsui Yanosuke (who later became President of one of C. Itoh's many affiliates) as "Supreme Advisor" to Ataka. Sumitomo and C. Itoh would engage in a second bruising round of negotiations in the fall of

1976; but before that drama unfolds, there is yet another story to tell.

Act Three: Enter the Labor Union

Ataka & Co. had no union until the crisis. Big as it was, Ataka was essentially a family business, and its employees were presumably firm in their allegiance to the company's owner, Ataka Eiichi. It came as something of a shock, then, when Ataka employees — predominantly white collar — banded together suddenly into a labor union in an effort to stave off the tie-up with C. Itoh.

Job security was the main impetus behind creation of a union. Ataka employees feared that their company would be overwhelmed by the larger partner. Given the traditional Japanese hiring practices based upon lifetime employment and the sense of competition between corporations, employees are highly sensitive both to their own position within the company and to their company's position among business rivals. Ataka employees were concerned that, as late-comers to C. Itoh, they would not be given the same opportunities for advancement as those who had started out with C. Itoh. Even in a merger between equals, one of the two normally dominates the post-merger organization; this domination was bound to be all the greater with Ataka openly treated as the supplicant in the merger. Seen in this light, the Ataka employees' fear of discrimination after a merger is understandable. Even worse, a merger would force many Ataka employees to lose their jobs.

At their inaugural meeting, union members passed unanimous resolutions opposing the business tie-up with C. Itoh and calling for a 100% Ataka-managed corporate rehabilitation program. Within a week, 87% of all Ataka employees had joined the union. Within a month, however, the general fear of C. Itoh had subsided, and as employees began thinking more calmly, a faction emerged within the union (primarily employees in the steel and chemical sections who were unlikely to lose their jobs in the event of a merger) favoring the tie-up with C. Itoh.

Facing an imminent schism within the ranks, the union leadership was forced to shelve the resolution opposing the merger. Hardly another month had gone by, however, when the leaders turned more radical, reviving their opposition to the merger and expelling the 89 members who supported it. By April 1976, the union had begun an all-out campaign, this time with the backing of Zenshōsha (Federation of All Japan Trading Labor Unions), the central union organization of trading house and other commercial firms. The union's major bone of contention was the Ataka management's attempt to elicit early retirements, and it carried its protest to Sumitomo's doorstep.

Sumitomo Bank, irked by these unforeseen difficulties, decided that the only way to push through Ataka's merger with C. Itoh was to take over Ataka's management. In June of 1976, the bank appointed its Managing Director Komatsu Kō as President of Ataka, despite the general feeling that Matsui Yanosuke, the Supreme Advisor whom C. Itoh had installed with such fanfare, would be Ataka's next president. Matsui was instead kicked upstairs to Chairman of the Board. Sumitomo had in effect declared to the world that it was assuming total responsibility for Ataka's management, including negotiations with the Ataka union. The Bank was now in complete control.

On August 31, President Komatsu told union leaders that Ataka wanted 1,000 early retirements within three weeks. Sumitomo believed it necessary to reduce Ataka's 3,600-man work force by about a third in preparation for the merger, and the 1,000-man cut was the first step in streamlining the personnel rolls. Komatsu's proposal encountered fierce union opposition.

We should note here in passing that personnel cuts in Japan are carried out in a radically different manner than such cuts in the West. Lifetime employment is the norm in Japan, especially in a large corporation, and companies which are forced to cut their personnel rolls in preparation for a merger generally solicit early retirements by offering more than the normal severance pay and by finding jobs for employees who leave (although these new jobs may not be as good as the ones they had). Such care is considered to be part of a company's responsibility to both its employees and to society at large, no matter how close to bankruptcy it may be.

By the three-week deadline, 850 employees had applied for early retirement on preferential terms. More than a third of the applicants were over forty, a sign that a substantial number of older employees had decided to abandon ship despite the difficulties many would encounter when finding new jobs. (No matter what their skills, they would lose all seniority when they moved.)

This first skirmish between Sumitomo Bank and the Ataka union left both sides unsatisfied. It was a setback for the union because so many employees responded to the bank's call for early retirements, and a setback for the bank because 850 applicants was still considerably short of its goal. Sumitomo had hoped to pare the Ataka work force down to size by the end of the September term and complete the merger by the new fiscal year (April 1977). Its schedule was in trouble from the very start.

In late December of 1976, however, Sumitomo, C. Itoh, and the Ataka management finally reached an agreement concerning the merger (the details of which are described below), and the union decided to change its tactics from all-out opposition to compliance based on certain conditions. These were:

1. The union shall approve the transfer of Ataka employees to C. Itoh on the condition that they be treated the same as C. Itoh's present employees.
2. Ataka employees not wanting to be transferred to C. Itoh shall be given three times the normal severance pay.
3. The Ataka management shall be responsible for finding new jobs for displaced Ataka personnel who are unable to find jobs for themselves.

Sumitomo and Ataka immediately approved the first and third demands, but rejected the one calling for triple severance pay. (Management ended up giving a 25% increase over the normal severance pay.) Nevertheless, the negotiations were successful, and the union received high praise from business circles for modifying its hard-line stance. How did the union itself regard its change of heart? The sanguine reflections of union chairman Miyazaki Shūzō are perhaps typical. "The union made the right decision by halting its opposition to the merger and its demand for Ataka's self-rehabilitation. We were not that strong to begin with, and adapting ourselves to the changing trends rather than opposing a *fait accompli* [i.e., the agreement between Ataka, Sumitomo, and C. Itoh] for opposition's sake was simply the smart thing to do." In short, pragmatism won out over principle.

In March 1977, President Komatsu called for 800 more early retirements and got 620, bringing the total number of retirees to nearly 1,500. Sumitomo had in fact surpassed its original goal, although even this number was to prove insufficient.

Act Four: Sumitomo vs. C. Itoh

Negotiations between Sumitomo Bank and C. Itoh concerning the merger with Ataka began on October 12, 1976. At stake were the price tag on Ataka's trading rights and concessions, and the number of Ataka employees C. Itoh could absorb. The lower the price tag on Ataka's trading rights and the fewer employees C. Itoh was required to take, the better of course for C. Itoh. Conversely, the more that could be gotten for Ataka's business rights and the more employees C. Itoh could be persuaded to take, the smaller the burden on Sumitomo. While the talks began in a mood of general concern about the affair's potential threat to Japan's international credibility, they quickly bogged down over these two practical questions.

At the opening round of negotiations, Sumitomo proposed that C. Itoh pay ¥900 billion for Ataka's trading rights and take in 2,400 Ataka employees. Despite repeated requests for a reply, C. Itoh was silent for more than a month after that, during which time the trading house conducted its own investigation of Ataka's business. On November 17, C. Itoh finally announced that ¥300 billion was a fair price for Ataka's trading rights and that 700 employees were all that it could absorb. Both figures were only a third of what Sumitomo had asked. Early in December, Sumitomo responded with a revised offer: ¥550 billion for Ataka's trading rights and 1,600 employee transfers to C. Itoh. C. Itoh promptly turned this proposal down, and prospects for a merger appeared doomed.

For Sumitomo the situation was critical. One false move now and the long months of negotiations would go for naught. As early as November, C. Itoh's president had hinted that his company might wash its hands of the affair, and following Sumitomo's second proposal, most of C. Itoh's board of directors opposed the merger altogether.

By this time, however, Ataka was long past self-rehabilitation. Bankruptcy was the only alternative. News of the impasse threatened to undermine the company's trading rights. A trading company's rights and concessions are founded necessarily upon the company's credibility; once that starts to deteriorate, trading rights crumble like a castle of sand. A failing company's trading rights are considered fair game by other companies, and Ataka's traditional positions in pulp, lumber, machinery and other areas were now at the mercy of other firms seeking to expand their influence. In an effort to counter this trend, Sumitomo quickly set up two new companies, Ataka Textiles Co., Ltd, and Ataka Kenzai Co., Ltd., to guard Ataka's textile and lumber trading rights — rights which C. Itoh did not want because both were losing propositions. Spinning off these two unprofitable divisions, however, did virtually nothing to stave off impending doom.

It was just at this time, when the situation appeared bleakest for Sumitomo, that an interesting development occurred. A groundswell of opinion against C. Itoh emerged among government and business circles alike. It is not clear even today who engineered it — perhaps Sumitomo Bank, or some government bureaucracy like the Finance Ministry or the Bank of Japan. Such general criticism by parties not directly involved in an affair may have no particular effect in other countries, but it has an immediate impact on businesses in Japan. In the face of this criticism, C.

Itoh's president called a meeting of the board of directors and obtained a carte blanche to negotiate the merger. The authority in his own hands, he reopened the talks with Sumitomo.

There could be no agreement, however, without the spirit of compromise. The negotiations between Managing Directors Higuchi Hirotarō of Sumitomo Bank and Aoyagi Kenji of C. Itoh got nowhere. But others were working quietly behind the scenes, old acquaintances who were well grounded in the rules of give and take. C. Itoh Chairman Echigo Shōichi met with Sumitomo Bank Chairman Hotta Shōzō; C. Itoh President Tozaki Seiki met with Sumitomo Bank President Ibe Kyōnosuke; and C. Itoh Vice-President Sejima Ryūzō met with Sumitomo Bank Vice-President Isoda Ichirō frequently outside the negotiating room, and they were eventually able to effect a merger. Formal agreement was reached on December 28, 1976, after two and a half months of talks. The main articles of the agreement are as follows:

1. Ataka's viable trading rights shall be assessed at ¥400 billion.
2. C. Itoh shall take in 1,000 Ataka employees.
3. AC Sangyo Co. (named after Ataka's "AC" brand) shall be established to take over Ataka's unprofitable assets for liquidation.
4. Banks shall write off loans made to Ataka which cannot be recovered as bad debts.

Both Sumitomo and C. Itoh had made concessions, but the final assessed value of Ataka's trading rights and the number of Ataka employees C. Itoh agreed to take were much closer to C. Itoh's initial demands than to Sumitomo's. Sumitomo obviously gave up more than it got. As one Sumitomo executive (recalling that C. Itoh Vice-President Sejima Ryūzō, perhaps the most important negotiator, had been on Imperial Army's General Headquarters staff during World War II) remarked wryly afterward, "We were outgunned by General Headquarters!"

Finale: Sumitomo vs. the Quasi-main Banks

How to divide up ¥200 billion in bad debts? This was Sumitomo's next headache. Granted, Ataka's two main banks, Sumitomo and Kyowa, would have to shoulder most of the burden. But other banks too were involved, including four major creditors (quasi-main banks): Mitsubishi Bank, Mitsui Bank, Bank of Tokyo, and Sumitomo Trust and Banking.

Even as Sumitomo was putting the final touches on the agreement with C. Itoh in December 1976, it was girding for battle with the other banks, for it anticipated even tougher negotiations than those with C. Itoh. The four quasi-main banks had been following the negotiations closely and were well aware of the bills they would get following Ataka's liquidation. Accordingly, they launched a first-strike offensive, heaping criticism on Sumitomo even before negotiations between the banks had formally begun. One bank claimed that Sumitomo had reneged on its promise because it had assured the other banks a year earlier, when they had formed a consortium to bankroll Ataka (at the request of the Finance Ministry and the Bank of Japan), that they would not have to take any of Ataka's domestic losses. Another bank insisted that Sumitomo's ignorance about trading company rights had played right into the hands of C. Itoh, and that Sumitomo ought to foot the bill for its own mistakes.

On January 19, 1977, Ataka's two main banks met with the four quasi-main banks, first to brief them on the negotiations with C. Itoh and the December 28 agreement, and second to make a general appeal for help in absorbing Ataka's ¥200 billion debt. On February 10, the two main banks announced that they absorb 78% of the total debt and asked the other four banks to absorb the remaining 22%. The quasi-main banks were outraged. As they saw it, the proposal was an affront to common sense. They argued that the Bank of Tokyo had absorbed more than 90% of Gosho's debts when Gosho was taken over by Kanematsu in 1967, and that this example had become something of a precedent. Why should they have to pay 22% when Ataka had *two* main banks?

Mitsubishi and Mitsui, Sumitomo's arch-rivals, were particularly adamant. Sumitomo Trust and Banking, which was part of the Sumitomo group, and the Bank of Tokyo, which had invested heavily in Ataka's worthless overseas ventures, were not as critical. Sumitomo officials, on the defensive from the start, made no public rebuttal, but they were wondering privately why the other banks were unwilling to pay part of the bill for protecting their country's credibility, which affected all of them, especially when they were already reaping the benefits.

The dispute over bad debts was quite plainly exacerbated by the banks' common desire to cut their own losses. Yet the further the dispute escalated and the longer a solution was delayed, the worse Ataka's problems became. A bank settlement on Ataka's ¥200 billion in bad debts was written into the merger agreement, and the six banks' failure to come to terms threatened to bring all progress to a standstill.

It is at such moments, however, when the bureaucracy steps in. In early April, when the banks had reached an impasse, the Finance Ministry and the Bank of Japan acted as arbitrators to end the long dispute. On April 20, the two main banks again invited the four quasi-main banks to discuss a revised allotment of Ataka's debts. This time, the meeting was successful. The agreement included two main clauses. First, Ataka's bad debts would be assessed at ¥230 billion. The two main banks would cover just under 81% of the total, the four quasi-main banks just over 17%, and ten other banks which had also loaned substantial sums to Ataka just under 2%. Second, the bad debts of AC Sangyo (the company set up as a repository for Ataka's obligations) would be assessed at ¥300 billion, which AC Sangyo would pay off in installments over a period of seven years. To insure prompt repayment, the main banks would extend guarantees to cover the principal.

Under the revised plan, the main banks were assigned 3% (or ¥6,900 million) more of Ataka's debts, and the quasi-main banks 5% (or ¥11,500 million) less, with the difference allotted to a group of ten banks that were not even a part of the original plan. It was a major victory for the quasi-main banks. And although the ten other banks, essentially bystanders in the dispute, must have wondered why they too had to pay for Ataka's failure, the sum was not enough to quibble about. They could say they had done their part for the nation's credibility and write off their losses as entertainment expenses.

With this agreement in the books, the last obstacle to the C. Itoh-Ataka merger had been overcome. The two companies signed a formal contract on May 31, 1977, setting the date of merger for October 1, 1977. Ataka shareholders were given one share of C. Itoh stock for every five shares of Ataka stock they owned.

The final curtain was rung down on the Ataka affair. In retrospect, Sumitomo Bank was perhaps the biggest loser. Settling its accounts for the six-month term ending September 30, 1977, Sumitomo wrote off an unprecedented ¥113,200 million in bad debts from Ataka. To make matters worse, the bank was faced with the dismal prospect of having to bail two other major client corporations out of trouble: Toyo Kogyo, the automobile manufacturer; and Itoman, the textile company. Thus, only one year after having become the most profitable bank in the land, Sumitomo yielded first place to Fuji Bank. The bank's decline in fortunes meant a drop in standings for the entire Sumitomo group. The retirement of Board Chairman Hotta Shōzō on June 29, 1977, after nearly 30 successful years at the bank's helm, was in a way symbolic of this change in fortunes.

For C. Itoh, however, the Ataka affair was a dream come true. Thanks to the merger, it had been able to diversify into hitherto untapped areas: it had acquired Ataka's interests in the steel and chemical fields and thereby strengthened its heavy industrial products division; it had acquired roughly ¥400 billion worth of trading rights outright; and it had overtaken Marubeni as Japan's third largest trading company. This is not to say, however, that the merger has given C. Itoh no headaches at all. The trading house went into the red in the six-month term ending March 1978. While this poor showing may simply reflect the general decline in business which affected all trading companies during this period, it might also be ascribed to difficulties that C. Itoh has had in absorbing the Ataka employees and getting the fullest use out of them: it is hard to say exactly which. Yet the future is hardly bleak. Despite the sometimes heated arguments with Sumitomo, the trading company, especially if it is operating in the red, can look forward to preferred financing from that bank, since it was after all the only company to listen to Sumitomo's pleas for help. Once the short-term difficulties are ironed out, C. Itoh can no doubt look forward to a period of substantial growth.

Epilogue

By way of conclusion, it is worth taking a closer look at the role played by the government in the Ataka affair and reviewing the criteria which influenced its decision not to let Ataka default. Although the bureaucracy generally kept a low profile in the affair, it nevertheless managed to do the right thing at the right time. When the news of Ataka's impending bankruptcy first broke in December 1975, the Bank of Japan called an unusual Sunday press conference to declare its support of Ataka & Co. and its intent to maintain international confidence in the Japanese economy. And when negotiations concerning the allotment of Ataka's bad debts reached a stalemate in the spring of 1977, both the Central Bank and Finance Ministry adroitly arbitrated the dispute between Ataka's main and quasi-main banks.

Even in the absence of such specific intervention, banks, trading companies, and other leading firms are acutely aware of the government's views. Businessmen keep in constant touch with Finance Ministry and Bank of Japan officials through regular consultations, informal conversations, and other exchanges. Theirs is an easy, open, and well-cultivated relationship.

Two questions remain to be answered. First, why did the Bank of Japan not grant Ataka the emergency loan that it did to Yamaichi Securities in 1965? To this question, Sumitomo Bank President Isoda Ichirō replies: "We did not want emergency financing from the Bank of Japan. To have accepted such a loan would have been tantamount to being declared incompetent, and everything would then have had to be cleared with the Bank." Stirring words, to be sure, but they are not the whole story. It is common knowledge that Sumitomo Bank's stocks and other securities were worth a total of about ¥400 billion more than their paper value in 1975, and the bank should therefore have been able to handle three or four Atakas without undue trouble. The Finance Ministry and the Bank of Japan no doubt took these under-declared assets into consideration when deciding that Sumitomo could shoulder the burden on its own, without the Central Bank resorting to emergency financing.

In 1965, Yamaichi's three main banks, Fuji, Mitsubishi, and the Industrial Bank of Japan, were unable to absorb the securities company's deficits. But only a decade later, a group of private banks led by Sumitomo was able to absorb its client's debts. It is clear that the city banks had achieved a phenomenal increase in their capital holdings and overall financial strength during those years.

The second question is, how does the government decide which companies may be allowed to go bankrupt and which may not? My own study of the major business failures and subsequent rescue operations, from 1965 (Yamaichi Securities) to 1978 (Sasebo Heavy Industries), suggests three main criteria.

First, the government will prevent a bank or other financial institution's failure, whatever the cost, in order to avoid widespread panic. The Finance Ministry Banking Bureau's main job is to insure that no bank, credit union, insurance or securities company, or major trading house (for, as we have seen, trading companies do much financing on their own) goes under.

Second, the government will not let any large corporation fail, since such a failure would have a harmful effect on Japan's international business reputation. In the words of one leading city bank executive, "The failure of a major Japanese corporation in any field would have such widespread repercussions that its creditors would not be allowed to handle the affair on their own." The shipping industry, which has suffered from chronic structural recession of late, is a good example of this rule. No one batted an eye when two relatively small shipping companies (Terukuni Kaiun, Ltd., and Oyama Shipping Co., Ltd.) went bankrupt, but it would be simply unthinkable to let a major firm like Japan Line or Sanko Steamship go under.

Third, the government will not let a large regional corporation fail when to do so would incapacitate the local economy. Sasebo Heavy Industries (Nagasaki Prefecture) and Toyo Kogyo (Hiroshima) are two typical examples. Government and business joined forces to save Sasebo Heavy Industries from seemingly inevitable bankruptcy; and Sumitomo Bank, with government encouragement, kept Toyo Kogyo afloat.

Given this wealth of examples, it is reasonable to conclude that no company coming under any of the above three categories will be allowed to fail in Japan. Not so in other capitalistic countries. West Germany may let a prestigious camera company such as Leica go under, and the United States may abandon once-mighty Penn Central to its fate. But capitalism as it is practiced in Japan is of a different breed. Prestigious corporations, from Nikon to JNR (Japanese National Railways), can expect a privileged destiny.

222 APPENDIX

An Abbreviated Genealogy of Postwar Parties

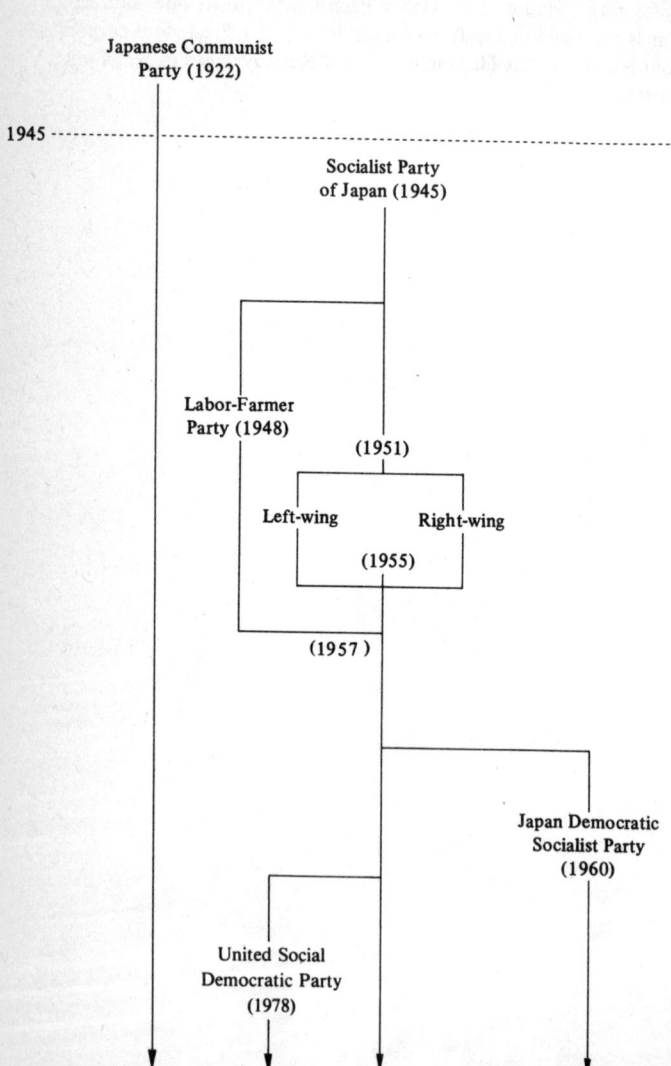

APPENDIX 223

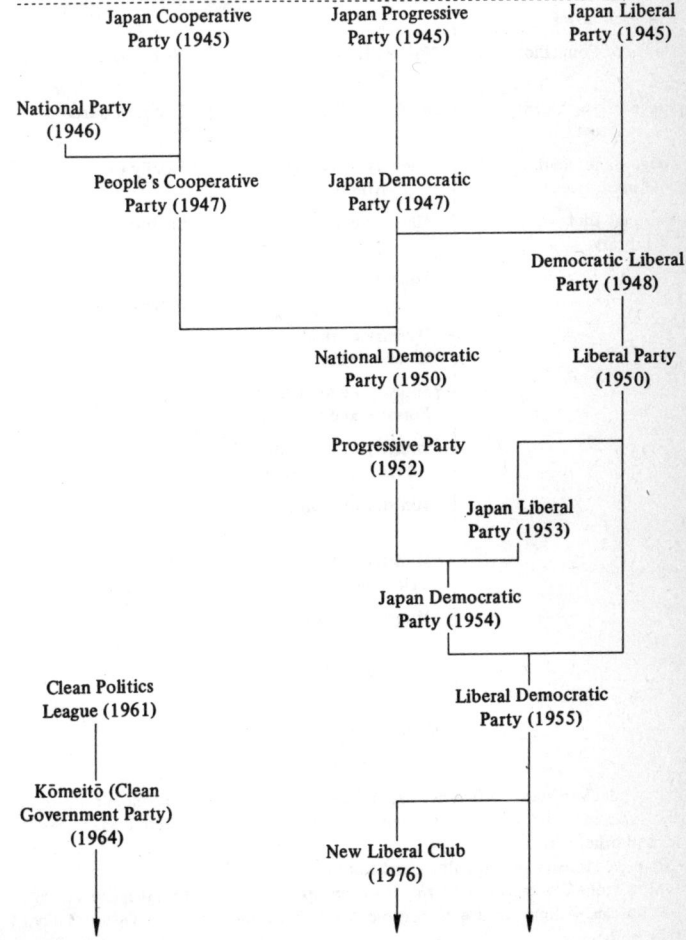

APPENDIX

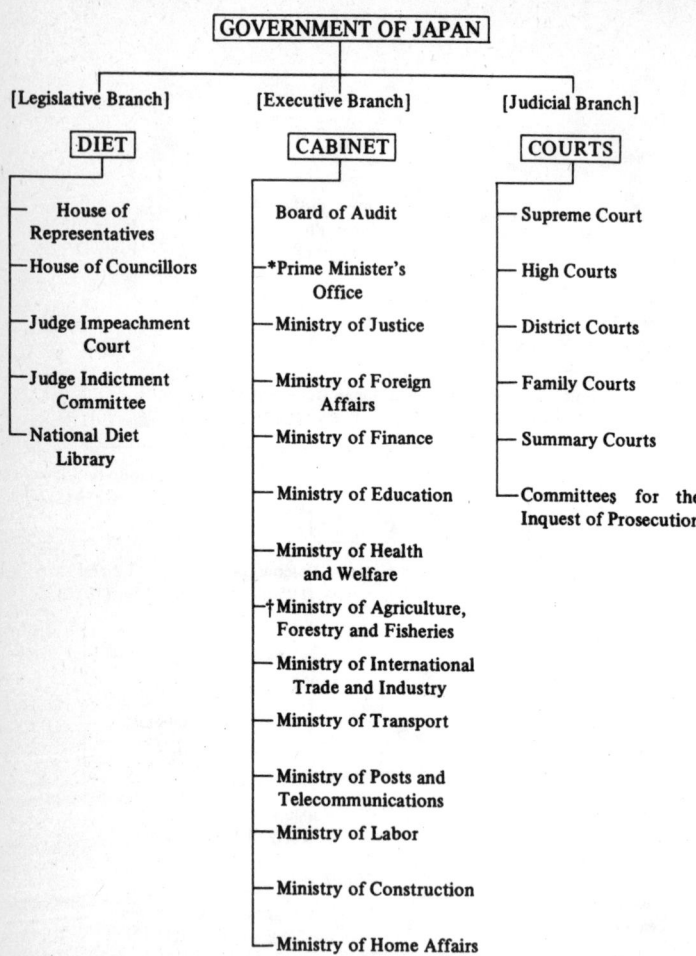

*The Prime Minister's Office consists of the Defense Agency, Economic Planning Agency, Science and Technology Agency, Environment Agency, Fair Trade Commission, and other offices.

†Formerly, Ministry of Agriculture and Forestry.

Adapted from *Organization of the Government of Japan*, Administrative Management Bureau, Administrative Management Agency, Prime Minister's Office (Tokyo, 1978), p. 2.

Bibliography of English Language Publications

Politics

Baerwald, Hans H. *Japan's Parliament: An Introduction.* London: Cambridge University Press, 1974.

Beardsley, Richard K., ed. *Studies in Japanese History and Politics.* Ann Arbor: University of Michigan Press, 1967.

Cole, Allan B.; Totten, George O.; and Uyehara Cecil H. *Socialist Parties in Postwar Japan.* New Haven: Yale University Press, 1966.

Curtis, Gerald L. *Election Campaigning Japanese Style.* New York: Columbia University Press, 1971.

Hellmann, Donald C. *Japanese Foreign Policy and Domestic Politics: The Peace Agreement with the Soviet Union.* Berkeley: University of California Press, 1969.

Maruyama, Masao. *Thought and Behaviour in Modern Japanese Politics.* Edited by Ivan Morris. London: Oxford University Press, 1963.

Scalapino, Robert A. *The Japanese Communist Movement, 1920-1966.* Berkeley: University of California Press, 1967.

–, ed. *The Foreign Policy of Modern Japan.* Berkeley: University of California Press, 1977.

Thayer, Nathaniel B. *How the Conservatives Rule Japan.* Princeton: Princeton University Press, 1969.

Watanuki, Jōji. *Politics in Postwar Japanese Society.* Tokyo: University of Tokyo Press, 1977.

Ward, Robert E. *Japan's Political System.* Englewood Cliffs: Prentice-Hall, 1967.

–. *Political Development in Modern Japan.* Princeton: Princeton University Press, 1968.

Economics

Abegglen, James C. *The Japanese Factory: Aspects of Its Social Organization.* New York: The Free Press, 1958.

–. *Management and Worker: The Japanese Solution.* Tokyo: Sophia University, 1973.

Caves, Richard E. and Masu, Uekusa. *Industrial Organization in Japan.* Washington, D.C.: The Brookings Institution, 1976.

Cole, Robert E. *Japanese Blue Collar: The Changing Tradition.* Berkeley: University of California Press, 1971.

Denison, Edward F. and Chung, William K. *How Japan's Economy Grew So Fast: The Sources of Postwar Expansion.* Washington, D.C.: The Brookings Institution, 1976.

Dore, Ronald P. *Land Reform in Japan.* London: Oxford University Press, 1959.

–. *British Factory-Japanese Factory: The Origins of National Diversity in Industrial Relations.* Berkeley: University of California Press, 1973.

Hadley, Eleanor M. *Antitrust in Japan.* Princeton: Princeton University Press, 1970.

Hanley, Susan B. and Yamamura, Kōzō. *Economic and Demographic Change in Preindustrial Japan, 1600-1868.* Princeton: Princeton University Press, 1977.

Hayami, Yūjirō. *A Century of Agricultural Growth in Japan: Its Relevance to Asian Development.* Tokyo: University of Tokyo Press, 1975.

– and Ruttan, Vernon W. *Agricultural Development: An International Perspective.* Baltimore: Johns Hopkins University Press, 1971.

Hirschmeier, Johannes. *The Origins of Entrepreneurship in Meiji Japan.* Cambridge: Harvard University Press, 1964.

– and Yui, T. *The Development of Japanese Business 1600-1973.* London: George Allen and Unwin, 1975.

Klein, Lawrence and Ohkawa, Kazushi, eds. *Economic Growth: The Japanese Experience Since the Meiji Era.* Homewood: Irwin, 1969.

Levine, Solomon B. *Industrial Relations in Postwar Japan.* Urbana: University of Illinois Press, 1958.

Lockwood, William W., ed. *The State and Economic Enterprises in Japan.* Princeton: Princeton University Press, 1965.

–, ed. *The Economic Development of Japan: Growth and Structural Change.* Princeton: Princeton University Press, 1968.

Ohkawa, Kazushi; Johnson, B.F.; and Kaneda, H., eds. *Agriculture and Economic Growth: Japan's Experience.*

Princeton: Princeton University Press, 1970. Also Tokyo: University of Tokyo Press.
—. and Rosovsky, Henry. *Japanese Economic Growth: Trend Acceleration in the Twentieth Century*. Stanford: Stanford University Press, 1973.
Ōkōchi, Kazuo; Karsh, Bernard; and Levine, Solomon B., eds. *Workers and Employers in Japan: The Japanese Employment Relations System*. Tokyo: University of Tokyo Press, 1973.
Patrik, Hugh T. and Rosovsky, Henry, eds. *Asia's New Giant: How the Japanese Economy Works*. Washington, D.C.: The Brookings Institution, 1976.
Taira, Kōji. *Economic Development and the Labor Market in Japan*. New York: Columbia University Press, 1970.
Takahashi, Kamekichi. *The Rise and Development of Japan's Modern Economy: The Basis for "Miraculous" Growth*. Translated by John Lynch. Tokyo: Jiji Tsūshinsha, 1969.
Yanaga, Chitoshi. *Big Business in Japanese Politics*. Yale Studies in Political Science, No. 22. New Haven: Yale University Press, 1968.
Yoshino, M.Y. *The Japanese Marketing System: Adaptations and Innovations*. Cambridge: M.I.T. Press, 1971.

Society and Culture

Austin, Lewis, ed. *Japan: The Paradox of Progress*. New Haven: Yale University Press, 1976.

Beckmann, George M. *The Modernization of China and Japan*. New York: Harper and Row, 1962.
Befu, Harumi. *Japan: An Anthropological Introduction*. San Francisco: Chandler Pub. Co., 1971.
De Vos, George A. *Socialization for Achievement: Essays on the Cultural Psychology of the Japanese*. Berkeley: University of California Press, 1973.
Dore, Ronald P. *Aspects of Social Change in Modern Japan*. Princeton: Princeton University Press, 1967.
Gibney, Frank B. *Japan: The Fragile Superpower*. Tokyo: Charles E. Tuttle, 1975.
Lebra, Takie Sugiyama. *Japanese Patterns of Behavior*. Honolulu: University Press of Hawaii, 1976.
— and Lebra, William P. *Japanese Culture and Behavior: Selected Readings*. Honolulu: University Press of Hawaii, 1976.
Murakami, Hyōe and Seidensticker, Edward G., eds. *Guides to Japanese Culture*. Tokyo: Japan Culture Institute, 1977.
Nakane, Chie. *Japanese Society*. London: Weidenfeld and Nicolson, 1970.
Reischauer, Edwin O. *The Japanese*. Cambridge: Harvard University Press, 1977.
Vogel, Ezra F. *Japan's New Middle Class: The Salary Man and His Family in a Tokyo Suburb*. Berkeley: University of California Press, 1971.
—, ed. *Modern Japanese Organization and Decision-Making*. Berkeley: University of California Press, 1975.

INDEX

Names

Abegglen, James C. *111*
Akita Daisuke *49*
Aoyagi Kenji *216*
Arisawa Hiromi *179*
Ashida Hitoshi *7–8, 36, 39, 145*
Ataka Eiichi *210, 212*
Ataka Yakichi *207*
Bell, Daniel *vii*
Bismarck *121*
Brzezinski, Zbigniew *94n*
Chou Ęn-Lai *14*
Dokō Toshio *69–70, 75*
Echigo Shōichi *216*
Eda (Saburō) *56*
Eisenhower, (Dwight D.) *14*
Fujiyama Aiichirō *14–5, 66, 72*
Fukuda Takeo *17–20, 43–6, 48, 54–5, 66, 77*
Fuwa Tetsuzō *60*
Giscard D'Estaing, Valéry *120*
Hara Takashi *4–5*
Hatoyama Ichirō *3–4, 7–13, 66*
Hayakawa (Takashi) *45*
Hedberg, Håkan *94, 111*
Hewes, Laurence I., Jr. *190*
Higashikuni Naruhiko *3, 6*
Higuchi Hirotarō *216*
Hirota (Hirotake) *8*
Hori Shigeru *44*
Hotta Shōzō *210, 216, 218*
Ibe Kyūnosuke *216*
Ikeda Hayato *3, 14–6, 19, 39, 40, 44, 66, 68, 77, 90, 194*
Inukai Tsuyoshi *5*
Ishibashi Tanzan *3, 12–4*
Ishii Mitsujirō *13–4, 45, 54*
Ishikawa Ichirō *61*
Ishizaka Taizō *67–9, 74*
Isoda Ichirō *216*
Itō Hirobumi *4*
Iwasa Yoshizane *75*
Izaki Kyūtarō *207*
Jameson, Sam *46n*
Jones, F.C. *108*
Juliana, Queen *120*
Kahn, Herman *111*
Kakizawa Kōji *91*
Katayama Sen *144*
Katayama Tetsu *3, 9–10, 36*
Katsumata (Seiichi) *56*
Katsura Tarō *4–5*
Kawashima Shōjirō *20, 41, 44*
Kido Kōichi *7*
Kikawada Kazutaka *74*
Kishi Nobusuke *10, 12–6, 33, 39, 66, 77, 90*
Komatsu Kō *213–4*
Kōmoto Toshio *20*
Kōno Ichirō *11, 14, 16, 19, 83, 97, 99, 103*
Kōno Yōhei *19, 63*
Konoe Fumimaro *5*
Kuraishi (Tadao) *55*
Ladejnsky, Wolf I. *190*
MacArthur, Douglas *4*
Masumi Junnosuke *22, 94n*
Matsui Yanosuke *211*
Matsumoto Zenmei *60*
Matsumura Kenzō *14*
Matsuoka Komakichi *144*
Miki Bukichi *9*
Miki Takeo *3, 14, 18–9, 21, 41, 45, 49, 54–5, 66, 77, 115*
Minobe (Ryōkichi) *36*
Miyajima Seijirō *15, 65–6, 68, 70–2, 77*
Miyamoto Kenji *60*
Miyazaki Shūzō *214*
Miyazawa Kiichi *20*
Mizuno Shigeo *71*
Mizuta (Mikio) *54*
Moroi Kanichi *74*
Nagano Shigeo *72–5*
Nakamura Umekichi *49*
Nakane Chie *132*
Nakasone Yasuhiro *17, 20, 45, 47–8, 53–5*
Nakayama Sohei *74*
Nishio Suehiro *9, 22, 144*
Nixon, Richard M. *18*
Obuchi (Keizō) *48*
Ogata Taketora *10*
Ōhira Masayoshi *17–20, 41, 45, 49, 54–5*

Ōkuma Shigenobu 5
Okuno (Seisuke) 54
Ōno Banboku 14
Osgood, Robert 94n
Ōtsuka Banjō 74
Perry (Matthew C.) 112
Reischauer, Edwin O. 38
Saionji Kinmochi 5, 7
Sakurada Takeshi 72, 75
Sasaki (Kōzō) 55
Satō Eisaku 3, 14-7, 39-40, 44, 66, 68, 77
Scalapino, Robert A. 22
Sejima Ryūzō 216
Shibusawa Eiichi 72
Shidehara Kijūrō 6, 39
Shiga Yoshio 36
Shigemitsu Mamoru 98-100, 106
Shiina (Etsusaburō) 54
Shimomura Osamu 16
Shone, Sir Robert 122-3
Sonoda Sunao 45
Suzuki Bunji 144
Suzuki (Kantarō) 6
Takahashi Korekiyo 5
Takane Masaaki 5
Takano Fusatarō 144
Takeuchi Tsuna 8
Tanaka Kakuei 3, 17-20, 39-41, 44-6, 48, 54-5, 66, 69, 77
Taniguchi Zentarō 61
Tōjō Hideki 7-8, 12
Tozaki Seiki 216
Ueda Kōichirō 60
Uemura Kōgorō 68-9
Umeda Masaru 61
Vogel, Ezra 86
Wakatsuki Reijirō 5
Yamagata Aritomo 7
Yamaguchi (Tsuruo) 48
Yokoi Tokiyoshi 188
Yoshida Shigeru 3, 6-13, 15-6, 38-40, 66, 70, 77, 102, 107
Young, Arthur 191-2

Political Parties

Cooperative Party 21
Democratic Party 7, 9-10, 38, 96-7
Japan Democratic Socialist Party (DSP) 22, 32, 55-6, 62-3, 70, 150
Japanese Communist Party (JCP) 21-2, 32-3, 36, 40, 44, 46, 49, 55, 60-3, 69-70, 73, 114-5, 150, 153, 156
Kōmeitō (Clean Government Party) 22-3, 33, 45, 61-3, 70
Liberal Democratic Party (LDP) 11-20, 22-3, 32-3, 36-41, 44-6, 48-9, 54-60, 62-3, 70, 80, 89, 93, 95, 108, 108, 114-156, 199
Liberal Party 7-10, 12, 38, 96-7
Minseitō (Democratic Party) 21, 65
New Liberal Club (NLC) 63
People's Cooperative Party 9-10, 19, 21
Progressive Party 7
Seiyūkai (Political Friends' Association [or Society]) 10, 21, 65
Social Populace Party 9
Socialist Party of Japan (SPJ) 3-4, 7, 9-10, 14, 21-3, 32, 37-8, 45-6, 48-9, 55-63, 70, 73, 89, 99-100, 114, 150, 155-6
Tosa Liberal Party 8

Labor Unions

All-Japan Federation of Industrial Organizations (Sanbetsu Kaigi: Zen-Nihon Sangyōbetsu Kumiai Kaigi) 145, 151
All-Japan Prefectural and Municipal Government Workers' Union (Jichirō) 156
All-Japan Seamen's Union 145, 151
All-Japan Trade Union Congress (Zenrō: Zen-Nihon Rōdō Kumiai Kaigi) 148
Association for the Formation of Labor Unions (Kiseikai: Rōdō Kumiai Kiseikai) 144
Chūritsu Rōren: see National Federation of Independent Unions
Council of Japanese Labor Unions (Hyōgikai: Nihon Rōdō Kumiai Hyōgikai) 144
Council of the Public Corporations and Government Enterprise Workers' Unions (Kōrōkyō: Kōkyō Kigyōtai-tō Rōdō Kumiai Kyōgikai) 153
Democratization League (Minshuka Dōmei) 145
Dōmei: see Japan Confederation of Labor
Federation of All Japan Trading Labor Unions (Zenshōsha) 212
Fraternity Society (Yūaikai) 144
General Council of Trade Unions of Japan (Sōhyō: Nihon Rōdō Kumiai Sōhyōgikai)

INDEX

Names

Abegglen, James C.   *111*
Akita Daisuke   *49*
Aoyagi Kenji   *216*
Arisawa Hiromi   *179*
Ashida Hitoshi   *7-8, 36, 39, 145*
Ataka Eiichi   *210, 212*
Ataka Yakichi   *207*
Bell, Daniel   *vii*
Bismarck   *121*
Brzezinski, Zbigniew   *94n*
Chou En-Lai   *14*
Dokō Toshio   *69-70, 75*
Echigo Shōichi   *216*
Eda (Saburō)   *56*
Eisenhower, (Dwight D.)   *14*
Fujiyama Aiichirō   *14-5, 66, 72*
Fukuda Takeo   *17-20, 43-6, 48, 54-5, 66, 77*
Fuwa Tetsuzō   *60*
Giscard D'Estaing, Valéry   *120*
Hara Takashi   *4-5*
Hatoyama Ichirō   *3-4, 7-13, 66*
Hayakawa (Takashi)   *45*
Hedberg, Håkan   *94, 111*
Hewes, Laurence I., Jr.   *190*
Higashikuni Naruhiko   *3, 6*
Higuchi Hirotarō   *216*
Hirota (Hirotake)   *8*
Hori Shigeru   *44*
Hotta Shōzō   *210, 216, 218*
Ibe Kyūnosuke   *216*
Ikeda Hayato   *3, 14-6, 19, 39, 40, 44, 66, 68, 77, 90, 194*
Inukai Tsuyoshi   *5*
Ishibashi Tanzan   *3, 12-4*
Ishii Mitsujirō   *13-4, 45, 54*
Ishikawa Ichirō   *61*
Ishizaka Taizō   *67-9, 74*
Isoda Ichirō   *216*
Itō Hirobumi   *4*
Iwasa Yoshizane   *75*
Izaki Kyūtarō   *207*
Jameson, Sam   *46n*
Jones, F.C.   *108*
Juliana, Queen   *120*
Kahn, Herman   *111*
Kakizawa Kōji   *91*
Katayama Sen   *144*
Katayama Tetsu   *3, 9-10, 36*
Katsumata (Seiichi)   *56*
Katsura Tarō   *4-5*
Kawashima Shōjirō   *20, 41, 44*
Kido Kōichi   *7*
Kikawada Kazutaka   *74*
Kishi Nobusuke   *10, 12-6, 33, 39, 66, 77, 90*
Komatsu Kō   *213-4*
Kōmoto Toshio   *20*
Kōno Ichirō   *11, 14, 16, 19, 83, 97, 99, 103*
Kōno Yōhei   *19, 63*
Konoe Fumimaro   *5*
Kuraishi (Tadao)   *55*
Ladejnsky, Wolf I.   *190*
MacArthur, Douglas   *4*
Masumi Junnosuke   *22, 94n*
Matsui Yanosuke   *211*
Matsumoto Zenmei   *60*
Matsumura Kenzō   *14*
Matsuoka Komakichi   *144*
Miki Bukichi   *9*
Miki Takeo   *3, 14, 18-9, 21, 41, 45, 49, 54-5, 66, 77, 115*
Minobe (Ryōkichi)   *36*
Miyajima Seijirō   *15, 65-6, 68, 70-2, 77*
Miyamoto Kenji   *60*
Miyazaki Shūzō   *214*
Miyazawa Kiichi   *20*
Mizuno Shigeo   *71*
Mizuta (Mikio)   *54*
Moroi Kanichi   *74*
Nagano Shigeo   *72-5*
Nakamura Umekichi   *49*
Nakane Chie   *132*
Nakasone Yasuhiro   *17, 20, 45, 47-8, 53-5*
Nakayama Sohei   *74*
Nishio Suehiro   *9, 22, 144*
Nixon, Richard M.   *18*
Obuchi (Keizō)   *48*
Ogata Taketora   *10*
Ōhira Masayoshi   *17-20, 41, 45, 49, 54-5*

Ōkuma Shigenobu 5
Okuno (Seisuke) 54
Ōno Banboku 14
Osgood, Robert 94n
Ōtsuka Banjō 74
Perry (Matthew C.) 112
Reischauer, Edwin O. 38
Saionji Kinmochi 5, 7
Sakurada Takeshi 72, 75
Sasaki (Kōzō) 55
Satō Eisaku 3, 14-7, 39-40, 44, 66, 68, 77
Scalapino, Robert A. 22
Sejima Ryūzō 216
Shibusawa Eiichi 72
Shidehara Kijūrō 6, 39
Shiga Yoshio 36
Shigemitsu Mamoru 98-100, 106
Shiina (Etsusaburō) 54
Shimomura Osamu 16
Shone, Sir Robert 122-3
Sonoda Sunao 45
Suzuki Bunji 144
Suzuki (Kantarō) 6
Takahashi Korekiyo 5
Takane Masaaki 5
Takano Fusatarō 144
Takeuchi Tsuna 8
Tanaka Kakuei 3, 17-20, 39-41, 44-6, 48, 54-5, 66, 69, 77
Taniguchi Zentarō 61
Tōjō Hideki 7-8, 12
Tozaki Seiki 216
Ueda Kōichirō 60
Uemura Kōgorō 68-9
Umeda Masaru 61
Vogel, Ezra 86
Wakatsuki Reijirō 5
Yamagata Aritomo 7
Yamaguchi (Tsuruo) 48
Yokoi Tokiyoshi 188
Yoshida Shigeru 3, 6-13, 15-6, 38-40, 66, 70, 77, 102, 107
Young, Arthur 191-2

Political Parties

Cooperative Party 21
Democratic Party 7, 9-10, 38, 96-7
Japan Democratic Socialist Party (DSP) 22, 32, 55-6, 62-3, 70, 150
Japanese Communist Party (JCP) 21-2, 32-3, 36, 40, 44, 46, 49, 55, 60-3, 69-70, 73, 114-5, 150, 153, 156
Kōmeitō (Clean Government Party) 22-3, 33, 45, 61-3, 70
Liberal Democratic Party (LDP) 11-20, 22-3, 32-3, 36-41, 44-6, 48-9, 54-60, 62-3, 70, 80, 89, 93, 95, 108, 108, 114-156, 199
Liberal Party 7-10, 12, 38, 96-7
Minseitō (Democratic Party) 21, 65
New Liberal Club (NLC) 63
People's Cooperative Party 9-10, 19, 21
Progressive Party 7
Seiyūkai (Political Friends' Association [or Society]) 10, 21, 65
Social Populace Party 9
Socialist Party of Japan (SPJ) 3-4, 7, 9-10, 14, 21-3, 32, 37-8, 45-6, 48-9, 55-63, 70, 73, 89, 99-100, 114, 150, 155-6
Tosa Liberal Party 8

Labor Unions

All-Japan Federation of Industrial Organizations (Sanbetsu Kaigi: Zen-Nihon Sangyōbetsu Kumiai Kaigi) 145, 151
All-Japan Prefectural and Municipal Government Workers' Union (Jichirō) 156
All-Japan Seamen's Union 145, 151
All-Japan Trade Union Congress (Zenrō: Zen-Nihon Rōdō Kumiai Kaigi) 148
Association for the Formation of Labor Unions (Kiseikai: Rōdō Kumiai Kiseikai) 144
Chūritsu Rōren: *see* National Federation of Independent Unions
Council of Japanese Labor Unions (Hyōgikai: Nihon Rōdō Kumiai Hyōgikai) 144
Council of the Public Corporations and Government Enterprise Workers' Unions (Kōrōkyō: Kōkyō Kigyōtai-tō Rōdō Kumiai Kyōgikai) 153
Democratization League (Minshuka Dōmei) 145
Dōmei: *see* Japan Confederation of Labor
Federation of All Japan Trading Labor Unions (Zenshōsha) 212
Fraternity Society (Yūaikai) 144
General Council of Trade Unions of Japan (Sōhyō: Nihon Rōdō Kumiai Sōhyōgikai)

INDEX 229

32, 71, 145, 148, 150, 153–6
Greater Japan General Federation of Labor Fraternity Society (Dai-Nippon Rōdō Sōdōmei Yūaikai) 144
Industrial Patriotic Association (Sangyō Hōkokukai) 145
Ironworkers' Union 144
International Metal Workers' Federation-Japan Council (IMF-JC: Kokusai Kinzoku Rōren Nihon Kyōgikai) 150, 155
Japan Coal Miners' Union 151
Japan Confederation of Labor (Dōmei: Zen-Nihon Rōdō Sōdōmei) 148, 150, 155
Japan Council of Chemical and Energy Industry Labor Unions (Nihon Kagaku Enerugī Rōdō Kumiai Kyōgikai) 150
Japan Federation of Textile Workers' Unions 145
Japan General Federation of Labor (Nippon Rōdō Sōdōmei) 144–5, 148, 151
Japan Postal Workers' Union (Zentei) 156
Japan Teachers' Union (Nikkyōso) 155–6
National Federation of Independent Unions (Chūritsu Rōren: Zenkoku Chūritsu Rōdō Kumiai Renraku Kaigi) 150, 155
National Federation of Industrial Organizations (Shinsanbetsu: Zenkoku Sangyō-betsu Rōdō Kumiai Rengōkai) 150
National Railway Workers' Union (Kokurō) 156
Printers' Union 144
Railway Engineers' Union 144
Shinsanbetsu: *see* National Federation of Industrial Organizations
Sōhyō: *see* General Council of Trade Unions of Japan
Spring Struggle Committee (Shuntō Kyōtō Kaigi) 155

Organizations

AC Sangyo Co. 216, 218
Anti-war Youth Committee (Hansen Seinen Iinkai) 58
Ataka America 204–6
Ataka & Co. 204–20
Ataka Kenzai Co., Ltd. 215
Ataka Textile Co., Ltd. 215
Bank of Japan (Central Bank) 81, 113,
 204–5, 209, 217, 219–20
Bank of Tokyo 205, 208, 216–7
Chief Cabinet Secretary 9, 44
C. Itoh & Co. 205, 209–19
Dai-Ichi Bank 123
Dai-Ichi Kangyo (group) 138
Dai-Ichi Kangyo Bank 211
Dai-Ichi Life Insurance 67
Democratic Association of Merchants and Industrialists (Minshu Shōkōkai) 73
Economic Planning Agency 54
Fair Trade Commission 126
Federation of Electric Power Companies 67
Fuji Bank 75, 209
Fuji (group) (= Fuyo Group) 71, 138, 209, 218, 220
Fuyo group (= Fuji group) 209
Gosho 217
Government Mint Bureau: *see* Ministry of Finance
Hitachi 70
Hitotsubashi University (Tokyo Higher Commercial School; Tokyo University of Commerce) 19, 207
Home Office 113
Honda 138
House of Councillors (Upper House) 41, 98, 155
House of Representatives (Lower House) 10–2, 15, 17, 19, 22–3, 32, 39, 41, 44, 46, 49, 55, 61, 63n, 155
Imperial Steel Works 207
Industrial Bank of Japan 74, 220
Industrial Issues Study Council (Sanken: Sangyō Mondai Kenkyūkai) 75
Itoman 218
Iwai & Co. 207
Japan Automobile Manufacturers' Association 67
Japan Chamber of Commerce and Industry (JCCI) 66, 72–5
Japan Chemical Industry Association 67
Japan Iron and Steel Federation 67
Japan Line 220
Japan Monopoly Corporation's Alcohol Division 148
Japan-Soviet Friendship Society 103
Japan Specialty Steel Pipe Co. 74
Japan Tobacco & Salt Public Corporation

230 INDEX

148
Japanese National Railways (JNR) *148, 153*
Kanematsu *217*
Kanematsu-Gosho *207*
Kangyo Bank *123*
Keidanren (Federation of Economic Organizations) *23, 65, 67-9, 115-6*
Keizai Dōyūkai (Japan Committee for Economic Development) *23, 65, 68, 74-5, 77*
Kyoto University *3, 15*
Kyowa Bank *209, 210, 216*
Labor Relations Commission *150*
Lord Keeper of the Privy Seal *7*
Marubeni *207, 209-10, 218*
Matsushita *138*
Meiji University *19*
Minister of Agriculture and Forestry *83, 97*
Minister of Education (Education Minister) *8, 14, 54*
Minister of Finance (Finance Minister) *13, 15-7, 19, 81*
Minister of Foreign Affairs (Foreign Minister) *6, 8-9, 17, 46, 98*
Minister of Health and Welfare *10*
Minister of International Trade and Industry *13, 19, 46*
Minister of Justice *69*
Minister of State *46, 55*
Ministry of Agriculture and Forestry (Agriculture and Forestry Ministry) *14, 16, 54-5, 81*
Ministry of Agriculture, Forestry, and Fisheries *126*
    State Forestry Service *148*
Ministry of Commerce and Industry *12, 39*
Ministry of Communications *67*
Ministry of Finance *15, 17, 19-20, 32, 39, 54, 81-2, 84, 86-7, 91, 113, 119, 125, 205-6, 217, 219-20*
    Banking Bureau *88, 208, 220*
    Budget Bureau *88*
    International Finance Bureau *88*
    Mint Bureau *148*
    National Tax Administration Agency *81*
    Printing Bureau *148*
    Tax Bureau *88*
Ministry of Foreign Affairs (Foreign Ministry; Gaimushō) *8, 39, 54, 104, 106*
Ministry of Health and Welfare *81*
Ministry of Home Affairs *85*
Ministry of International Trade and Industry (MITI) *32, 54, 68, 73, 85, 113, 118-9, 125-6, 137*
Ministry of Labor *137*
Ministry of Posts and Telecommunications *81*
Ministry of the Interior *85*
Ministry of Transport *81*
Ministry of Transportation (Transportation Ministry) *15, 39*
Mint Bureau: *see* Ministry of Finance
Mitsubishi *65, 75, 138, 189, 209-10, 217, 220*
Mitsubishi Bank *216*
Mitsubishi Corp. *207, 210*
Mitsui *15, 65, 75, 138, 189, 209-10, 217*
Mitsui & Co. *205, 207-8*
Mitsui Bank *216*
Mitsui Financial conglomerate *15*
Mitsui Mining's Miike Coal Mine *71*
National Council for the Restoration of Diplomatic Relations with China and the Soviet Union *103*
National Students Federation (Zengakuren) *61*
National Tax Administration Agency: *see* Ministry of Finance
Nichimen *208*
Nichiren Shōshū *61*
Nikkeiren (Japan Federation of Employers' Associations) *23, 65, 70-2, 74-5*
Nippon Steel *123, 72, 75, 207, 210-1*
Nippon Telegraph and Telephone *148*
Nissan Motors *70, 123*
Nisshin Spinning *67, 71*
Nissho-Iwai *207*
Nōkyō (agricultural cooperatives) *191*
Oji Paper Co. *207*
Oyama Shipping Co., Ltd. *220*
Petroleum Association of Japan *67*
Policy Affairs Research Council (Seichōkai) *55*
Postal Service *148*
Prince Motors *123*
Printing Bureau: *see* Ministry of Finance
Sanko Steamship *220*
Sasebo Heavy Industries *220*
Shipbuilders' Association of Japan *67*

INDEX 231

Showa Denko *10*
Small Business Finance Corporation *73*
Sōka-Gakkai (Value Creation Society) *22, 33, 61*
Sony *138*
State Forestry Service: see Ministry of Agriculture, Forestry, and Fisheries
Sumitomo (group) *138, 206, 209, 210-1 213-9, 226*
Sumitomo Bank *205-6, 208-11, 213, 216, 218-220*
Sumitomo Metal Industries *119*
Sumitomo Shoji *209-10*
Sumitomo Trust and Banking *216*
Suzuki & Co. *207*
Takashimaya-Iida *209*
Terukuni Kaiun Ltd. *220*
Tōhō Movie Company *70*
Tokyo Chamber of Commerce (Tokyo Shōhō Kaigisho) *72*
Tokyo Chamber of Commerce and Industry *72-3*
Tokyo Electric *74*
Tokyo (Imperial) University. see also University of Tokyo *8-12, 55, 66-7, 86, 88, 144, 188*
Tokyo Municipal Assembly *11*
Tokyo University of Education *36*
Toshiba *67, 69-70*
Toyo Kogyo *218, 220*
Toyota *137*
University of Tokyo (Tōdai): see also Tokyo (Imperial) Univeristy *4, 18*
Waseda University *11, 13*
Yamaichi Securities *204, 219-20*

Laws, Treaties and Statistics

Agricultural Cooperative Societies' Act *191*
Agricultural Land Law *189, 198*
Anti-Monopoly Law *112, 114, 118, 126*
Basic Agricultural Act *196-7, 199*
Basic Survey of Employment *163*
Census of Manufacturers *158*
Census of Works *158*
Chambers of Commerce and Industry Law *72*
China-Japan Treaty of Peace and Friendship *19*
Deconcentration Law *207*
Economic Survey of Japan *192*
Economic White Paper *180*
First Rationalization Programs *117*
Five-Year Plan for Fostering the Synthetic Textile Industry (Gōsei-Seni Ikusei Gokanen Keikaku) *117*
Food Administration Act *191*
Foreign Exchange and Foreign Trade Control Law *81*
General Agreement on Tariffs and Trade (GATT) *121, 196*
General Plan for the Liberalization of Trade and Foreign Exchange (Bōeki-Kawase Jiyū-ka Keikaku Taikō) *118*
ILO Convention No. 87 *153*
Labor (Trade) Union Law *144, 150, 152*
Law on Extraordinary Measures for Special Depressed Industries (Tokushinhō) *68, 119*
Law to Promote Small Business Modernization *180*
Local Employment Act *124*
Partial Nuclear Test Ban Treaty *36*
Political Contribution Control Law *40, 69*
Potsdam Declaration *6*
Public Corporations Labor Relations Law *153*
Public Peace Police Law *144*
San Francisco Peace Treaty *7, 9, 11, 13, 145*
Saudi Economic Development Program *120*
Second Rationalization Program *117*
Small Business Law (Chūshō Kigyō Kihonhō) *180*
Soviet-Japan Peace Agreement *66*
Special Law for the Synthetic Rubber Industry (Sekiyu-Kagaku Gōsei-gomu Seizō Tokubetsu Sochihō) *117*
Temporary Demand and Supply Adjustment Law *117*
Temporary Law for the Promotion of the Aircraft Industry *117*
Temporary Law for the Promotion of the Electronics Industry (Denshi-kōgyō Shinkō Rinji Sochihō) *117*
Temporary Law for the Promotion of the Machinery Industry (Kikai-kōgyō Shinkō Rinji Sochihō) *117*

Third National Comprehensive Development Plan 199
U.S.-Japan Security Treaty 13-4, 35, 48, 105
War Indemnity Special Measures Law (Senji Hoshō Tokubetsu Sochihō) 207

General Terms (English and Japanese)

agrarian reform 188-9, 199
amakudari 89
batsu 37, 62
buchō 21
Class A (part-time) farmer 187-8
Class B (part-time) farmer 188, 198
daimyō 4
dual structure 167, 170, 178-180
Engel's coefficient 202
enterprise unions viii, 143-4, 150-2, 155
faction: see also habatsu
  ix, 11-3, 37-8, 40-2, 44, 49, 62-3, 95
gakubatsu 37
genrō 5, 7
gunbatsu 37
ha 95
habatsu ix, 37, 95-6, 99, 106
han 4, 84
heimin 4
hōjin kigyō 168
hoshu-kei 22
ie viii, 133-8
"ittō-nanaraku" 40-1n
Japan, Inc. x, 68, 94, 111-26, 128, 130, 141-2, 205
jiei-gyō 162
jishu-dokuritsu rosen 60
kakushin 22
kakushin-kei 22
kanbatsu 37
kanryō 39-40
Kasumigaseki 91
keibatsu 37
keiretsu viii, 132, 137-41
kidōtai 59
kōenkai 32
kojin kigyō 168, 174
kuge 4-5
land reform 184, 189-92, 197-8
liberalization of capital and trade 113, 118, 122, 125, 131, 174, 180, 203
lifetime employment: see also permanent employment system 88, 133-4
Lockheed Scandal 69, 82, 209
main bank 205-6, 216-9
Meiji Restoration 4-5, 84-5, 91, 188
Minamata disease 45
National Income Doubling Plan 16, 68, 90, 193
Occupation 6-8, 11, 21, 38, 60, 85, 93, 96, 106, 113, 145, 188-9
oil crisis 18-9, 69, 71, 92, 111, 117, 143, 182
oyabun 40
oyabun-kobun 62
Permanent employment system 136
Principal Seminar A-Class Examination 86
purge 8, 38
quasi-main bank 216-9
Red Purge 22, 153
ringi 134, 136, 141
ryōtei 21
samurai 4-5, 84
SCAP (Supreme Commander Allied Powers) 6-9, 11, 70, 85, 112, 116, 145, 189-90
seiji-shikin 40
seniority (wage) system 128, 134, 137, 143, 197
shizoku 4-5
shuntō 71, 155
tansan 50, 151, 154
tōjin 39-40, 54
"Three-chan farm" 195
"Two-chan farm" 195
vertical society 132-3
Yawata-Fuji merger 75, 123
zaibatsu viii, 37, 112-3, 116, 189
zaikai viii, 64-78
zaikai-jin 64-78